The 100 Kilo Case

The True Story of an Irish ex-NYPD Detective
Protected by the Mafia, and one of the most
infamous drug busts in New York City

Peter Daly was born in Ballyshannon, Donegal in 1933. He moved to New York in 1952 and returned to Donegal, Ireland in 1981 where he now lives.

James Durney is a graduate of NUI, Maynooth. He was born in Naas, Co. Kildare, in 1961 and is married with two grown-up children. An award-winning writer, he has written extensively on Irish affairs, including award-winning books on organised crime in America and the Irish revolutionary period.

James has also worked on several radio and TV documentaries and was a consultant on TG4's *Mobs Mheiriceá (American Mobs)*.

The 100 Kilo Case

The True Story of an Irish ex-NYPD
Detective Protected by the Mafia, and
one of the most infamous drug busts in
New York City

Peter Daly with James Durney

HACHETTE
BOOKS
IRELAND

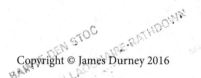
A CIP catalogue record for this title is available from the British Library.

ISBN 978 1 473636583

Printed and bound by CPI Group (UK) Ltd, Croydon, CR0 4YY
Typeset in Garamond by redrattledesign.com
Photos from collections of Peter Daly and James Durney
Map of Manhattan Precincts ©Andriy Yankovskyy

Hachette Books Ireland policy is to use papers that are natural, renewable and recyclable products and made from wood grown in sustainable forests. The logging and manufacturing processes are expected to conform to the environmental regulations of the country of origin.

Hachette Books Ireland
8 Castlecourt Centre
Castleknock
Dublin 15, Ireland

A division of Hachette UK Ltd
Carmelite House
50 Victoria Embankment
London EC4Y 0DZ

www.hachettebooksireland.ie

Peter Daly: Dedicated to my family, Rita, Shane, Finola, Conor and Evan and my silent partner, Detective Joseph Novoa.

James Durney: Dedicated to my father, Jim Durney, from whom I inherited a passion for the printed word.

AUTHOR'S NOTE

I first made contact with Peter Daly in early 2005 while interviewing Korean War veterans for my book *The Far Side of the World: Irish servicemen in the Korean War 1950–53*. Peter had served in Korea just after the signing of the armistice and despite the fact that both North and South Korea were on high alert, Peter's tour of duty was an uneventful one.

During our interview, Peter confided that he had a better story to tell.

As a New York detective, he had made one of the biggest narcotics seizures in police history – bigger than the celebrated French Connection haul. He duly sent me a newspaper clipping and photograph of his Special Investigating Unit (SIU) team posing with the drugs cache. Having written about American organised crime for years, I was intrigued. Peter Daly was a man who had been on the street and knew many of the big players. As he was on first name terms with Jimmy 'The Gent' Burke and Henry Hill, I interviewed Peter for a revised and updated version of my first book *The Mob: The history of Irish gangsters in America*.

Peter's story, however, merited more than just a couple of pages in another book – he had been mentioned in several publications about the NYPD, most notably the bestselling *Prince of the City* by Robert Daley. I had read the book and seen the movie years before I knew Peter, and it had made a big impact on me. Peter had known Bob Leuci and had been a partner of Detective Carl Aguiluz, who Leuci had turned. I pressed Peter for more information. In reply, he said he had written it all down to clear his head when he'd come back to Ireland in the mid-1980s – it had been a sort of therapy for him. We developed a good friendship over the years and, eventually, Peter agreed to co-operate on a book based on his life story.

We began working together in March 2009, when Peter handed over much of his written material. Peter had written much of this story in the late 1980s, when he changed names to protect those still alive. This book, however, is a true story, a work of non-fiction, based entirely on factual material and Peter's written reminiscences.

Some of the names of the characters have been changed – not to protect the person, but to protect their innocent families. Several characters asked not to be mentioned or asked for their names to be altered. Peter insisted that no one should be harmed by these writings, especially an innocent family member. After all, that was the reason he became 'the Quiet Man', so as not to send anyone to prison.

As an outsider looking in – on the workings of the NYPD and organised crime – I have tried to maintain impartiality in the presentation of Peter's story. However, no memoir can be entirely accurate, it is just not possible. This is Peter's story told from his view of how events occurred.

Precinct Map of Manhattan

CONTENTS

PROLOGUE

Bad day at Liverpool

My troubles, and I had a lot of them, really began in Liverpool in England, in December 1974. I was sitting down for breakfast looking out the window when two cars pulled up at the kerbside. Two plain-clothes cops jumped out of the first car, quickly followed by two uniforms. My bowels began to tighten and I could feel a shiver running down my spine. I knew what this was. After twelve years on the streets of New York, I'd seen it all. I knew when shit was going down and I knew my luck had run out.

A month earlier, I had travelled over to London to see my sister, Maeve. While I was living in New York, Maeve had had a big falling out with the family and had run off to London. I had been away for twenty years but, now that I was home, I took on the responsibility of healing the rift and getting the family back together again. I flew to Cardiff airport and took the train to Bristol, calling on my old school friend Fr Herbie Bromley. Many people from Ballyshannon would call to see Fr Bromley. It was what you did: you had a cup of tea and a chat with the local priest then went on about your business. Little did I know that Fr Bromley was also having a chat – with the British Special Branch.

That was my first trip over, and when I called to see my childhood friend on this, my second trip, he told the Special Branch that I would be returning to Ireland by way of Liverpool. I have often asked myself why he did what he did but, in all these years, I've yet to figure it out. My brother was a prominent Irish republican and maybe he thought I was involved too. I happened to be travelling with my cousin, Danny, who was a sales representative for a dynamite company. He was completely legit, but sometimes two and three make four and not five.

I had picked the worst time to travel to England. In February 1974, nine soldiers and three civilians had been killed in a coach bomb on the M62; then the Guildford pub bombings in October had four soldiers and a civilian dead; while the worst atrocity had occurred in November when two Birmingham pubs had been bombed, killing twenty-one people and injuring 182. Public revulsion at this slaughter and the continuing violence in Northern Ireland had led the IRA to declare a truce on 21 December, but the IRA had ordered a number of active members to travel to England in case the ceasefire broke down, and Bristol was a regular entry point for bombing teams travelling to Britain.

My mind raced back over the previous few days. We had booked into a small hotel, but immediately noticed a lot of strange activity around us. That evening a detective stopped us on the stairway and asked for our passports. He checked them out, handed them back and said nothing. Alarm bells started ringing in my head, and I was glad to be leaving England. Or so I thought.

The cops came straight up to our table and told us we were being arrested under the Prevention of Terrorism Act. We were taken to the local police station, at Huyton outside Liverpool. Danny was released without charge and brought the news of my arrest home to Ireland. It was obvious that it was only me they were looking for. Years later, when I was in Lewisburg Penitentiary, I received an unclassified US Embassy document that said that Fr Bromley had contacted the Special Branch and offered full co-operation in my arrest.

The British Special Branch was responsible for matters of national security, so this was no ordinary arrest. Detective Inspector Michael Atkins and Detective Constable John Bennie visited me at Huyton Police Station. Atkins asked if I was Peter Daly, to which I said I was, and then he told me he was in possession of a warrant issued on behalf of the US authorities in connection with the theft of illegal drugs in New York. He then read the warrant and cautioned me that I was not obliged to say anything unless I wished to do so, but what I said might be used in evidence against me. I read the warrant and said I had nothing to say. Atkins and Bennie left, but returned the next morning, took me from my cell and brought me to Liverpool Railway Station where we boarded a train to London. To say I was in deep trouble was an understatement.

PART I
RISE

Honour can be construed in many ways. Part of being honourable is the capacity to fall, without taking others with you, and get up again to face the world head on. Part of being honourable is the ability to see and hear, and not repeat things that may be damaging to others.

Sam Badillo, former NYPD detective

CHAPTER 1

I, citizen

My story starts where it finishes, in County Donegal on the northwest coast of Ireland. I was born in the little town of Ballyshannon on 22 August 1933. My father was Patrick J. Daly, the local doctor, and, as part of his duties, he was the medical surgeon to the American armed forces stationed near Enniskillen in County Fermanagh, during the Second World War. After each visit there, he would return with many gifts, such as chewing gum and canned beer, unheard-of items at that time in Ireland. My mother, Sarah, was the daughter of an ex-Royal Irish Constabulary man from Clare Island, and she had family connections to Grace O'Malley, the famed pirate queen. I was the first-born of five children, and had one brother, Anthony, and three sisters, Maeve, Fidelma and Grainne.

I had a happy childhood with all the freedom that living in a small town brings. Plus we were reasonably well-off because of my father's position. However, both my parents drank a lot, and there were plenty of house parties with people staggering around. I took a dislike to alcohol and what it did to people – or, rather, what it brought out in people – so I never drank. At the age of fifteen, after a convent and Christian Brothers education, I spent a year at the

Franciscan College in Multyfarnham, County Westmeath. But I had no interest in furthering my education, or staying in Ireland. I had set my sights on England or America. Travelling and seafaring was in my blood and I wanted to see the world.

When I was sixteen, I found some money hidden in the house and took a train to Belfast where I signed up to the Royal Air Force, but when they found out I was underage, I was returned home to my parents. They were furious that I had taken family money. Some years later my brother Anthony did something similar, only he was successful and ended up serving in Cyprus and other places with the RAF.

In 1951 my uncle, John Daly, arrived home from New York for a holiday, and I begged my father to allow me to return with him to America. I was only eighteen and my father refused but I bided my time until I was nineteen when my uncle claimed me out – at that time, you had to have a sponsor to go to America – and on 5 September 1952, fourteen days into my nineteenth year, my mother accompanied me – my father was too busy – on the bus to Sligo town, from where I would take the train to Cork and a bus to the port of Cobh. My father was reluctant for me to go, as was my mother, but she wanted to make sure I got on the train. She was quiet until it was time for me to board, then she broke down. It was emotional for me, too, as our family did not usually express our feelings. All my siblings emigrated and seemed destined not to stay at home.

At Cobh I boarded the liner the MV *Georgic* bound for New York. It was full of young Irish emigrants heading to America for a new life – 1952 was a big year for emigration. It seemed everyone was leaving and the mode of transport then was the ship. I spent my first night sleeping outdoors on the foredeck of the ocean liner, gazing at the stars. As I sailed across the Atlantic, I threw a silver dollar overboard and uttered an old Irish toast: 'May you live as long as you want, and never want as long as you live.'

———————•———————

The ship arrived in New York eight days later, gliding past the Statue of Liberty and the array of towering skyscrapers, dominated by the triumphant spire of the Empire State Building. It was a breathtaking sight. To me, there was no greater metropolis than New York City. My uncle picked me up and I went to live with him and his wife, Bridie, in their cramped apartment on University Avenue in the Bronx. It was an area known as Mott Haven and was an all-Irish community then.

My uncle worked as an electrician on the West Side docks and immediately found me work at the Atlantic and Pacific Tea Company stores. They called me if needed – unloading delivery trucks and putting goods in the storage area below the supermarket, and then stacking shelves in the shop. But I soon tired of this and my next job was at a Bronx housing complex called Fordham Hill, where I was employed as a porter, earning $48 for a seven-day week. This allowed me to move out of my uncle's home to an apartment, which I shared with fellow Donegal natives the McNelis brothers.

After a few months, a union representative came in and reduced the working week to six days and I got paid extra for the seventh day. I received $300 in back pay and felt secure enough to quit that job and go to work for Grimbles furniture warehouse on Long Island. The work there was brutish and intense, so I went to work as an elevator operator at the Bank of Manhattan Company at 40 Wall Street. It was a dull job, but it was a total change in terms of environment and workload.

In my free time, I began playing Gaelic football for New York's Donegal Football Club at Gaelic Park in the Bronx. My favourite pastimes were football and dancing. I don't drink alcohol but enjoyed dancing at the old Madison Avenue Tuxedo Ballroom, the Roseland and the Yaeger House on 86th Street.

I loved being in New York – there was so much freedom compared to back home. For the first time in my life, I was meeting people of different races, even of different sexual persuasion. I remember the first time I met a transvestite, when I was on the beat – he was one of the best-looking women I'd ever seen!

The food in America was also very different and colourful. In Ireland, food was just bland. The first time I saw a pizza, I thought someone had got sick on a plate! But it became one of my favourite foods. The only thing I never got used to was coffee, and I remained a tea drinker. With my new friends and money in my pocket, I really enjoyed everything this wonderful place had to offer – movies, dancing and American sports, like baseball and football. I loved the Americans and everything about this great country. Americans were so open and welcoming, which was so refreshing after the repressiveness of Irish society – they would tell you their problems at the drop of a hat and wanted to hear yours, too. And the women were so colourful – all of them looked like movie stars to me.

When I arrived in America, all emigrants had to sign the Selective Services Act, and faced the very real possibility of service in the armed forces. Many of my friends and acquaintances from Ireland had been drafted into the US army, which, at the time, was engaged in the Korean War, which had started in 1950. Several Irish emigrants were killed in the war and at one point, eight Irish-flag-draped coffins were pictured in a warehouse at Idlewild airport on their way home to Ireland, as they were not citizens of the United States. Irish-American politicians were outraged by this and a new law, the Dunne Act, named after Martin Dunne, an Irishman wounded in Korea, was enacted for the remaining period of the Korean War. It stated that any foreign national who served in the American armed forces was entitled to apply for citizenship after ninety days of basic training. Ultimately, this legislation would have a huge bearing on the rest of my life.

I realised that I would most likely be conscripted, so I contacted the draft board offices, who said I could volunteer for the usual two-year draft and pick my time to go. So, on 27 October 1953, a little over a year after arriving in America, I was inducted into the US army at Whitehall Street in Manhattan. The army was a fast-track to American citizenship, and the re-employment rights at the time assured any draftee that their job would be available to them when they were discharged.

I received a full medical examination, including a variety of injections, and was bussed to Fort Dix, New Jersey, to begin basic training. My fellow recruits called me 'Pete', or simply 'Irish'. Basic training was tough, but it bonded us – rich and poor and from different backgrounds – together. Much of everything we did was teamwork. There were a few other Irishmen there, and one Irish family living on the base invited me to their home for dinner on several occasions. There were also a lot of Hispanics in the army, immigrants like myself. I tried to get back to New York as much as possible, where I was still playing football with Donegal, Cavan and Tyrone teams.

Basic training lasted about ten weeks. Then I took an aptitude test, qualified for radio repair school and was transferred to the US Signal Corps Training School in Fort Manmouth, which was also in New Jersey, for instruction on radio repair on used field equipment. After that, I did another course in microwave radio equipment. This took about six months. Finally, I was sent on to

Fort Lewis, in Washington state, for a two-week course in survival behind enemy lines. We were shown how to eat the farmers' food when on the run – not to pull the vegetable out of the ground but to dig a small hole and take out the vegetable itself, leaving the top greenery in place. The farmer would see nothing wrong; some days later the greenery would turn brown, by which time we would be well away.

Corporal Peter Daly, US Army, 1955

Patrolman Peter Daly, 1962.

CHAPTER 2
Land of the morning calm

When my training was complete, I was assigned to Headquarters Company, 2nd Battalion, 35th Regiment. They were known as the Cacti regiment and were part of the 25th Tropic Lightning Division. My next stop was Korea.

In February 1954 our troopship left San Francisco for a two-week journey to Asia. Troopships were not designed for comfort. Canvas bunks were one above the other, four and five high. We had to lie flat on our backs or stomachs. Space was so tight that if we rolled on our sides, we would hit the bunk above; between the tiers of bunks, the space was so narrow that we had to walk sideways, over crammed aisles of sea bags and packs. Lighting and ventilation was poor, so we spent as much time as possible on deck. We read books and newspapers, played cards, told stories and sang songs, but most sat listlessly, whiling away the hours until it was time to go back below deck again. The more energetic, like myself, ran around the deck in a frantic effort to keep fit.

After fourteen days, I came on deck to see land looming over the horizon. The troopship was approaching the American naval base in Sasebo, Japan. We spent two days in Sasebo, which had an utterly American feel to it with hamburger joints and stateside-style bars, then the transport sailed on to Korea, anchoring in Pusan, Korea's main port. The town was a sprawling slum with flimsy and filthy wooden shacks everywhere. I could see dozens of Koreans, mainly women, squatting and sitting along the walls of the dock sheds. They were dressed in sacks and their faces were downcast and sorrowful.

Although an armistice had recently been signed, tensions were still high and we landed in full gear with rifles at the ready. It was monsoon season and the tent where our food was served had bullet holes in it and we were soaked through despite our ponchos. We joked that it was the only place you could eat and take a shower at the same time. The tin plate I ate from was covered by a mound of rice, topped with a thick slice of bread with margarine, and plenty of ketchup, salt and pepper. Before our meal we had to take several pills – the army made us sign our consent, which was witnessed by an officer – that were a safeguard against all sorts of diseases because in Korea the rice and other crops were planted in human fertiliser.

Outside the tent, I could see up to the United Nations graveyard. The area was covered with thousands of small white crosses in long rows, up and down and across. It was a sight that I couldn't help but dwell on, like all newcomers to Korea.

A few hours after arriving in-country we were given an official reception by UN personnel followed by a performance from a US army band, then we marched to a siding near the railway station where a train was waiting to take us northward to Camp Casey. The engine pulled six long carriages. Progress was torturous at times and the train laboured up even the slightest of slopes – it was so slow, you could exercise by getting out and walking alongside. The seats inside were wooden and the carriages were crowded to capacity. The smell of wet bodies and clothes drying *en masse* added to the glorious scent of the human fertiliser in the passing paddy fields. Fear, cold and discomfort brought everyone together – people from all walks of life.

Young barefooted kids ran along the razor-sharp stones and railway track to catch up with the slow-moving train and climb onboard. During the journey, we heated and ate the pre-cooked C rations and these kids offered, and gave, sexual favours to some for the canned food. There are always the few who take advantage of someone else's misery and I remember little girls, mere children, disappearing with men into the dark recesses of the train. Then the kids would bite the cans open with their teeth.

It took sixteen hours for the train to get to its destination, a journey that would have taken three to four hours on an American railroad. When we disembarked, we had to walk two miles through pitch darkness to meet the canvas-covered trucks, lined up to take us the rest of the way. Assignments and names were read out from the lighted cab of a truck. When the first group was ready, they moved out, with half-lights on. Then the next group of names were called out and onto the next truck, until the full battalion was mobile.

The trucks brought us to Camp Casey – a sprawling mass of tents – the end of our journey. We jumped out to the cacophony of shouting platoon sergeants. This was where I was to spend the next few months. It was a miserable country. For the rest of my life, no matter how many problems I seemed to have, I could always counter them by saying to myself, 'Remember Korea! Remember the thousands who died, the smell of the paddy fields and the starving young kids.' Anything was bearable in comparison.

———•———

The smell of shit in Korea was up before you every morning, especially the hot mornings. The smell was in your tea, in your clothes and, when you slept, it was one of the last things you noticed before you nodded off.

I learned a lot about human nature in Korea and witnessed the good and bad of my fellow human beings. My religious beliefs did not go unchallenged. I saw contraceptives and hypodermic needles in the cigarette-butt cans outside the church entrance and outside the command post. Some of my fellow soldiers indulged in regular intercourse with local women and girls, while others injected easily available heroin. Coming from a strict Catholic background, I steered clear of the prostitutes and drugs, and instead played soccer with the Korean kids who worked around the camp.

The Koreans took our dirty clothes, which were usually left on the floor near the stretcher-type beds, down to the river to wash them. They beat the dirt out of the clothes on the stones in the middle of the river, dried and folded the clothes and placed them neatly on each man's bunk. The clothes always came back very clean, and I was surprised given the conditions they had to work in. For this service, which was such a help to me, the Koreans were paid a pittance, but for them it was the difference between eating or going hungry.

The division had been in Korea since July 1950 and from that time there were rumours of a withdrawal home to its original base in Schofield Barracks in Hawaii. The rumours had, apparently, been going around for years and little credence was given to them, but it was nice to think about it, and it also helped keep morale up, but the day came when the rumours finally came true. I had been in Korea for about eight months and now it was nice to be leaving. Many of the old hands spoke about the beauties of Hawaii, so I was looking forward to my next posting. We were kitted out in combat gear and steel helmets for what was known in military jargon as a 'strategic withdrawal'. Landing craft took us out to the ship troop carriers, where we were packed in so tight that some men passed out, but they were left where they were until it was time to climb up the rope ladders to the larger ship.

The return voyage to the United States took sixteen days. Because of the bad weather, there was no hot food for several days, only cold sandwiches. As we were sailing through hurricanes and stormy seas, ropes were tied the length and breadth of the transport for the men to hold on to, as they moved back and forth through the driving rain. Some of the men were found almost frozen to death, lying on deck with their hands solid in a folded position across their chest.

When we finally reached our destination – Oahu, Hawaii – every man dressed in his parade uniform as if we were returning heroes. As each of us stepped off the gangplank onto Hawaiian soil, we were greeted by a 'hula-hula girl' who put a 'lai' of colourful flowers around our necks, then gave us a kiss on the lips.

We boarded open-topped trucks and travelled to Schofield Barracks to the waves and cheers of the locals. There were no rice paddies, only pineapple fields as far as the eye could see. The movie *From Here to Eternity* was filmed at Schofield and the barracks was just as I remembered it from on the big screen. The wooden buildings were a welcome sight after the tents in Korea – and there were spacious mess halls and dry beds. We were given three weeks on R&R and I went to all the tourist sights. I went out to Waikiki Beach as often as possible and saw Hollywood stars like Red Skelton, Bud Abbott and Lou Costello sunning themselves on the golden sand. Later, the division spent some months near the town of Hilo, and we did military exercises high up on the volcanic mountains.

In September 1955 I returned by ship to the US mainland, to San Francisco. I had been overseas one year, six months and twenty days. From the west coast I travelled across the US in a twin-propeller engine plane with wooden seats and no safety belts. One engine caught fire and the interior lights went out, and when anyone lit a match to have a cigarette, everyone was afraid that it was the other engine going on fire. Landing at Salt Lake City airport, we were sent to a local hotel where we showered, ate the best food on offer and slept on soft mattresses with white cotton sheets. The next day, we resuméd our flight to Dover military airport in New Jersey and, from there, to Fort Dix and back to military life again – barrack living, drilling, weapons training, etc.

I was looking forward to leaving the army even though I was not sure what my next step would be. I am basically a traditional old-fashioned Irish male and was ready to settle down and have a family. The disciplined structure of the army suited me and I thought of joining the police force, but I was really undecided what I would do when the time came.

As my initial time of service reached its close in the autumn of 1955, I was offered a deal to stay in the army – a sergeant's commission and extra money, plus an assigned area of my choice in the US – but it wasn't enough to make me re-enlist for another four years. When my time was up, I was processed out of the army at Fort Dix and honourably discharged on 8 October 1955. I received the National Defence Medal, the United Nations Service Medal, the Korean Service Medal and Good Conduct Medal. Much more importantly, I received $300 mustering out pay and was granted American citizenship – three years and three months after I arrived in America.

I went back to my job at the Manhattan Bank, working the four–twelve shift, making the long subway-train trip to my apartment in the Bronx in the early hours. When I asked for a month's holiday so I could make a trip to Ireland to see my family, the bank refused, so I quit. I had saved plenty of money in the army and was able to return to Ireland for six months. Back in my hometown I played football for Ballyshannon, but we lost the County Donegal Championship final to Dungloe.

In January 1957 I returned to New York only to come back six months later for the wedding of my brother Anthony. At the reception, I saw Rita Moore, my childhood sweetheart. I had known Rita since we were kids and had had a crush on her for as long as I'd known her. Her father was a sergeant in An Garda Síochána, the Irish police force, and had been based in Ballyshannon for some time. Rita and I had gone out together when we were young teenagers. And at my brother's wedding I asked her to come back to America with me – you could call it a marriage proposal – and so we decided to get married.

On 6 June 1958, we were married in a small, simple ceremony in my local church. We had a small wedding breakfast in my home with a cake provided by Michael Burke, a friend who owned a local bakery. The next day we headed to Rita's family home in County Laois.

Upon our arrival at Rita's home, we found her father seated in front of the large open-hearth fireplace, poking at the smouldering turf in the grate. Taking a moment out from his fireplace duties, he raised the long black iron poker into the air as a gesture of welcome to Rita and her 'friend'. He bellowed a greeting and told his wife, Annie, to make up two beds as Rita's friend would be staying the night. In a polite voice I replied, 'Just make up the one bed, we got married yesterday!'

Rita's mother rushed across and with tear-filled eyes wished us both the very best and embraced her daughter.

Within days I returned to New York, while Rita got her passport in order. I rented a furnished apartment beside Yankee Stadium in the Bronx. It was a cold-water flat and pretty run-down. Rita arrived some two months later. Our life was hard and my career was going nowhere and, it turned out, things would prove too hard for our marriage to survive.

She found it difficult to adjust to life in the big city and we had several marital break-ups. Our first child, Shane, was born on 7 June 1959 and that same year I bought my first car, a 1949 Dodge. Our second child, Evan, was also born in New York, while our twins, Conor and Finola, were born in Mullingar Hospital, in 1961, because Rita had left me and returned to Ireland.

I got two weeks' leave from the police academy and followed her to Ireland, and was there when the twins were born. Rita's father was now stationed in Kinnegad in County Westmeath and she had moved back to his house. I returned to New York after the twins were born, but Rita stayed on for about a month while she recovered from the births, and then returned to New York. We had a troubled marriage, which eventually ended in a bitter divorce.

After my discharge from the army, I had undertaken some schooling, paid for by the GI Bill of Rights. I'd gone to a six-month night school course at the New York Institute of Criminology, where I studied investigative techniques, and graduated with honours. I'd had an interest in becoming a private investigator, but decided I'd be better off joining the police force.

I was a good prospect for the police force: I did not drink alcohol, I played sports regularly and was married with responsibilities. As an ex-serviceman, I was entitled to two points on any exams. I also had a cousin in the NYPD, Inspector John Barry. Both of John's parents had died in a fire, and my uncle and aunt, John and Bridie Daly, had taken John into their family and cared for him. John Barry was president of the Superior Officers Union of the NYPD, which catered for policemen with the rank of captain and above.

When I took the Civil Service Police Academy examinations in the autumn of 1960, I was relatively confident I'd get in.

At that time, an average of 50,000 people took these annual exams and new appointments had to be made from the long list of successful applicants. I was officially advised that I had passed and was on the civil service list for the New York Police Department, the New York City Transit Police, the Housing Police and the Sanitary Department. At that time New York City had three separate police departments – Housing, for the projects; Transit, for the subways; and the NYPD. But the department could only take so many people at a time. My dream of becoming a police officer in New York was on hold for a time, but in early 1961 I received a letter asking that I present myself at the police academy in Manhattan for a physical examination.

CHAPTER 3
NYPD Blue

On 18 January 1961 I joined the ranks of the NYPD. As an Irish emigrant, it was a position of respect and standing in the Irish-American community, an admirable transition into the American mainstream. My Irishness meant I fitted easily into the NYPD. For more than a hundred years, the Irish had used the NYPD as a sort of patronage system and, by the early 1960s, they still had a dominant presence not only in the police department, but also in the fire department and in street politics. On top of this, the Irish community had just captured the most powerful position in the world – the presidency of the United States of America. The Irish were one of the major and most important ethnic groups in New York and even with minority hiring initiatives, 42 per cent of NYPD officers were Irish-Americans.

Becoming a cop was hard work and it took the best part of a year before I got to wear the NYPD blue. Before starting training, I had to go through the final series of physical exams and psychological tests. I then spent six months in classes, and needed a 72 per cent average in every course. If you failed one of the major exams and did not make it up, you were asked to leave. I attended the classes at the police academy, which was based in a run-down building on Hubert Street, on the Lower East Side. It was a very old, dilapidated warehouse building that the NYPD used for training. Daily classes consisted of police instruction, the law, judo, boxing and self-defence, firearms training, and driving. Gym combined running and callisthenics with self-defence, first aid and CPR. A high level of fitness was required – we ran, did press-ups, jumping jacks, swimming and so on – I'd done all of this in the army and I still played football and ran a bit, so I was quite fit. There were different instructors for each subject and each of them stressed that his subject was the most important part of the job.

For academic classes, I had to fill out biographical forms detailing my education, work and military experience, languages (I should have put down my ability to speak Irish!) and other special skills. The academy had a large swimming pool and we had to be competent for an emergency in the Hudson or East rivers. Many of the recruits were military veterans and were up to the required standard on firearm usage. My time on the pistol range was productive and I came first in my class, scoring 282 out of 300.

Like all graduates I was to make a speech at the end of the course, mainly about why I wanted to be a cop. I started off by saying that, to me, New York was the greatest city in the world and that, at some stage, I was going to be mayor! I wanted to emulate the career of Bill O'Dwyer, who'd been born in the little village of Bohola in County Mayo and had gone from being a labourer and patrolman to be the mayor of New York. This was the man that inspired me. If he could do it, so could I.

I was twenty-seven when I joined the NYPD, slightly older than the other recruits, who were mainly in their early twenties. I was six-foot tall and weighed 180 pounds. Like all new recruits, for my first year I was a probationary patrolman. This was a weeding-out period. If the NYPD put a gun in your hand, they wanted to see how you would use it. They wanted to see whether or not you were serious, how you spent your time off, if you drank and so on. I wore a grey uniform for the first full year until I passed my training, worked only at night while I was attending classes and could use my own car. Probationary cops were not allowed to be on the streets after midnight or to visit places that served liquor.

During that first year, I learned the basics of the streets. How to approach a crime scene without disturbing the evidence, how to make mental observations about entering premises and to take note of people who might have witnessed a crime. I enjoyed the fieldwork, actually observing cops on the job after being in the classroom. A training officer accompanied me on field training and for my last two months I was on the street on different shifts and in different areas to ensure maximum exposure to police work.

On 6 January 1962 I graduated as a patrolman at a ceremony held in the old Madison Square Garden. It had been a long year, but now after all the classes and exams this was one of the proudest days of my life. In my new blue uniform, which along with my equipment I had to pay for out of my own pocket, I sat listening to Police Commissioner Michael J. Murphy telling me I had received the best and most intensive police training in the world, that I had studied the law, the science of police work, police tactics, (as well as the criminals' tactics) and that I was now fully prepared to engage in the war against crime, to put what I had learned into practice on the streets of the city. I would be expected to discharge my obligations fairly, respecting every person equally.

I savoured every word the police commissioner uttered and couldn't wait to hit the streets. Some newcomers wanted to settle in as quickly as possible, maybe get a steady seat in a sector car with free meals and quiet late tours, but I wanted to get in on the action straight away. I decided that if I was going to rise through the department, I had to get a posting in a tough district. My instructors at the academy had spoken of some precincts in the quieter residential areas of the city, particularly Staten Island and parts of Queens that were 'country clubs'. They'd also spoken of the 'action precincts' like Harlem, Fort Apache and Bed-Stuy. 'You'll learn more in an action precinct in three months than you'll learn in a country club in three years,' I was told. I got my wish and was assigned to the 7th Precinct on Manhattan's Lower East Side, a tough area that housed many economically deprived families.

The day after I graduated from the academy, I walked through the doors of the 7th Precinct on Clinton Street. I was carrying a clothes bag and a satchel with gun belt, nightstick, flashlight and extra ammunition. I walked up to the huge desk, which ran almost the length of the wall on the right, and looked up at the uniformed desk sergeant. He sat alone behind his high desk, reading the paper. 'Patrolman Pete Daly reporting for duty,' I announced.

The sergeant raised his eyes reluctantly. 'Down the hall and see the roll call man,' he said disinterestedly. 'First door on the left.'

I went to the roll call man, who directed me to the locker room. I put on my uniform and pinned on my badge, number 7347 – I was ready to face my first assignment.

I was assigned to a squad of about eight men and this determined my duty hours. I worked one week on a day tour, from 8 a.m. to 4 p.m., and the next week from 4 p.m. to midnight, and midnight to 8 a.m. There were about 200 men in the precinct divided between cops like the roll call man and desk lieutenant, who hardly ever left the building, patrolmen and radio-car men. My squad – foot patrol was for new recruits – were given their posts, which averaged a five and a half city block, and the radio-car men – there was about six radio cars – their sectors. I was given a map of the precinct, with its various posts and sectors. Because of the high crime rate, patrolmen were required to call into their station house every hour; a late or forgotten call would bring out a search party.

Every new cop was assigned to a veteran cop. Mine was John Furey, an Irish-American from the Bronx, and my first shift on patrol began with him uttering the proverbial words, 'Forget everything you learned in the academy, kid, this is the real world.' A tough, fair cop, Furey taught me a lot: to forget the civilians and the bosses, only another cop could be trusted; never express an opinion on religion or politics; never 'rat' on another cop; and always rush forward with club swinging to back up another cop who was in trouble, no questions asked. I gained an understanding of the old-time cops who broadcast a message of respect with a stern word, or a nightstick. It was from veterans like John Furey I learned the meaning of trust and loyalty. On patrol he brought me up on the rooftops of tenements and told me to smash any bottles found on the roofs of buildings into small pieces with my nightstick so they could not be dropped on any other cops patrolling below. Rocks and bricks found on rooftops were also thrown down into the alleys behind the buildings. We called into shops and businesses on our beat where Furey introduced me to the owners.

I still remember vividly my first night on the job and my first collar. I was patrolling my post not long after coming to the 7th Precinct, and noticed some movement in a clothes shop through the front window. I quickly jumped back into the shadows where I could see and not be seen. Two men were gathering up clothes and bringing them to a hole in the wall. It later transpired that the two burglars had broken into a disused building adjoining the clothes shop and broken a hole in the wall to gain entrance to the shop, thereby not setting off any alarm. I called the radio car and told them to come with siren off. We got the two burglars in the act, and I got my first collar.

Police work to me held so much promise. I was optimistic, full of myself, but I also discovered a dark side to police work, which was prevalent right from the beginning. This was most definitely not dealt with in training. One of the first things I was told was, 'Always take care of the sergeant.' Soon I would learn what that meant. Desk sergeants handled the civil service side of police work. After roll call, all that desk sergeants had to do was drink coffee and read the paper. Recruits soon became aware that the buck stopped with the sergeant, so it was good to be in favour with him, and the roll call man, who made up the daily schedule. A few bucks slipped their way could give a cop a good post. An older cop asked me what post I had and he told me it was a good post, saying I could eat at the deli 'on the arm', have a drink or collect a 'flute' – a Coke bottle filled with whiskey – if needed. I didn't know what all this meant, but I learned quickly enough.

Some of the older cops were happy to mark their time on the beat for what was known as 'twenty and out' – retirement after twenty years' service with a decent pension. While I didn't blame them, I was young and full of vigour, and couldn't understand how they could be so apathetic. I vowed that my time was going to be as active as possible.

When the prescribed six weeks assigned to patrol with my experienced cop were over, I was free to make collars on my own. Rookies needed collars to boost their statistics, and I was out to make arrests.

In the 1960s the Irish virtually ran the police department by virtue of numbers. Next came the Italians and then African-Americans and Hispanics. Every group had its own ethnic association – the most powerful, of course, was the Irish officers' Emerald Society; the Italians had the Columbia Association; the Germans, the Steuben Association; the Jews, the Shomrim Society;

the Latinos had the Hispanic Association; the Poles, the Polaski Association; and the St George Association was for everyone else. Being one of three native-born Irishmen in the 7th Precinct, I got a lot of radio messages like 'Hee-haw, hee-haw', and comments like, 'Keep the chickens outta the kitchen.'

In American cities, cops were home-grown, and from the working-class neighbourhoods. I became a cop at a time when policemen were respected, or at least feared. It was a time of massive racial unrest. There were many newcomers to New York, mostly migrants – Puerto Ricans and African-Americans from the rural south. They came for work and to have a better life, but they were not wanted and were resented by the mostly white residents of areas like the Lower East Side, a traditional Jewish neighbourhood.

Colour never mattered to me. I treated anyone who committed a crime the same. Everyone was equal in my eyes. I had an easy manner and was free of attitude, which went down well with cops and the public alike. Co-existing with this attitude was the Irish sense of humour and natural empathy with the underdog. I had a natural compassion for the weak, needy and indisposed. Walking the beat, twirling my nightstick, I learned the names of the storekeepers, smiled at the mothers and kids and made a point of helping elderly ladies across the street. I am essentially outgoing and love people, and I made an extra effort to say hello, to stop and talk when I could, and learned to ignore it when people looked away or said nothing back. I acquired the who-doesn't-belong-here radar of the professional cop. When I heard a shout of 'Julio' or 'Raoul', I linked it with a specific person and filed it in the back of my mind. I talked to the street kids and showed them I cared, but let them know that I was the new cop on the block – and if they messed up my beat, I would come looking for them. I was soon on a first-name basis with anyone worth arresting.

When you walked a beat like the Lower East Side, the criminals got a quick sense of how much they could get away with, which was as much as you let them. On the street, respect is everything. Your word was law.

The 7th Precinct in the 1960s was one of the most violent districts of the city. It was said that six months on the streets of the Lower East Side was as good as five years in another force. The Lower East Side was once the home of Irish, German and Italian immigrants, and then later the Eastern Europeans, but by the time I arrived on the scene, the Eastern Europeans that had filled the apartments and run the stores had mostly moved on, and had been replaced by African-Americans and Puerto Ricans.

There were also street gangs such as the Puerto Rican 'Dragons', African-American 'Sportsmen' and the 'Mayrose', a mixed gang of Irish, Italian and Jewish youths. Armed with fists, sticks, flick-knives and 'zip-guns', they regularly engaged in turf battles.

It quickly dawned on me that most of the city's police work was being done by a small cadre of cops. In court, I kept seeing the same group of police officers responsible for a big share of all the arrests. Arrests, of course, meant overtime. I spent many hours in court and typing up reports, as my arrest rate went up and up. This was what I'd wanted when I joined the NYPD, to make a difference. This was the only way I could make it to the top and that was where I was heading.

CHAPTER 4

The streets of New York

A 10–13 was the radio call for an officer in trouble, and would bring out all available police officers. Squad cars from as many as three separate precincts would get to the scene with as much noise as possible, their blaring sirens often preventing the loss of a police officer's life.

I had been on foot patrol for a few months when one evening some Puerto Rican thugs broke some bottles on the steps of the Jewish synagogue on Henry Street during a Sabbath service. The episode could potentially have deteriorated into a full-scale race riot, as it was a very hot summer night and everyone was out on the street. I was on street patrol with a hairbag, Julian Holden*. Inside the synagogue, there was a large gathering of Jewish worshippers while outside there was an equal number of junkies, winos and Henry Street gang members. The ordinary citizens, happy to escape the stifling heat in the tenements, were playing games of dominos, standing on corners, sitting on stoops and lounging in doorways.

A shopkeeper pointed out the two youths who had broken the bottles among a small group of teenage boys and girls. 'C'mon,' I said to my partner and we headed over to arrest them. I took out my notebook, asked the two youths their names and said I was arresting them for disorderly conduct. Julian Holden was fit and a weightlifter, but when I turned around, I found I was alone struggling with two youths and realised I was going to have a major problem trying to cuff them and bring them in on my own. Suddenly, all hell broke loose. The men who were losing at dominos decided that the screaming and cursing was enough to distract them from their games. They threw over the makeshift boards, which were supported by wooden milk boxes or cinder blocks, and joined in the fray. Quick punches were thrown at anyone in general. The two youths decided to make good their escape and struck out at me, while their girlfriends also decided to join in. I was soon swinging, left and right. But I knew, sooner or later, the hoods would turn from fists to knives or zip guns.

A girlfriend of one of the youths got both of her hands around my throat, a vice-like grip I had to break with a punch to her chest, a chop to her throat and a quick leg behind hers to knock her over. I continued bashing skulls deftly with my nightstick. Getting hit with one of these sixteen-inch cocobolo hardwood batons was like being hit with a cast-iron frying pan. I could hear the clonks just as if it were water melons I was hitting. A shock ran up my arm as the nightstick connected. I was in full swing, but I could see that there was no way I was going to come out on top.

I had taken a severe blow to the nose and left eye. However, I knew that the longer I stayed in the one place, the more time it gave them to finish me off. I had to make a move to save myself so fought through the crowd of twenty or more, towards a glass-panelled telephone box. To some, it was just another night-time street show, while others were egging those involved to do this and that, and a few more were waiting to get in a lick or two. From the rooftops, about four large glass bottles, filled with water for added weight, exploded on the sidewalk area I had just left. These were known as 'airmail'. I couldn't see upwards but fired two shots from my revolver up into the open sky, making sure they wouldn't strike anyone. It was a message to those above about the seriousness of their actions.

Battling my way forward, I got into the phone booth and left the folding glass door open. I placed my revolver on the little shelf next to me for quick access if necessary and put in the dime I always kept for emergency calls, quickly informing the operator that I was a police officer and needed to call in a 10–13 at Henry and Clinton streets. Just then, bricks shattered all the glass in the booth, spraying me and the street with tiny shards. At the same time, I could hear the sweet sound of sirens rising in the distance as patrol cars flocked to the scene.

I came out of the shattered telephone booth with my gun drawn. My nightstick and hat were missing. Most of the street people disappeared when they heard the wailing sirens and the place was soon swarming with cops. I even managed to rearrest one of the two thugs who had started the whole affair. Holden reappeared claiming he had made a telephone call for assistance. I looked at him sceptically. Some more airmail rained down on the radio cars and a cobblestone bounced off the roof of one. I was brought to the hospital for medical attention to my eye and nose.

The following night as I turned out for patrol, my fellow officers suggested that I should take more time off but I knew I had to go right back to the street to show the thugs they had not got the better of me. The desk lieutenant had changed my posting to a quiet spot, but I explained my position. The lieutenant told me that if I could come up with a legitimate reason why I should return to the scene of the previous night's affray, then he would be forced by the rules of procedure to grant the request, otherwise his orders were that I go to the newly assigned spot. I said that I wanted to go back to arrest the second thug wanted for assault on a police officer and I was the only one who could identify the perpetrator. My request was granted. I went back to that same block, walking under the fire escapes as protection from airmail. I then went up on the rooftop of a tenement near the synagogue. Often when someone was caught up on the rooftops they received, and expected, a good beating.

From my vantage point, I could see the apartment across the street where one of the two troublemakers lived. An old-timer, Sergeant Johnson*, accompanied me. He threw a brick through the window, smashing a guitar that was lying near the bed. The occupants cursed us, but there was little else they could do. We wanted them to know we had returned. Later, I spotted the other young instigator of the rumble and with Sergeant Johnson, arrested him and brought him to the station house.

I was asked, 'Was this the motherfucker who assaulted you?'

When I answered, 'Yes,' several cops stood and escorted me outside the room and closed the door. The cops beat and kicked the youth without mercy and put him upside down into a trash barrel. When I took him upstairs to be fingerprinted and processed, he could hardly walk.

There were unwritten rules that every cop lived by – first-time offenders who had not hurt anybody were treated gently; professional criminals were treated as one combatant would treat another; smart-ass punks and vicious thugs could expect a going-over. Anybody who laid a hand on a cop expected, and was given, a good beating. When I asked what had happened, the defendant said that he had fallen down the steps of his apartment house just before he was arrested. He was aware that things would be made worse if he said anything about what had actually happened but, in my eyes, he was redeemed. This had always been my measuring of a man – one who could take his medicine and not rat on others, no matter what the consequences were. I asked him his name.

The kid's name was Peter Longonne and he was eighteen years old. He had been charged with assault on a police officer and possession of a switchblade. I knew he did not have a knife on him when he was arrested and that my fellow cops were making sure the kid went down. This was the kid's first arrest and his mother was in court with him. Peter Longonne copped a plea and was given a suspended sentence. I spoke up for him in court saying that he had got caught up in the action. 'This youth,' I told the judge, 'has got a job since his arrest and has had regular conferences, at his request, with me. He is a better person than his appearance in court depicts.'

I became good friends with Peter Longonne and I checked from time to time on his progress.

Because I was quite active in making arrests, after about a year I was transferred from foot patrol to one of the 7th Precinct patrol cars. There were several sector patrol cars, or RMPs – radio mobile patrols – in the precinct. This was a prized transfer and there was a verbal test given by the sergeant that each driver had to pass. The most important question in the test was: 'What's a half share of ten dollars?' You had to read these questions properly as there was a kind of code spoken, nothing was ever spoken direct. The correct answer was two. If the applicant gave the wrong answer, he didn't get the position! I, of course, gave the right answer, so I was in. Nothing much was said – a drawer was opened and I knew that I was to place something in it. How much was up to my discretion, but I had to be sure it was enough. Obviously, it was and I was assigned to a sector car.

A radio car had a driver and a recorder, who handled the communications and record-keeping. Duty in a radio car was divided evenly – four hours apiece – between the driver and the recorder. Partners in a patrol car were like a married couple in their devotions, decisions and everyday conversations. They sat side by side for eight hours, five days a week. They faced the street together and the sheer size and variety of what they encountered intensified their bond. It was central that they got on with one another, though that was not always the case.

One sector RMP was always designated the 'gofer' car and was responsible for bringing sandwiches and beer to the station house's administrative and clerical personnel, and 'flutes' to the lieutenants and sergeants. There were a number of bars within the 7th Precinct area which were well-known organised crime hangouts. When I was collecting a flute I would vary the calls to spread the hospitality equally. I became well known in these places for 'looking the other way' to the many fights that took place 'outside', because if they happened inside the bar it would have to be officially recorded and the bar would not get its liquor licence renewed. This is how I got to know some organised crime figures.

One of my first RMP partners was Jack Sirocco*, whose father was a lieutenant in the NYPD. When he'd been a motorcycle cop, Sirocco would pull over drivers on the West Side Highway and 'forget' their automobile violations for ten or twenty dollars. He carried a stamped addressed envelope with his own postal address and, when he was given money, he posted it straight away to his home address. Alternatively, he'd roll the money into a tiny brick and swallow it. Internal Affairs detectives regularly pulled Sirocco in, but never found any money on him. Eventually, many years later, Sirocco was caught and to save his skin, he ratted out his fellow officers in a precinct in Queens.

I had less than half a dozen partners while on RMP patrol. Partnerships stayed together unless there was a problem that could not be resolved or your partner was bumped up for promotion or transferred to the plainclothes division. My next RMP partner was Joseph O'Donnell, known as 'Smokey Joe' – his hair was jet black and he had a slightly dark complexion, he'd be what was called 'black Irish'. He stood over six foot and was built like a professional footballer. Ours was a good partnership and we got on well – we both had an easy-going attitude. Smokey Joe was a great person for playing pranks on other cops and we lightened up our work day by doing so.

Most days and nights the streets had plenty of action, so there was little chance of patrolmen getting bored, but they did need ways to let off some steam and keep their sanity. For instance, one time cops on the opposite shift filled our car up to the roof with garbage and we retaliated by putting a large rotten fish under the back seat of their car. Another time I got little packets of mustard from a deli, and just as we were handing the car over to the other shift smeared the mustard on the back of the steering wheel. The other cops thought it was shit and we got a great kick out of the joke. There was never any animosity about these pranks. Most cops saw the humour in them.

CHAPTER 5

Grease

Despite its reputation as a hard city, I found New York a very welcoming place. I loved the Americans, their sense of humour, acceptance of others, their progressive ways and their sharing of wealth. The latter was very important. I liked the openness of America, especially after the repressiveness of Irish society. As a cop, I enjoyed every minute of my work – the good and the bad.

From the early days of the police department, the taking of bribes was a widespread practice. Some cops availed of it, some did not. However, nobody said anything about it. If a cop didn't want to take money, his share was divided among those who did. There were always a few tests you had to take. I was asked to get a 'flute' for a desk sergeant. When I came back with the flute, and asked no questions, I knew I had passed the first test. There were other tests, like having to cover for incompetent or drunk cops. I did not drink alcohol and was always available as a driver for others who did. Like the majority of cops, I slipped into 'the system'. The attitude of superior officers seemed simple: 'Just don't get caught.' Graft and corruption had become so entrenched in the department that few even thought of it as corruption. It was easier to go along than to try and change things, like Frank Serpico did.

Police officers belong to an exclusive club. We protected each other and expected an absolute bond of loyalty from one another. Cops need to be sure their partners are there to watch their back. When you worked all day with cops and socialised with cops, you became dependent on them. You got to know the names of their children, their wives and girlfriends. You ate with them, shared dreams with them, told them your problems and they told you theirs. You became genuinely reluctant to detract from even the most incompetent cop in your precinct. You never knew when this cop would one day be called as your backup.

The police department, in some ways, mirrored my home – the worst thing you could say to an Irishman was that he was an informer. Even to be suspected of being one in the police department made a cop a pariah. In the early years of the NYPD, when Irish-born cops held sway in most of the station houses, the seeds were planted for what became known as 'the blue wall of silence'. It was a cop's omerta. The penalty for breaching the blue wall of silence was isolation, retribution and, in some cases, violence.

I discovered early that there were perks to being a policeman. It had been happening from the days of the first cop on the beat. It started with a free cup of coffee – or tea in my case – a haircut, a favour here or there. These things might be frowned upon by civilians, but cops looked at these as a benefit of the job. Whether it was a meal or a traffic-ticket bribe, most cops had simply come to expect it as their natural due, and probably never gave it a second thought. Besides, Joe Public was to blame – shopkeepers and tavern owners were happy to see a cop on patrol and eager to show their appreciation. They knew that if they had a problem, it would be sorted out. A traffic offence could be quickly cleared up with a few dollars. A cop might as well get the cash instead of the city.

There was a saying among cops at the time, 'As you grease you ride.' It was part of the culture and if you weren't in, you were out. It was that simple. Most cops would have preferred to be honest, but they were forced to be dishonest by the system of corruption that existed. Young policemen became corrupt because of peer pressure. I'm not saying everyone was corrupt, but many availed of what was on offer, be it money or a simple favour.

I began to share – as well as understand – the disillusionment around law enforcement that lay behind the cynicism of so many police officers. It was the assistant district attorneys, lawyers and judges who ran the system, and the whole thing from top to bottom was in question. Cops spent long days and nights on the streets and additional hours in court, but found their defendants released and back on the street before they even got out of the court building. Usually, this happened because the fix was in.

When we testified on a case in court, we were advised to watch the judge's reaction to our testimonies. If he stared out the courtroom window, we were being advised that the fix was in and the case was to go out the window. Nothing was ever said to us, but we had to read the many movements and facial features of the main players in the case. We were being advised about how things were going to go, regardless of what you said! We had to read the situation ourselves. So a cop was either in or out.

When someone did you a favour, or a person was pulled over for a traffic violation, or whatever the situation was, they would say, 'That was a nice thing you did for me. I'd like to buy you a hat.' It was an inside way of asking if a bribe could be arranged. It was usually just a small amount of cash. But it worked both ways. Cops tipped all sorts of people in the system – the precinct clerical man, and the day and night court clerks to call their cases faster than they normally would have. It was to move your situation ahead; whether it was lunch money, the cost of this or that, or tickets to a game or show, they all got you through your situation faster, regardless of what it was. Some cops paid desk officers to book prisoners in their particular precinct to avoid long trips from other outlying precincts. When you had a long day on the beat or on surveillance with no sleep or hot shower, you learned that a little 'grease' made life a lot easier.

CHAPTER 6

Mad Dog and Red

About two years after being on the force, I met legendary mobster Samuel 'Red' Levine, a member of the notorious Murder Incorporated, which had been the enforcement arm of the Italian/Jewish syndicate in the 1930s and 1940s. According to legend, Levine, an Orthodox Jew, did not commit murders on the Sabbath. He was reputed to be one of the hitmen on two of the most famous Mafia murders: Joe Masseria in a Coney Island restaurant in 1931 and Salvatore Maranzano, the Mafia Boss of Bosses, some months later.

Many of the killers working for Murder Inc. went to jail or the electric chair, but Red Levine was not one of them. He disappeared off the radar but in the 1960s he ran bookmaking and loan shark rackets on the Lower East Side from Sammy's Bar on Forsyth Street. I first met Red Levine when two police friends were dismissed pending an investigation into bribe-taking. Red got both of them, who had large families, full-time jobs with a trucking firm on the West Side. The two cops had been set up for bribe-taking by an informer, Willie Ox. Eventually, the case was thrown out and the cops went back to work, but they did not forget their benefactor. Red's friendliness was well known to many cops in the area, who never forgot a good turn.

This friendship was cemented when I arrested Mad Dog Frank Falco, who was working for Red as an enforcer. Falco also worked as a leg-breaker for the Aiello* brothers who ran numbers and loan shark rackets from the Madison Street Bar & Grill on Catherine Slip in Little Italy. Borrowers who didn't get up the weekly 'nut' with the interest added were given a warning and, if they didn't cough up, a broken arm or leg was Falco's reminder. Falco was a loose cannon and it was his aggressive attitude and penchant for violence that earned him his nickname Mad Dog.

It was this attitude that got Falco into trouble when he drove through a red light at East Broadway and Jefferson Street. Falco felt he had some ownership of the roads in his area and it was not unusual for him to drive with no intention of stopping, or looking left or right. Smokey Joe and I were sitting in Car 813 to the west of the Old World Library building, looking out directly into East Broadway, when Falco flew by in his big-finned black caddy. It took us a few blocks to get him to pull over, and it was only when I stuck my .38 revolver out the driver's window into his face that he pulled in to the kerb.

I said to Smokey Joe, 'This scumbag is going in for anything. If he as much as spits, he's a gonner!'

I approached warily. I never went up to an occupied car, as the door could be pushed out at me or a gun fired through the window. Like most cops, I was never foolish enough to put my arm in an open car window and be dragged away. I always made sure the engine was turned off and the keys given out to my extended left hand and would order the driver out to stand with his arms folded over the top of his head.

'Throw out the keys and exit the vehicle!' I ordered, pointing my revolver at Falco's sneering face.

Falco looked at me menacingly, but turned off the engine and threw the keys on the ground. He slowly got out of the car and did as ordered – assuming the arrest position of legs spread and hands on the roof.

'Why didn't you stop when you heard the siren?' I asked.

'Sorry, officer,' Falco said. 'My hearing's not too good. Probably damaged from the war.'

'Cover this punk,' I said to Smokey Joe. 'And shoot him in the ass if he moves. Maybe that'll get his attention.'

Falco suddenly changed his attitude and a smile lit up his good looks. 'Hey, no hard feelings, officer. I was only kidding.'

O'Donnell covered Falco while I looked in the car. I thought there must be something wrong, as it was a total change of character for Falco to be nice. I found nothing suspicious in the car, but still felt Falco was guilty of something. When I asked him his name, he said, 'Joe Amoto', and when I asked for the keys of the trunk, he gave me a key, but it didn't open the trunk. He produced another key and when the trunk was opened, it revealed a large box containing about 150 pornographic movies. Falco was arrested and brought to the station house where he was charged with the transportation of pornographic movies for distribution and sale. It was here that 'Joe Amoto' was revealed to be Frank Falco. He was a suspect in the murder of a Chinese businessman, shot dead in an argument over a parking space in Chinatown. To make matters worse for Falco, the Cadillac was not his, neither were the goods seized. The car and the goods belonged to the Aiello brothers. When they heard the news, they wanted their car back immediately, but they were told that that was out of the question because the car was being held as evidence.

Red Levine was approached by the Aiellos to set up a contact for the car and the case. Red got in touch with me, through a contact in the 7th Precinct station house. I was delighted to hear the news, as it put Falco in the shit with his own people. The car would go, but the rest of the charges – dangerous driving, resisting arrest and possession of pornography for sale – were going to stick. Falco secured his bail through his father, who was a bail bondsman. If Falco kept his mouth shut, I would see that the car was released with the DAs signature, as I knew the right words to say. However, Falco had to pay for his conduct towards me. A sum was agreed and Red Levine organised the payment.

A week later, Frank Falco was up before an Italian court judge. I presented the case and soon had the DA eating out of my hand, but Falco was to do time, no matter what. However, the car was to be eliminated from the case. The car owners had no 'knowledge' that Falco was transporting such items. Of course, that was all bullshit, given that Falco was working for the Aiellos. The case was called. Falco was told to be cool and allow the car to be released. But instead of doing what he was told, he became furious that an Italian judge was sitting on the bench passing judgement on him, a fellow Italian, and treating him as a criminal. The judge called a recess and stormed out to consult with the defence and prosecution. All three returned and the furious judge put the case off for another two weeks so that the defendant could reconsider his position in a more serious light. Under these circumstances, the DA could not even consider releasing the car.

I headed back to the 7th Precinct, but stopped off at Sammy's Bar to see if Red was there. There was no sign of him, so I then went to Mendell's Bar, where I found Red enjoying a meal of matzah balls, a Jewish soup dumpling made from a mixture of matzah meal, eggs, water and oil. He motioned for me to join him. I waited as the same dish was ordered for me. Red had a very hoarse voice. He no longer had the red hair that had given him his nickname and looked like an old retired gentleman, but he talked like you would expect a real old-time wiseguy to talk. Red said that matzah balls were good to eat and often saved lives.

'When cops or mobsters who have just eaten them are shot in the chest,' he said, 'the matzah balls prevent the bullets from going further and killing them.'

So Red reasoned everyone, in both his and my occupation, should take a daily dose of matzah balls. I, of course, agreed.

The conversation turned to the car, as Red had the funds at hand waiting for the papers' release. I told him of Falco's actions in front of the judge and the packed courtroom, the result of which was that the car would be held for another two weeks. When he heard this, Red nearly choked on his matzah balls. He got up and made a phone call. When he came back, he told me that when Falco went back to the court the next time, it would be different. The Aiello brothers were going to talk to Falco and they were sure the problem could be solved and the DA would then release the car. We finished our meal, shook hands, and I left.

The case was held two weeks later. When the judge sat at his bench, a pal of Falco's went out to the corridor to tell him to appear. As Falco stepped forward, I was shocked by his appearance – he had two black eyes, a cut on his lower lip and his right wrist was in a plaster cast complete with names and autographs. Falco started by apologising to the judge and the court for his previous outburst and unacceptable behaviour. He assured the judge that it wouldn't happen again and he was ready for whatever punishment the court felt was just.

The DA said, 'Your Honour, the first matter before the court is the release of the car used in this case, as it was loaned to the defendant and was not part of the case.'

The judge agreed and ruled that the necessary release papers were to be given to the arresting officer so that he could convey them to the rightful owner of the car, who, in turn, would then take them with the proper registration and ownership papers to the police pound and collect the car. When I took the car's papers to Red Levine, I received a nice 'thank you' for them.

Frank Falco pleaded guilty to the possession of the pornographic movies and was sentenced to do some time in prison. Given that he pled guilty and saved the court valuable time, he was given a lesser sentence but, nevertheless, his sentence began that day.

That was not the last time I heard of Frank Falco. About eight months later I was on patrol when I received reports of a body in the East River at South and Montgomery Street in the 7th Precinct. This was my first sight of a dead man taken from the river, and when a body has been in the water for a time it is not a pretty sight. The body was identified as that of Bobby Monroe. He'd been shot twice in the side of the face. The immediate area was cordoned off and hair from the victim, marks where his body had been dragged along the ground and tyre tracks were found. Later investigation revealed Bobby Monroe had been shot dead by Frank Falco, who had walked into the bar with a companion, past the patrons sitting at tables or at the bar, and gone straight to the rest rooms. He had come back out with a pistol drawn, gone directly up to Monroe and fired two shots into his face. As Falco and his companion had dragged the well-built labourer's body along the sawdust-covered floor to the rear entrance, he'd warned the witnesses that the same fate awaited anyone who talked.

Not long after the Monroe killing, Falco and some friends were celebrating an armed robbery they had orchestrated in Brooklyn by drinking and carousing with their girlfriends in a roadside dive in Lodi, New Jersey. One of the thugs, Tommy Trantino, sat at the bar drinking himself into oblivion. Detective Sergeant Pete Voto and Patrolman Gary Tedesco, an unarmed probationary policeman, responding to a noise complaint at 2.30 in the morning, walked into the bar. The sergeant found a gun wrapped in a towel on the bar. Trantino jumped him from behind and disarmed him; he gave the policeman's service revolver to Falco and ordered the two police officers to strip. They were taunted and pistol-whipped, then shot in the head, execution-style. The murderers fled the scene.

Frank Falco was already a murder suspect and it was advised to police and the general public that he was armed and extremely dangerous. Cops hunting for Falco were told to take no chances, and frankly cop killers were not going to be treated nicely. When one of our own was murdered, cops were generally up in arms. Two days after the double killing, Lieutenant Thomas Quinn and the 7th Squad detectives got word that Falco was staying at the Manhattan Hotel, near Times Square. Using a pass key to enter his room, they found Falco lying on the bed asleep, with beer bottles scattered around. Lieutenant Quinn placed his pistol to Falco's head, but the gangster woke suddenly, pushed the gun away and jumped up. Quinn fired and then kept firing until he put six bullets in the cop killer. A few hours later, Tommy Trantino turned himself in. He was tried and sentenced to death in New Jersey's electric chair but, on appeal, was given life. He was released in 2002.

CHAPTER 7

Gold shield

The goal for many patrolmen was to become a detective. A good detective began his career as a good patrolman and I was constantly reminded that 'The only thing better than being a New York City patrolman is being an NYPD detective.'

Making detective was the way to get ahead in the police department and the only target that mattered to me was getting my gold shield; in the autumn of 1966 I was interviewed for a place in the detective division, along with 300 others. I had proved my worth with a string of convictions against drug dealers, armed robbers and other criminals. Making the bosses look good with strong statistics was the best insurance a cop had in the department. Normally, if a patrolman made 150 arrests in a three-year period, he would be interviewed.

The interviews were at police headquarters and were held over a period of a few days before a board consisting of five captains. I brought along a file I had made up dating back to the day of my first arrest right up to the present. It also contained the charges, dates, the defendants' names and the final outcome of each case. A friend who was a detective had advised me to do this as the board would be impressed with the fact that I was an organised person and good at filing the facts and circumstances of each case. I also included that I had fired my revolver in a previous arrest. This incident, and how I handled what could have been a controversial shooting, had brought me to the attention of the higher-ups.

For his career to flourish, a cop needed a sponsor – known as a 'rabbi'. This could be a politician, a businessman or a judge. I went to Inspector Pat Lonergan* and two friends – criminal court judges Matthew Touhy* and Tom Cassidy* – who were to be my sponsors. I was confident I would get the detective placement because of my arrest rate, and, of course, my 'connections'. An appointment to detective usually required an exam and promotion to sergeant, but I did not take any exams and bypassed the promotion.

———◦———

My partner Eddie Galente and I came across a woman who'd been the victim of a handbag snatch. We ran after the two young black muggers on foot, calling on them to stop, but they ran faster. So I got down on one knee and, as I had been taught to shoot in the dark in Korea, aimed and shot one inch lower to allow for wind breakage of the bullet and movement of the target. My bullet hit the running youth in the buttocks. The distinctive sound of the .38 revolver shot and the echo through the buildings sounded like a bomb going off, and the youth hit the ground probably more from fright than pain. The other kid continued to run as Galente fired off several unaimed shots. We found the injured youth on the stoop of a brownstone where he had tried to crawl up the steps.

'You shot me in the ass!' he gasped unbelievingly.

'Well, now you have two assholes,' I said.

It was only a flesh wound. The injured youth was arrested, and confessed to robbing the handbag and gave a description of his accomplice. By the time we got back to the squad car, the woman complainant had gone. We brought the injured youth to Bellevue Hospital on First Avenue, where the attending doctor signed the confession, which I had written down.

We made our way back to the precinct, aware that the station house could be picketed because we had shot a young black kid. There was a lot of tension in the neighbourhood – the previous year there had been a major riot when a white cop shot dead a black youth. In a situation like that, when a police officer fired his revolver, it had to be reported to the station house desk officer, then to the department's ballistics unit, along with the gun's serial number, and a search of the area had to be made to find the bullet in case of civil liability – claims of personal injury or accidental property damage.

When the chief of detectives Pat Lonergan arrived at the 7th Precinct to interview us, he was very angry because he had been out on the town with his wife when he'd got a call to come down to the station house. When he read my report detailing the perpetrator's accomplice, which even included the colour of his socks, he assumed I was making it up. He asked, 'What really happened?' He said he didn't want any trouble from the locals and told me to quit the bullshit and give him the real story. I began to describe the incident, but when the chief heard my accent, his whole demeanour changed.

'Where are you from?' he asked.

I told him I was from Donegal.

Lonergan shook his head and smiled and added that his wife was also from Donegal. I told him about the other youth, the one who got away, but Lonergan had heard all this before – there was always 'one' who got away. He then asked if I'd fired any shots and I replied I'd fired one, which had wounded the youth. Chief

Lonergan also asked Eddie Galente the same question and he said he also only fired one shot. The chief seemed happy and left.

We remained in the station house for some time in case of a riot. I asked some of the 7th Precinct squad detectives if there'd been any progress on the missing perp, but they just fobbed me off. Detectives were the royalty of the station house and did not warrant questions from a mere patrolman. 'C'mon,' I said to my partner. Armed with the address of the kid we had arrested we went over to his home. When we were admitted to the apartment, we discovered the other youth, dressed exactly as his accomplice had described him and with a cut on his finger from the lady's handbag. He was arrested and brought down to the station house. With that second arrest, the mugging case was cleared up.

When Chief Lonergan heard the case had been cleared, he couldn't believe it. I had been telling the truth. The chief said if I wanted to be in the Detective Division I was to get in touch with him.

That is how I made a connection – a 'rabbi' – and how I became a detective.

CHAPTER 8

Narc

New detectives were either dispatched to precincts around the city or to special assignment squads, such as Burglary, Safe, Loft and Truck (responsible for investigating major commercial robberies and hijackings), and Narcotics. I was assigned to Narcotics. It was where all the action was.

On the day I was assigned to the 1st Precinct station house at Old Slip on South Street, a stone's throw from the Fulton Fish Market, I wore my best suit. The station house was a three-storey, rectangular building, which would later be used in the classic cop movie *The French Connection*. The outside was a drab masonry grey; the inside a dingy police green. I looked out of place in my good suit as most of the people I met inside were dressed like bikers and junkies. The third floor was where the clerical sergeant interviewed each of the dozen or so new arrivals and then gave them their assigned groups. I was assigned to the Undercover Unit – Group 1 – which covered Manhattan South from 42nd Street, which included the Lower East Side area I'd covered with the 7th Precinct.

My first partners in the Undercover Unit were Jim Mulligan, Johnny Kai and Terry Gillerman. I was the fourth member of the field team. Jim Mulligan, a typical Irish type, was team leader, a detective first grade and the oldest in years and experience. Johnny Kai, also a detective first grade, had been born in Canton and spoke six different Chinese dialects. His parents owned several restaurants in Chinatown. He was tall for an Asian, being almost five foot ten inches. He had become a detective in 1955 and worked undercover for four and a half years; he was my partner for nearly three years. Johnny Kai became a well-respected member of the New York Chinese community and died of cancer in 2007. Terry Gillerman was a detective third grade. He was of medium height, a stubby Jewish guy from Brooklyn. His father owned a bar on East Heuston Street and one of his best friends was the writer Truman Capote. I met Capote at his father's bar several times, but was unaware of who he was at the time. Terry Gillerman died quite young. Once a week, Lieutenant Madigan summoned all the undercovers into his office for a no-holds-barred heart-to-heart meeting.

In my first year working with this team, I made sixty-five arrests and my three team-mates also made from five to ten arrests each per month, working mostly out of the 10th Precinct. There were a number of other teams working undercover and our work areas overlapped, but this was necessary as pushers and user-pushers travelled back and forth to avoid being caught in any given section of the city. Our team did most of the street buys (undercover buying of narcotics by detectives from drug dealers) in the 10th Precinct, on West 20th Street, but did a lot of work in the 4th Precinct (at Ericsson Place on the Lower West Side), the 5th Precinct (on Elizabeth Street in Chinatown), the 6th Precinct (on Charles Street in Greenwich Village) and the 9th Precinct (on East 4th Street). As the junior member of the team, I recorded the buys.

Our team worked on our own terms, largely picking our own targets. There were about twelve to fifteen undercover officers and they decided of their own accord what team of backup officers they wanted to work with, which was basically who they felt safe with. The undercovers had nights for buys and nights for pick-ups, and had to record two buys to prove that the sellers were actually dealers and not someone down on his luck.

I spent a few months looking around at who was who, and who the most capable leaders were. I soon found out who the 'nice guys' were – they were *not* good street guys. Our team were all slick, streetwise, intelligent and industrious detectives. While we were supposed to put in an eight-hour day, in practice we usually worked only when a specific arrest or surveillance was at hand. There were none of the restrictions placed on uniformed patrolmen, no roll call, no set times for duty. If a detective was late for work, he would simply call the squad room and say, 'I'm on the job.'

Narcotics detectives worked longer hours and mostly at night-time, as that was when all the action took place. We followed the buy-and-bust approach to rid the city streets of the growing number of drug dealers. It was a classic sting operation. The undercover pretends he's there to buy narcotics. He or she shows the target a 'flash roll' (the money), and when the target produces the goods, he is arrested.

I operated as a cover officer for over two years. It involved covering the street narcotics buys made by undercover male and female detectives on the street, known as the 'set'. An undercover cop would buy drugs with marked money and a backup team would make the arrest. The field team would handle the arrest so the undercover would not have to reveal his/her identity until – and unless – the case went to trial. My team members and I would watch the activities, keep note of each buy and then, at a later date, arrest the offender who had sold the drugs, as the passing of time would cloud the events and the actual sale would have faded from memory. Subjects were picked up days and even weeks after a buy, so the delay protected the undercover from exposure. It enabled an undercover to buy narcotics in the same precinct two or three times a week.

Kathy Burke was the only woman detective I worked with. One of her first buy assignments was with myself and my partners at the time – John White and Richie McGuire. This was my second narcotics team, when I was the team leader, in late 1967. A few months after this I had a communication that drugs were being sold in a local high school. Kathy was about five foot two, slightly built and looked like a teenager, and so fitted in in the high school very easily. I gave her the low down on the school, but felt that it might be a dead end, as the information was not too promising. Kathy was very eager to prove her worth, but after a few hours in class, she realised I was right. It was a definite dead end. The student body was primarily black and Kathy was white. She wasn't in the school ten minutes when she was pushed up against a wall and warned, 'If you're the man (a cop) you'll be sorry.' Of course, she did not admit to being a cop but left the school and told me what happened. I was calm and very understanding, reassuring Kathy that it was OK. In time Kathy Burke rose to be the most highly decorated female detective in the NYPD's history.

After the initial arrest, the booking and arraignment could be quite time-consuming – though this usually resulted in a larger pay packet for overtime. Putting confiscated drugs into evidence was also a laborious process. Each bag of drugs found on a dealer had to be counted out, individually labelled and initialled. The dope from the undercover's buy was then officially recorded and placed in an evidence envelope. The undercover signed his name on the envelope, in accordance with the established department procedure for vouchering undercover buys. The envelope was then signed by the covering officer, and the name of the seller was added – his regular name, his street name and any description (height, weight, what he was wearing, or if he had tattoos, etc.), the time and date and the location of the buy and the amount of money paid.

From there, the drugs would go down to the police lab for testing. If the numbers vouchered did not add up, the arresting officer was in for a hard time from a superior and risked a command discipline, which could range from a warning to loss of vacation days. If it happened too many times, Internal Affairs was called in.

The dealers and users were out on the street every day and every night. Heroin had become the dominant trade and popular drug of choice as its price was right. There was no shortage of heroin at the time. The night buys for our team would start at 30th Street and Tenth Avenue. This was a quiet, deserted area at the southern end of the High Line near the vacant railroad car lot. There was an old railway car converted into a hot soup and grill restaurant on the south side of 30th Street on the southeast corner set back onto the old redbrick warehouse building that surrounded it. There were two public telephone booths on the Tenth Avenue side. The dirty-brown railway protection wall stretched east to west along the north side of the roadway. There was also an elevated overpass where the empty barrow-like cars of all shapes and sizes and colours were shunted back and forth, and unhooked and then re-attached to incoming and outgoing trains.

Our team had the telephone numbers of the two public phone booths and kept a record of most of the call phones in the area by location. We were in the habit of having 'out-of-order' stickers, which were glued across where the coins were deposited, so that incoming calls were undisturbed. The doors were open and the ring was easily heard in the still evening air. A call would indicate where the undercover was and where the street action was.

For the straight-up addicts, their days and nights were an endless cycle of scoring junk, getting works to shoot it with, finding a safe place to cop and making enough money to get more junk. They came to the set to score, but they went anywhere and did anything they could to get the money they needed. It was a soul-less existence. They stole, mugged and prostituted themselves to buy heroin. Dusk and onwards was the best time for the open-street carrying and copping action. Junk was delivered during the evening rush hours when the streets were a bustle with the rush of the home-bound workforce.

Like the cops who pursued them, the sellers, dealers and holders worked in teams. The drugs were usually stashed two doors away from the seller or held directly across the street with one of the dealers. One was in possession of the package, while another sold the product and another took the money. There was also another scanning the action, looking out for police or knock-off artists. Buyers gave their money to the seller and picked the drugs up from the holding guy. The idea was that the seller getting the money was usually obvious to the police and, if confronted, no junk would be found on him, so it could not be proved that any heroin was physically handed over. The holder supplied the buyer from the hidden stash. The holder took most of the risks.

I soon learned to despise the big-time drug dealers, people who made a profit from other people's misery, but I was sympathetic towards the small-time dealers who were caught up in a cycle of selling to feed their own habit. Drugs dehumanised both the seller and the user.

I also learned that the business of establishing the correct legal conditions for a search or an arrest was ridiculous. The law required that the arresting officer observe the defendant operating in a suspicious manner on a corner known for drug trafficking and that, upon closer inspection, the officer noticed a glassine envelope sticking out of his pocket as well. In other words, there had to be a clear reason for the arrest. Easier said than done but, in the real world, a cop watched the suspect until he was sure he was dirty and then hauled him up, found the drugs and then created a legal justification for the arrest.

CHAPTER 9

Blackie and the Jap

The third narcotics team I worked with consisted of Blackie Ruzzo, J.C. Connors and Eddie 'The Jap' Rodriguez. This was around the beginning of 1968. We worked the area at 23rd and Eighth Avenue, 30th Street and Eighth Avenue, and then 15th Street and Eighth Avenue and all points in between. The area most active was Eighth Avenue from 15th Street – mainly north to 30th Street.

Judges would rarely send any first-time offender to prison, either for selling or buying small quantities of drugs. A sale of drugs to an undercover officer usually resulted in a suspended sentence or placement on a rehabilitation programme. Because of crowded judicial calendars, a prisoner was usually allowed to plead guilty to possession – a misdemeanour – and could count on a light or suspended sentence.

After a few months of busting low-level dealers I had realised that police activity against heroin traffic and addiction was futile and pointless. The key targets were the distributors, the *real* dealers – the dealers we arrested were really only small-time pushers and addicts, passing on an extra supply to other addicts. Their arrests made little difference and though the sale from one junkie to another of a bag of heroin – the smallest unit being traded at the time – qualified as a felony, what happened later on in court was of little consequence.

Making collars often felt pointless. A junkie dealer would be arrested on a Friday night and on Monday be back on the same corner. It was all about crime statistics – complaints, arrests and convictions detailed in graphs, spreadsheets and lists. I was making little difference here. It was the big-time suppliers I wanted to work against.

A cop on the street needed something to believe in to continue his work. For me, it was the action – the adrenalin rush of the arrests, the energy that radiated from the set. I got off on the danger, working undercover, making successful busts. The Undercover Unit became my home away from home, and I spent more time with my colleagues than I did with my family.

It was my job to observe the buy and there had to be two buys from the same dealer before an arrest was considered. The cover officers, all detectives, would carry out the arrest, usually when the junkie identified was walking away from the set. This was called a 'pick-up buy'. The dealer-junkie was brought to an unmarked car, where he met the undercover detective, who made the buys from him. The undercover sat in the front seat with a large brown grocery bag over his head with two eyeholes cut out so he could see the arrested junkie and confirm the buy. Then another bag, with no cut-out holes, was placed over the dealer's head and the undercover got out of the car in an unlit area. The dealer was then brought to the station house and placed in the lock-up cage. Sometimes, the undercover officer would get picked up and brought to the station house with other dealers. They would all be thrown into the open-view lock-up cage, and watched to see if they would get rid of any junk or a set of works they had on them. Each dealer was taken out of the cage and escorted into the large toilet where they were made empty their pockets and strip totally. Most were men.

Undercover cops would examine the dealers' ears, the roof of their mouths, their hair, which was gone through by hand, under their armpits and down the middle of their backs. The officers also noted where the dealers had shot the junk into their veins, some were in the joints of their arms, others the inside of their upper legs. Others couldn't do it themselves and had fellow junkies 'hit' them in the back of the shoulder blades or in the cheeks of their ass.

Women didn't like the needle marks to show when they wore short sleeves or hot pants, so they would use the lower thigh, or the back of the shoulder, the ass or back of the hand.

Most junkies carried a set of works – an addict's lifeline – consisting of a spoon, syringe, and matches or a lighter. Powdered heroin was cooked on a bent spoon, so the junkie could hold it on his knees. The powder was put on the spoon and mixed with a tiny drop of water or saliva. It was then heated to make it all into one liquid. To rid it of the impurities the heroin was filtered through a cigarette filter tip and drawn into the syringe. A belt was tied around the arm to cut off circulation to the upper arm and make the veins more prominent. Hardcore junkies jacked the plunger in and out to get a potent mix of junk and blood going from syringe to vein.

An undercover cop could not be well-dressed or groomed or wear a watch or ring, as all those items meant money to a junkie, and money meant junk. No junkie would have any property as he'd have sold everything to support his habit. Besides, if he had such items, they would attract other junkies to rob him.

To make the arrest more realistic and not blow my partner's cover, I would inflict a fake beating and a false finding of a set of works on the undercover. I would go through a big deal that I hadn't time for junkies and that I was only interested in sellers. Eddie 'The Jap' Rodriguez was one of the best men I ever worked with as an undercover officer. He was a master of disguise and looked like a lowlife junkie. Later, when Rodriguez worked in the Bureau of Special Services (BOSS), a secret branch of the NYPD's Intelligence Division, he broke up a huge Cuban ring that had plans to blow up the Statue of Liberty and other government buildings. The Jap was so well in with the group, they bought him a pearl-handled pistol in Florida as a gift. As part of his street disguise, Rodriguez would wear a kamikaze-type pilot's leather fur cap. He wore thick-lens glasses and carried a half bottle of blackberry wine in his hip pocket. Rodriguez would be arrested with the other dealers or junkies, he'd be smacked around and fall all over the middle of the street or hallway and curse the arresting officer with the worst Spanish swear words he knew. I would take the Jap's cigarettes out and throw them all around the hallway floor and make him show his needle marks. Rodriguez, and other undercover officers, arranged black marks on their forearms before they went onto the street, just in case they ended up in a group and had to shoot up. At times, Rodriguez would be locked up in the cage and have to go to court, but he would be brought to another 'court'.

Some pick-ups could turn violent. One junkie, whom I had arrested previously, tried to hit me with a long umbrella when I was again arresting him. I parried the blow, took the umbrella from him and placed it at the back of his neck. Then I quickly bent it to the front and took both ends of it in one hand and escorted him to the waiting car. Some months later this same man was on the crowded sidewalk of 21st Street, between Eighth and Ninth avenues, walking with a few friends, when he noticed me pulling up in my car, looking in his direction. Knowing the inevitable was about to take place, he threw himself onto the sidewalk and rolled over onto his back and started to kick his feet and wave his arms about furiously, screaming, 'Help! Help!

La Hara! La Hara!' (Street legend has it that La Hara is what the Puerto Ricans called the police, as when they came to New York all the cops seemed to be named O'Hara.) I quickly got out of the car, bent over the skinny junkie and got a good tight grip on his belt buckle and a fistful of the clothing under his chin and carried him to the car where I threw him into the back seat. When we got to the 10th Precinct station house, he decided to make a run for it, only to discover that I was faster than him. I swung him around, gave him a quick knee in the groin and said, 'You want to run now, go ahead.' Naturally, he didn't. 'Now follow me,' I said. The junkie, holding his balls, hobbled painfully behind me into the station house.

There were times, however, when being undercover was very dangerous work. Three junkies once made Blackie Ruzzo when he was undercover in a back tenement hallway on the Lower East Side (i.e. they blew his cover). One of them noticed his silver automatic in its ankle holster and assumed he was a cop. Blackie got a bad beating and suffered two broken wrists and numerous cuts and bruises from being stomped. One of his assailants tried to shoot him with the automatic, but didn't know how to get the safety off. Blackie was found by police officers from the 7th Precinct and rushed to Bellevue Emergency. Two days later, the three assailants and an accomplice who had bought Blackie's gun from them were arrested. They were badly injured from the fight they put up 'while resisting arrest'.

Many drug raids involved crashing into apartments. I thrived on this action, but it was a tricky, dangerous job and could easily go wrong. At times, cops were in possession of a court-obtained search warrant, but we were aware that if we knocked to gain entry, the goods would be flushed away or thrown out a window. So a 'no-knock' law was brought into effect, where cops could crash the door without announcing their presence. This was one of the most dangerous parts of police work – the how and when to crash the door and what might be waiting on the other side.

Given all the resources and risks that a raid involved, it made a lot of sense to do some double-checks and verifications before carrying out a forced-entry operation. The usual checks were made to assure the suspect was inside. There were many ways that this was done, depending on the area, the location and other factors. The most common were making telephone calls or pretending to be a female sales lady or store representative or watching the lights in the house. Things were done according to the individual circumstances at the time. This was where street knowledge – the sixth sense – and the know-how came into play. If an empty apartment was hit and no damage was done to the doorway, long hours of patient waiting inside would eventually pay off, when the occupiers turned up.

CHAPTER 10

Scarface meets Dick Tracy

Many cops on the street had a handle, or nickname. Most junkies called me 'Dick Tracy', while my fellow officers called me 'The Hawk' because I was noted for studying a situation with patience until I felt the time was right to take my prey.

Once, I was sitting in my street clothes on the front-entry steps of a West Side tenement surrounded by junkies when I heard one say, 'You know when you were young your mother told you that God was everywhere? Well, she was wrong – Dick Tracy is everywhere!' I smiled to myself, knowing it was me the junkies were talking about, but I said nothing. I was waiting for a dealer to arrive on the scene and when he did, I pounced on him. The junkies were right – Dick Tracy was everywhere!

A tactic of mine was to jump out of a car and run quickly into a restaurant or pool hall, as another officer stood at the front door. I walked around with my pick-up leather jacket on. Everyone present knew me and knew why I was there. The junkies and dealers knew that when I appeared, I had only one reason to be in their midst – someone was going down. They would look threateningly at me. Some could be armed with a gun or a knife, so they were tense situations. However, I was well-armed too. I always carried two revolvers – one in an underarm holster and the other in an ankle holster. The street hustlers knew I would never pull out my revolver just for show – if it came out, it would be used. My reputation was enough. I didn't have to say anything. Everyone knew Dick Tracy was crazy, 'loco'.

A junkie's first objective was self-preservation, and I used psychology in the crowded pool room or restaurant. I would fix on one person and stare directly at him as I walked across the room; all the way between the tables my eyes would not leave that person. To the others, it was obvious who I was going to collar, and they were all just glad it wasn't them. They would get all emotionally aroused that 'Juan' was being collared but they were of two minds: angered for Juan's sake but relaxed for their own. This relaxed emotion was important; when I got near Juan, I quietly changed my attention and picked up 'Raul'. I had diverted all of their attention from themselves to another so when I picked 'Raul', they were relaxed and shocked and had no fight in them. Everything had to be done swiftly and deliberately with a demonstration of strength and will. No handcuffs were used, as their noise and appearance would break the trance and cause a break in concentration. I would make a quick exit as the door team member took up the rear. The pick-up was usually seen at some point by the undercover as they left the building to the unmarked car and this was when the junkie was identified.

I had devised my own quick-fire method of handcuffing and would place my hand on a junkie's shoulder and tell him in Spanish 'meda, meda', which means 'look, look', and I would have him put both hands up on the counter top and then tell him to interweave his fingers. Then I would grab his fingers with my fist so he couldn't move them. It was the quickest way to cuff someone with his own hands, and I took him backwards out the door to the car.

On the way out, I would walk around to this person who

had given me a particularly malevolent look and say, so everyone would hear me, 'Thank you, Indio, call me later.' I'd have had no connection with the guy but everyone now thought he was the rat. No one would touch him now either, selling or buying.

I would do the same thing to a street-corner pusher. I would walk up to him and say, 'Give me a call in an hour', and walk away. Nobody would go near him after that. He would have to go somewhere else to deal – Harlem or over to the West Side. I burned anyone who gave me bad vibrations. When two uniform cops told me that a Puerto Rican drug dealer named Benny Guzman, known as 'Scarface', had threatened to shoot a cop if he didn't 'fuck off' from The Big B, the restaurant from where he operated, I was furious. Threatening a cop with violence was not on. The uniforms asked me to pick up Scarface for serious drug sales and put him behind bars, but I told them I'd do better than that. 'Anyone known to be such a cop hater, or shooter, would make a great street informer.' The uniform cops laughed, thinking that this tough guy would never turn out to be a stoolie. 'Give me two weeks,' I said, 'and I'll have him working for me.' The uniformed cops just laughed louder.

During the following week, I made almost ten pick-ups from junkies for sales as they sat in The Big B. Junkies hung out at restaurants putting extra sugar in their coffee as they waited to score. To the trained eye, it meant that they were strung out, waiting around for someone to appear with their drugs. Some restaurants ran out of sugar, there were so many junkies waiting around to buy drugs. The sugar gave them a little high until they actually scored.

My pick-ups were all single collars – one or two in any night. Because I appeared for the pick-up, the street people knew Dick Tracy was working so the action set got too hot. But on two of those pick-ups, Scarface was sitting in The Big B. As I left with my prisoner, I would stare at Scarface and as our eyes met I would give him a nod of approval, or of appreciation, as if it was Scarface who had given me the tip-off. The job was about 90 per cent attitude. It was all about how you looked and conducted yourself. As the second week drew near, I collared another dealer and did the same to Scarface. It made it almost impossible for him to sell drugs on the street in that area.

Then one night, I went in to The Big B and made it look like I was going for another person, but instead plucked Scarface himself. My partner J.C. Connors picked up a second junkie. We took both of them to the station house and held Scarface on a make-believe possession. The second pick-up was released after the arresting officers pulled off a phoney line-up through a two-way mirror. His arrest was a ploy to carry the news about the arrest of Scarface back to the street and to let everyone know he was being grilled by Dick Tracy.

Benny Guzman was about twenty-five and had a reputation as a violent drug dealer and heroin user. He lived in the Henry Street tenements and had served time for dealing drugs and assault. He'd been slashed on the face by two black dealers, who later turned up badly beaten in an alleyway. On the street it was said that Guzman had beaten the two black dealers with a baseball bat. This incident cemented his reputation and the scar on his face gave him added menace.

I talked to Scarface about his problem – that he couldn't deal in his usual areas – and told him how he could repair the damage done to his reputation by passing on a little information. But Scarface was a tough guy and he wasn't for turning. He sat there with a sneer on his face. I let him go. Two days later, an undercover cop bought some heroin from him. Then late that night, I picked him up and put him into the back seat of the car with the detective who'd bought drugs from him. As usual, the undercover had a large brown grocery bag over his head with only his eyes showing.

Scarface was in the back seat of the car giving his tough-guy stare when I uncovered J.C. Connors. Scarface couldn't believe he had just sold drugs to a cop.

'All right, tough guy,' I said. 'Now is the time to choose: jail – and you're going down big time – or you work for me. The choice is yours, but you make it now. I'm not kidding around!'

Scarface was caught in a dilemma. Like most of those faced with the stark reality of jail or snitching, he chose to co-operate. So, within two weeks a potential cop shooter had become an informer, working with the cops he hated so much. Informers usually convinced themselves that they could use the cops to their own ends – that they weren't really snitching, but taking care of business in another way. All informers were the same. People involved in crime, and the drugs business in particular, who traded their friendship, loyalty and morality for money or to save themselves, were not known for their honesty. In official words, they were 'confidential informants', but to cops on the street they are known as 'stool pigeons', 'stoolies', 'snitches' or 'rats'. Cops never trusted a stoolie. You had to listen to everything they said with patience and not believe any of it until it was checked out thoroughly. You never want your case resting with a stoolie's testimony. In most cases, if you couldn't back up a stoolie's story in court with some corroborating evidence, your case went out the window.

Informants had to be registered with the police department, and under no circumstances could a registered informant be on parole or probation, but most cops didn't ask and didn't care.

Scarface became a good stoolie, but he was never fully trusted. He produced plenty of information, but stoolies also used their handlers – in his case, that was me – so you had to be very careful where to draw the line. They could not be an informant for too long before the real criminals knew who they were, so were expendable.

CHAPTER 11
A prince of the city

My arrest rate put me in line for promotion and, in late 1968, I joined the Special Investigating Unit. The SIU were not ordinary detectives, but the most aggressive and talented detectives in the NYPD. They were the elite, a breed apart from their brother officers. The SIU didn't bother with street junkies, they concentrated on the main players, the big heroin dealers. Each detective was hand-picked from all across the NYPD on the basis of talent, experience and accomplishment. They were detectives at the pinnacle of their careers. Their commanders felt that they got more production out of their men if they let them have their own lead. And it proved correct. SIU were responsible for the biggest seizures of narcotics in New York City.

In the early 1960s, a small squad of the best narcotics detectives had been thrown together for the French Connection case, which had led to the formation of the SIU, and every member of the unit worked non-stop to try to top Popeye Egan and Sonny Grosso's landmark bust of 66 kilos (a kilogram, or key, is equal to 2.2 pounds – this was enough to supply the entire American market at the time for eight months). No police unit in NYC probably bagged more hard drugs, busted more big-name dealers or created such chaos with the drug trade as the SIU.

The squad room for the SIU was an attic-type room on the fourth floor of the 1st Precinct building, which is now the NYPD Museum. Every room was panelled with dark wood, had high ceilings, and walls painted the depressing municipal green of all American public buildings. The squad room was drab, with a pockmarked wooden floor, ancient typewriters and old black standard phones on squat wooden desks. One end of the room was portioned into small cubicles with six-foot barriers for the SIU commanders and supervisory personnel. On the walls of the squad room were duty charts and rosters of the field teams. Newspaper clippings from the SIU's most important cases were also tacked to the walls, some with smart pencilled-in comments. The bulletin board held official police department memoranda and communications, but also handwritten notices announcing cars or suburban homes for sale, at prices no ordinary cop could afford.

I knew many of the detectives on the French Connection and other high-profile drugs cases. When the *French Connection* movie was being filmed, many of the SIU detectives got bit parts: Randy Jurgensen played the police sergeant who was in charge of the towing away of the Frenchman's car and asks him not to smoke; Joe Nunziata was the only one wearing a camel-hair coat – his own, of course – in the final shootout. When the movie was being filmed in the 1st Precinct station house, Sergeant Keating just happened to be on duty on the desk. He also just happened to hold an actor's equity card, so he got a bit part in the movie. Eddie Egan and others were given small parts too, and were technical advisers on other movies, like *The Godfather*. I got my copy of Robin Moore's book, on which the film was based, signed by Eddie Egan and Sonny Grosso.

The SIU detectives were known as 'princes of the city' because we operated with exemption, and with the arrogance of old Italian princes. We liked this description. We only worked the cases we considered important. I fell in love with SIU – the work and the people. We were all big, physical men in our twenties and thirties, who had served in the armed forces or had played high school and professional sports.

Some of the legendary detectives in the SIU at this time were Joe Nunziata, Les Dana*, Bob Leuci, Frank King, Eddie Codelia and Ray Viera. The most popular choice of attire was a three-quarter-length black leather jacket. We looked very stylish but, most importantly, we did not get dirty and did not smell. Some of the sharper detectives dressed like the gangsters they were working against with camel-hair coats draped over their silk suits and diamond rings on their pinkie fingers. They were sometimes known as the 'Pinkie-ring Squad'. Joe Nunziata was one of the snappiest dressers, always grooming his hair and checking his clothes. Frank King was a big, beefy Irishman, who dressed sharply and looked more like a mob guy than a cop.

The most common weapon used was the .38 revolver holstered on the hip, but some carried extra weapons – another pistol or a blackjack, a leather-covered hand weapon – and weren't afraid to use them. Eddie Codelia once shot four junkies who had jumped him in an undercover buy. The junkies had been armed with pistols and knives, but Codelia had fired first and shot all four. Two had died instantly – one shot in the head, the other shot in the heart – another had also received a head shot and was critically wounded, while the last assailant had been shot in the back as he was running out the door of the tenement.

There were many Irish cops in SIU during my time there, including Frank King, Dave Cody, Jack McClean, Captain Dan

Tange and Lieutenant John Egan. While the SIU detectives were the best in the business, the opportunity for corruption was rife and many took advantage of this – though not all detectives were crooked. A few of them conveniently looked the other way or had their own quaint notions of how to handle the problem.

When I arrived in SIU, there were rumours of pay-offs and actual drug dealing by detectives. The SIU were a law unto themselves and some detectives obtained money unlawfully by using their police authority to shake down narcotics suspects and extort, or steal, money or property from them. Sometimes an arrested drug dealer would offer a bribe in return for his release, and often that formality was bypassed: the detectives would simply take the money, voucher some for show and pocket most of the cash themselves.

I benefited financially at the time, but it was small change compared to what some of my colleagues made. Like every other working cop, I struggled to pay all my bills on my income and though the extra money helped, I got a bigger buzz from making quality cases. Sometimes I had several good cases going at once and I was working overtime trying to keep them all going. I had seen corruption and graft from my first days on the force, but to be accepted by other cops, you had to be like them. Some detectives would only show up at the precinct on payday dressed in their camel-hair coats and sporting diamond pinkie rings.

If you came into money, it wasn't the best idea to show it. If you didn't get too greedy, there was no trouble. Taking money from drug dealers was deemed justifiable by most cops. Most dealers would be out on the street on bail before the arresting officer was out of the court house, and they'd be right back dealing again. The drug dealers were so rich they could buy anybody – bondsmen, district attorneys and judges. They could be hurt or put out of business in only one way, and that was by taking their cash at the moment of arrest. Human beings are human beings. It doesn't matter what business you work in, there are no straight lines. There will always be shortcuts to financial gain or promotion. What man invents, man can circumvent. But I suppose that was then, now there are more safeguards put in place for cops to avoid the temptation of drugs and money.

In the SIU, the number of cases was not important, it was the quality of the case that counted. The eighty or so detectives in the SIU operated normally in small teams. While the team collectively picked the target of each investigation, one member of each team was usually acknowledged by the others as the team leader. The teams were their own bosses and made their own cases. Each team was composed of three, four or five male and female detectives operating under an experienced senior who was in turn responsible to a sergeant.

The SIU had a commanding officer, a deputy commanding officer, a captain, a lieutenant, and five sergeants – not nearly enough to exert supervisory pressure over so many detectives working in small teams throughout the city. Over the years, several commanders attempted to implement controls, all of which were resisted by the men, and all of which failed. The detectives and their superiors rarely came together as a unit.

The SIU detectives left their homes and met their team-mates at prearranged locations in the city. There was no supervisory control over the field teams, who only occasionally kept their superiors informed of their activities. Only a promotion, a transfer, Christmas party or the payday meeting brought the detectives into the squad room. The teams rarely used the office and usually met on the street.

CHAPTER 12

Busting Brothers

For my first assignment in the SIU, I was put with several other new detectives, or 'greenhorns', to investigate some lower-ranking drug dealers – this was to prove our worth. My first team members were two other Irish detectives, Pat McNeill* and Jim Thomas*. Both men were about ten years younger than me and dressed like hippies, with long, red, curly hair and handlebar moustaches. Both were from Irish cop families and Jim Thomas's father was a high-ranking officer in the NYPD.

A specialty of the SIU was 'Gypsy' wires – illegal taps on phones – as well as hidden recording devices. Using my army experience as a radio repairman, and learning from older detectives, I became something of a wiretapping and bugging expert. My field was dressing as a telephone repairman and making my way into a house or workplace to plant bugs. McNeill and Thomas had no experience of this, but were well versed as undercover men on the streets. We were given a file on major violators under investigation by the SIU and told to pick one.

I chose a wiseguy named Charlie Siena, also known as 'Charlie Brothers'. The only available photo of Charlie was from his youth rap sheet, which showed him with a black eye and other facial bruises. He had held up a drugstore, shot someone, got caught and then took a beating for his efforts. Brothers was connected to the Bonanno crime family, one of the five major New York mafia families. The Bonannos operated mainly in Brooklyn, Queens, Staten Island and Long Island.

We spent weeks investigating who Brothers' friends were and who he was connected to. I took some still shots of Brothers at his home in Queens, where he lived with his beautiful girlfriend. Every car he met was photographed and traced. Brothers turned out to be a well-connected individual – the Pan-Am Club in Queens was one of his favourite spots. I felt Charlie Brothers was well worth the extra surveillance, but he was a terror to tail as he drove like a madman on the highways and knew the city streets like a well-read book.

I decided to bug Brothers' car, but McNeill and Thomas got the bright idea that they could do this job themselves, probably to impress me. They went to the car and checked it and taped the bug into its place on the underside of the steering column. The three-foot-long copper-insulated antenna had to be extended, and this was usually stretched out along the folded-up lip end of the front dashboard; the regular radio antenna connection was then unscrewed so that the radio reception was mostly static, leaving the bug with a further transmission radius. So while McNeill and Thomas were fully preoccupied, Brothers came down the block and saw someone, as he thought, breaking into his car and yelled at them.

McNeill and Thomas took off in different directions as if they were on fire. If they were caught, they would blow the whole case and I knew our supervisors would be up in arms against them. They energetically jumped over hedges and fences as Charlie Brothers got into his car and took up the chase. Jim Thomas ran into a dead-end street, but then dashed into a front garden, rang the front doorbell, and when the door was answered, hurriedly flashed his detective shield. The owner couldn't believe his eyes and wouldn't move, until Thomas produced his gun. The owner let him in and Thomas locked the front door. From inside, he saw Charlie Brothers drive up, turn and go back down the street. The people in the house thought they were harbouring a criminal, but he told them to ring the 1st Precinct and get them to identify him. When the owner phoned and gave the detective's shield number, Thomas was identified. He then got on the phone and told the office to give the house address and phone number to me when I called in.

Thomas settled down as the owners brought him some coffee and goodies. He waited, for what seemed like an eternity, until the phone rang, and I asked for Detective Jim Thomas. Jim filled me in on what had happened and asked if Pat McNeill had got away. I said he had and that I'd be over to pick him up. It took some time for the heat to die down as the cops were also searching the area, believing the subject they were looking for was hiding in a back garden. All turned out well and, according to the team's tape, Brothers actually believed that it was a couple of junkie hippies who had tried to rob his car. Thomas and McNeill had to shave and cut their long hair for the duration of the investigation.

We next bugged the telephone in Brothers' apartment in Maspeth, Queens. The setup that I installed consisted of a little black box bug, which was attached to Brothers' telephone wire. The bug was located in the lobby ceiling and the wire was the same colour as any other running upwards. When the house phone was activated, the conversation, including the digits of the phone number the call was connected to, was recorded on a tape recorder. The tape was only activated when the phone was in use.

The team sat on the wire – sitting and listening, hour upon hour. It was long, tedious and mind-numbing work. Occasionally, we would glean nuggets of good information, but Charlie Brothers proved to be a wise phone operator. He never mentioned places or anything concrete on the phone and made most of his calls from public telephones picked, it seemed, at random. However, I detected that sometimes Brothers seemed a little high on the phone and thought he was probably smoking marijuana or snorting a little coke.

During the investigation, we discovered that the SIU had a registered informant, Manny Rivera, who was on the fringes of the Bonanno crime family, to which Charlie Brothers was connected. Word was put out that Manny Rivera was to be picked up, preferably on a possession charge. Several nights later, Rivera was arrested in possession of a small amount of junk.

The real mark of a detective is the interrogation, which is a matter of convincing a suspect to trust you. I became quite good at this, and I learned that suspects were much more manageable after they'd been sitting in a cell for a few hours with no means of communication and were told how expensive a lawyer would be or how much bail bonds cost. A suspect needs a friend or someone he can relate to. I came in on the interrogation and duly reminded Rivera that he was a registered informant and should not be dealing drugs, but that I would tell the Assistant DA that I deemed Rivera to be a well-connected street dealer, who was willing to co-operate further. We would supply a listing of the collars Rivera had previously given up and stress that without his help, our case would not have succeeded. We'd request a dismissal of Rivera's charges, which we knew the ADA would usually do. That's how it worked. Rivera would not have to appear in court or be confronted by the defendants at any time.

My tactic was to let Rivera think he was the centre of the universe, that he was very important and everybody cared about him. Rivera agreed and was released. He was not told that we'd tapped his phone and was not asked to give up Charlie Brothers, the real purpose of the operation.

I decided to push Rivera, but still didn't disclose what I wanted or that I was even aware of his connection with Charlie Brothers. Instead, I asked for information on someone other than Brothers, then came back a few days later and told Rivera that they were small fry and were of no interest, and that he'd have to come up with bigger fish, otherwise there was little good that could be reported back to the ADA who was handling his case.

A night or two later, Rivera turned up to meet me. He was high on drugs. I slapped him around a bit, nothing too much, but told him unless he gave me someone worth arresting this was his last night of freedom.

'There is this wiseguy,' he said, 'known as Charlie Brothers.' Rivera described how things worked. 'I never telephone him directly. I call an answering service. It must be a garage limo service or a contractor somewhere in Lower Manhattan, but you can leave a message that you called. You just leave your nickname, not your return number or anything because, if you did, he wouldn't know who you were and would never call you back. This way, you have given him your name, or what you are known as, and a number that you are always at for at least an hour. You will get a call back that day or the day after, but it is always within that set hour. He has a book where he puts your coded name, number and your set hour. Nothing is done right away. Then you set the night at wherever the delivery is to be made and he arrives at any time he feels like. Payment is on the spot. Money on consignment! He is reliable and usually has good-quality goods. On the heroin he supplies me, I can get three whacks at my end and I get no complaints from the dealers I supply to move it on the street. Of course, I also realise they whack their bundles and get out of my fifteen about twenty bags, so they can take care of themselves and make some profit.'

Rivera said Brothers was never armed but he usually had a heavy with him who was. He said he did not know where Brothers got his stuff from, but it sometimes smelled of boat diesel. Rivera felt it could be stored in a motor room or on a boat. Clever dealers soaked their narcotics packages in a bucket of diesel oil for a few moments, and then wrapped it in South American newspapers, which they could get from international paper stands, for a few days. This gave the buyers the impression the junk was fresh from South America. It was a misleading tactic and if the junk was seized, it could also fool the cops.

Some days later, Rivera phoned Brothers and waited for the return call, which came about 7.40 p.m. Rivera had to act really confident because, according to him, Brothers could detect any glimmer of doubtfulness in the tone of a customer. The drop was to take place in Alphabet City in the East Village. I parked my car on Avenue C, facing south, one block north of Rivera's block, which was a one-way street going east. McNeill and Thomas were parked at the kerb in a New Jersey registered car on the north side of Rivera's street, an equal distance between the corner of Avenue C and Rivera's apartment house. My car was responsible for the food and hot drinks and I had another cop, Tony Morello, with me.

The day passed slowly. I sat patiently, half down in the front seat where I could easily see the intersection. Experience had taught me that if I parked my car directly under the street light less of the interior was visible. I perked up when I saw a car approaching. Brothers was not alone, he had a front-seat passenger beside him. The car pulled across the intersection to enter Rivera's block and, on a signal, Thomas and McNeill's car pulled out on to the road. The car stopped suddenly and McNeill got out to look under the hood. Brothers' car pulled up a few feet from the stalled car and Morello and I jumped out of our car, either side of Charlie's, shields pinned to our chests in clear view, just in case the drug dealers thought it was a stick-up. At the same time, Thomas jumped out and, with McNeill, surrounded Charlie's car, guns pointing at each of the occupants. With revolver drawn, I ordered them out.

Brothers opened the door slowly. He put his hands in the air to show he was unarmed and was ordered to put them down, as there was no need to alarm the public. Brothers then turned to place his hands on the car roof. The passenger did likewise. The keys were handed to me and Brothers was quickly patted down. He was clean. His partner was searched likewise, and a small revolver stuck in his waistband was confiscated. They were both cuffed and escorted to the car with its hood up and put in the back seat. Morello was given the keys of Brothers' car and I went back to my own car. The cars drove one behind the other to a prearranged location at 14th Street, underneath the East River Drive.

When we reached 14th Street, Brothers and his partner were taken out and searched thoroughly. Brothers began acting very cocky, demanding to know what he was being arrested for. We found nothing on him and he became more belligerent. The cops had got his friend on a gun possession charge, but there was nothing on Brothers. However, I explained that possession of anything illegal in the passenger section of the car was presumptive evidence of possession by everyone in the car. Therefore, he as the owner and operator of the car was responsible for his passenger's firearm. It was enough to make an arrest stick – maybe not get a conviction, but the arrest was quite within the legal limits of the law.

We opened the trunk and found a shoebox with $25,000. The rest of the car was thoroughly searched – the spare tyre was taken out and checked, under the seats were searched, the back seat was removed, the hub caps taken off, door and ceiling panels were checked, along with the dashboard, glove compartment and ashtrays, even the plastic covers were taken off the interior roof lights.

The passenger gave his name as Thomas Marchione and confessed that he owed four years on a previous ten-year bank stick-up and that he would have to do these four years before he even started to do time on this charge. He asked me to throw the gun charge away. I didn't reply.

I took out a large newspaper-wrapped package. When Brothers caught sight of it, he grew quite nervous. I calmly displayed it to the other cops and turned to Brothers and said to him, 'Tell them what it is, Charlie.'

Charlie Brothers would not say what it was, so I said, 'It's the goods that he had on him when you got him out of the car on Avenue C!' Taking great delight in these revelations, I said, 'Tell them how you did it!' When there was no answer from Brothers, I said, 'Oh, of course, that's too much to expect of you, so let me tell them how you did it!'

I explained that Brothers had concealed the package inside a longer parcel, that had been put inside his trousers. When he had got out of the car in the darkness and stretched his arms upwards to show he was not armed, the package had dropped down the inside of his trousers and onto his foot, so he could kick it quickly under the parked car. However, when I'd gone back to my car after the superficial body search, I'd spotted the package under the parked car. I'd retrieved it and kept it for the right moment as a surprise for Brothers and his pal.

Brothers was arrested, although I knew that he would probably not be convicted, because the laws of search and seizure could not prove possession of the goods beyond reasonable doubt. We both knew he'd had it in his possession, but the law would not convict him. I would have to testify that I saw Brothers in physical possession of the package and also that he let it slide to the ground, but how could I see it as it passed under the material of his trouser leg? Brothers was brought to a night court and released on bail.

I took Tommy Marchione and spoke quietly to him, saying that he should not forget this favour. I hailed a cab and let him go free. I didn't see the point of putting him away for about ten years on the old gun charge and new narcotics charge. Besides, it was always good to be owed a favour, especially by a connected mob guy. When Brothers' case came to court, it was thrown out because possession of the drugs could not be proved. Brothers went free.

Initially my aim was to bust Brothers, but somebody like Charlie could be useful in the future. He might flip and give me that big case that every cop dreamed of. The end result was that I made a lifelong friend by actually telling the court the true facts of the arrest, that I did not actually see Brothers in possession of the package. We became mutual friends by my handling of the case – not trying to make the possession charges stick by lying. It was also not forgotten in certain circles that I had released Tommy Marchione, who would certainly have been convicted on a weapons charge.

CHAPTER 13
The Hotel Taft bust

In September 1969 I travelled home to Ireland on a three-week holiday to visit my family. While there, I received a telegram to say I'd been promoted to detective second grade, which added about $10,000 a year to my pay packet.

I returned to New York a well-rested and content man. Things were going well. Sure, I had marital problems, but who hadn't? I was looking forward to new cases. With some good collars under my belt, I was assigned to another team, which included Joe Novoa, who became a loyal partner and friend. Novoa looked Italian, but had been born in the Castilian region of Spain and, at five foot seven inches, he'd just made the height requirement for the NYPD. At first, we worked with several other SIU detectives, until Carl Aguiluz joined us in February 1970 and we became a three-man team. Aguiluz was about five foot eleven inches, and was quite dark and swarthy. He'd been born in Honduras and joined the NYPD in his late twenties having previously worked as an electronics technician and trained as an aeroplane pilot. After he joined the NYPD, Aguiluz worked undercover in New York for some time as a member of the Communist Party and had been assigned to the SIU in June 1969, the same month as Novoa.

Today in the narcotics division there are all kinds of sophisticated technologies for collecting information while undercover officers and informants penetrate criminal organisations, but in the 1960s and 1970s it was totally different. Our specialty was wiretaps. We used to bug houses, cars and just about anywhere we could to get recordings of drug dealers doing business. We used every trick in the book and a few that weren't, but that was the way it had to be done to get a conviction.

We planted bugs in the drug-mixing 'factories', in apartments that we broke into with a safe-and-lock expert when there was no one there. In these factories, all the wall sockets and light fixtures had been detached and were open to view so that no electrical bugs could be hidden within them or powered by their electricity. So it was a complicated procedure to bug them.

Federal law prohibited government agencies from monitoring telephones, and it was not easy to get a warrant to tap a phone. There had to be sufficient reason to believe, established by tangible evidence, that the telephones to be wired were being used by suspected criminals and could lead police either to their apprehension or to the prevention of further crimes. We also had to show that the telephones themselves were being used to further illicit criminal enterprises. This itself could be a bit tricky to substantiate, but most judges, depending on the circumstances and the applicants, would issue the warrants. The SIU, however, didn't seem to care about warrants – they used wires and bugs at every opportunity, and mostly without even applying for a warrant.

Information on one tape could lead to another wiretap and then another, and so on. Each tape recorder had to be attended to at least once a day – even at weekends. While Carl Aguiluz was an exceptional wireman and bugging expert, he was not as committed as the rest of us. He went home on Friday evening and came back to work on Monday morning. So Novoa and I checked the tape recorders and bugs on Saturday and Sunday, while Aguiluz was enjoying his time off with his family.

The team had to respond to information as it was gathered. Surveillance had to be set up and tails implemented. It was hard, painstaking work. We lived out of our cars – sitting on surveillance for days on end. Novoa and I became very close, but there was not so much closeness with Aguiluz. To me, he was a more detached person, not as warm as Novoa. Aguiluz always seemed to be thinking about something else, as if he had other things going on. There were rumours that he could not be trusted, that he had worked undercover with the feds, so many of the older hands in SIU were reluctant to work with him.

New York City was the main port of entry and the distribution centre for much of the narcotics that came into the country. Cocaine didn't make its mark until the mid-1980s. In the 1960s and 1970s, heroin was the main drug and it came in mainly from Peru and Colombia through airline flights or the shipping lanes.

There was a big difference between South American drug dealers and the Mafia. The Mafia had been in the drugs trade since the 1920s and had a limitless supply from the Far East and Europe. Their business was based on their capacity to deliver – always. Mafia dealers extended credit and waited for payment. Foreign distributors trusted them and were willing to wait for their money too. The South Americans had a different way of operating – their prices were lower and they moved through the narcotics trade with carloads of drugs and money. This made them easier to work against. Everyone in the SIU wanted to work the South Americans. Catching a Mafia drug dealer was hard work because they rarely came into personal contact with the drugs – it was usually farmed out to the lower echelons – but the South Americans carried both their drugs and money with them.

South American drug mules would arrive in New York and any other number of big cities, mostly on Sunday mornings when only a skeleton crew of officers were working at customs. There would be up to a dozen mules onboard South American airlines, in groups of three or four, all unknown to one another to prevent them giving up another party if they were caught. Most usually got through, though some were caught; it was an acceptable risk.

Other groups of smugglers took the goods from these mules to prearranged meets at crowded outdoor locations, like Grand Central Station. Each group had a different pick-up point that they didn't know about in advance. When a sale was made, one of the group was contacted and advised that the goods were to be picked up. The payment was made at another hotel unknown to the group members. Each group had a hotel room and location where no one resided. They would deliver the narcotics in a suitcase or shopping bag to the unoccupied room and leave it there. The paying customer was then given a key and would go alone to pick up the drugs.

How we knew all this was the result of our first big case on 31 March 1970. It was the seizure of twenty-eight kilos of pure heroin at the Taft Hotel, found in the room of Argentine businessmen Raoul Leguizamon and Alberto Diaz. The Taft Hotel, on the east side of Seventh Avenue between 50th and 51st streets, was once one of Times Square's best-known tourist landmarks. It offered low-priced and dependable tourist accommodation and, when it opened, it was the city's third-largest hotel, with twenty storeys and 1,750 rooms. Because of its size, it was easy for some of the rooms to be used for illegal activities.

We knew the *modus operandi* in this type of narcotics commerce. When the Argentineans produced the shipment ordered, the buyers, or receivers, had to make a minimum down payment. After they had successfully delivered the goods, they would complete the payoff to the crime syndicate involved – the Union Corse, a criminal syndicate operating out of Corsica and Marseilles, who were the primary organisers of what was known as the 'French Connection'. The wholesale price for twenty-eight kilos was about $300,000.

The lead for this case came from the Café Madrid, a bar and grill on the north side of 14th Street, just west of Seventh Avenue. One of its owners was Frankie Ramos. Another case – the McAlpin Wine Jugs Case – had been made from South American narcotics traffickers in this restaurant. Several of them were arrested in the McAlpin Hotel on Herald Square at the corner of Broadway and 34th Street. The traffickers had used wine jug bottles with the straw basket halfway up the bottle. The glass in the bottles was in two parts: the top section in view was filled with wine and the lower part held heroin, or cocaine. Two men under surveillance evaded arrest in the Wine Jugs Case, and one of them figured prominently in the Taft Hotel bust.

For months after the Wine Jugs Case, a telephone tap remained on the two public payphones at the Café Madrid. Most people in the narcotics business talked very little on a business or home phone but felt a little more secure on a public phone, as they were more difficult to tap. But SIU detectives sat in their cars and listened freely to the voices on the phones. Any moves and meetings were known in advance, and anyone arriving at the restaurant who had previously made an appointment was identified as they arrived or left. Binoculars were always on hand, and we had a special one keyed to see licence plates after dark.

Around 11.30 on a February night when the team members had just decided to call it a day, a white-haired, well-dressed South American male bounced to the sidewalk with all the muscle co-ordination of a well-trained athlete. His full head of white hair and grey silk suit made him stand out from the other late-night walkers. The man was later identified as Raoul Leguizamon, the missing Wine Jugs smuggler. On a hunch, I moved my car slowly to follow Leguizamon along the street where he suddenly waved a taxi down and slipped into the taxi's rear seat. I contacted Joe Novoa – who was in his own car with Carl Aguiluz – on the portable radio to tell him what was happening, and in case my car was made. The standard leapfrog surveillance would then be used – changing one car for another so as not to alert the suspects.

The taxi drove down 14th Street to Eighth Avenue north, on Eighth Avenue to 51st Street, then west to Seventh Avenue. I followed in one car, and Novoa and Aguiluz in their car. Leguizamon got out of the taxi at Seventh Avenue and walked under the well-lit overhanging entrance of the Taft Hotel. Aguiluz jumped out of the second car and went into the hotel lobby, while I found a parking spot and put my official Police Department card on display to avoid the tow-away parking restrictions.

I quickly found the all-night security officer, who turned out to be a cop buff, and was constantly up and down the floors on the lookout for hotel burglars, prostitutes and pimps and any illegal activities. The security man ran a check for the occupant I described and showed me the card he'd filled in: his name, where he came from, flight time and number, and that he had checked in earlier that day.

I asked the hotel security man to make a room available for us; he also provided coffee and tea, rolls, butter, bacon and scrambled eggs. Novoa arrived after parking his car and the team got down to work. The team's room was between Leguizamon's (Room 87) and his passage to the elevators. A coffee container lid was put in the room doorjamb to keep it open so that we could see easily all movements at that end of the floor. Aguiluz went to the security man and returned with a telephone record showing the calls made from Room 87. Especially important were those calls within the city area, but there were overseas calls too. I placed a call to our team sergeant, Gabriel 'Steph' Stefania, and notified him about where we were and the possibilities of a case.

Sergeant Stefania arrived early in the morning with two more men, so that when Leguizamon left the building, he would have two fresh tails on his heels. After breakfast, Leguizamon, wearing a dark overcoat, took a brisk walk in the snow-speckled streets up to the Sheraton Hotel, three to four blocks north on Seventh Avenue. He disappeared somewhere into the upper floors of the hotel, while his tails lingered in the lobby and the corridors. Many hotels in the area housed the staff of various overseas airlines, including those from South America, who spent their time off resting before the return trip. Fifteen minutes later, Leguizamon left through the main door on Seventh Avenue, but this time he was wearing a tan raincoat and was carrying a small leather pouch. He walked back to the Taft Hotel and took a seat on one side of the lobby.

A few minutes later, another man entered and Leguizamon stood up. They were some twelve or fourteen feet apart but it was obvious they knew each other. The new face on the scene went into the restaurant of the hotel bar and made a head motion to Leguizamon that he would be inside. Leguizamon then got into the crowded elevator, closely followed by his tail, and went directly to his own room, past our observation point. After about ten minutes, Leguizamon went back downstairs and entered the bar, where he went directly to a table where the other man was seated. Leguizamon had the brown leather pouch with him and placed it on the table. Sergeant Stefania and I were stationed outside the bar, in full view of the suspects' table.

Leguizamon pushed the pouch across the table to the other

man. As soon as he put his hand out and lifted the pouch, we stepped forward quickly and quietly, without attracting attention. We identified ourselves with our gold detective shields in the hollow of our left hands, leaving our right hands free for any quick movements. There were none. Both men were escorted to Leguizamon's room where we found sixty-two pounds of heroin in large plastic bags. The other man was identified as Alberto Diaz. He was taken to his room where we found several empty brown leather suitcases with Raoul Leguizamon's name on them.

We later learned that Raoul Leguizamon and Alberto Diaz were drug mules who had travelled to New York as tourists on several occasions. Raoul Leguizamon, a former Argentine soccer player, was sentenced to seven years, while Alberto Diaz's case was dismissed due to a lack of evidence of narcotics possession.

Evidence of Arrest: Twenty-eight kilos of heroin seized by Detectives Daly, Novoa and Aguiluz at the Hotel Taft, 31 March 1970.

Sergeant Gabriel Stefania, prisoner Alberto Diaz, Detective Peter Daly and prisoner Raoul Leguizamon at the desk in the 18th Precinct, 31st March 1970.

CHAPTER 14
The 105 Kilo Case

There are cases that all cops hope and train for – a case that opens the door to bigger and better things. When a cop went through the door, his life and career were made and he'd never have to worry again.

In April 1970, I went through that door.

My big case was the arrest of four South American drug dealers and the seizure of 100 kilos of heroin and cocaine at an address on West 19th Street. It was the biggest seizure of narcotics in NYPD history, dwarfing the sixty-six kilos of heroin seized in the French Connection Case. The day after the arrests, a newspaper photo went up on the SIU bulletin board of a group of detectives, including myself, Novoa and Aguiluz, standing behind a table on which reposed 100 kilos of narcotics. Over this photo was pasted a hand-lettered headline: 'Can You Top This?'

It began late in the evening of 14 April 1970. Myself, Novoa and Aguiluz were on surveillance at the Café Madrid in Lower Manhattan. We became suspicious of four people in a car with Florida licence plates. They were later identified as Emilio Diaz Gonzalez, Jose Luis Mulas, Jorge Rodriquez Arraya and Elena Risso. We had been on surveillance there for weeks and four newcomers to the Café Madrid stood out. They were wearing tropical light clothing, which brought them to our attention because April in New York is cold and rainy. Two of the men stayed in the car, while the other man and the woman went into the restaurant. I got out of my car, walked slowly by their car before returning to my own. I told Novoa there was something suspicious about them and radioed Aguiluz in his car that we were going to tail them.

Not long after, the man and woman walked out of the Café Madrid with some others, shook hands and got into the car. The woman drove. We followed, with Aguiluz in his car and Novoa and myself in mine. We used the usual leap-frog formation and kept in contact with two-way radios. The car stopped at an all-night deli and some of the passengers went in to buy groceries. I parked my car in an alleyway and Novoa followed them into the deli. Novoa had been born in Spain and understood what they were saying. 'Don't buy any bread,' one of them said, 'we have plenty of bread at home.' This meant they were staying in an apartment and not in a hotel. We followed the car as it made its way to a hotel in Chelsea, where it stopped and a bag of groceries was given to a man in the lobby.

The car made a u-turn and headed back west. They left Lower Manhattan and went up the West Side Highway and across the George Washington Bridge to the vicinity of Fort Lee in New Jersey. This was outside the jurisdiction of the NYPD, but if deemed in 'hot pursuit', action could be taken. We agreed to stop the car when our chance arose.

It looked like they didn't know where they were going or else they had made the tail and were deliberately misleading us. (Much later, I found out that the group had an apartment in New Jersey that they were possibly trying to prevent us from finding.) The car drove into the parking lot of the Toll Gate Motel in Fort Lee. I followed them in and, when I stopped the suspects' car, it took off again. We knew we had to stop them getting away. Aguiluz overtook their car, while I drove in tight behind and boxed them in. We got out and approached them carefully. One of the occupants asked what the problem was. I told them it was because they were acting suspicious at a late hour of night.

I had learned long ago that the only way to catch bad guys was to bend the rules – and if you were going to do that, you needed guys around you who were willing to do the same. We had to find some reason to get the suspects to return to New York where the car was registered and, more importantly, where we had jurisdiction. Aguiluz soon thought of a reason and asked for the paperwork of the car.

Elena Risso said the paperwork was in her handbag, which was in a suitcase in the trunk. When the suitcase was opened, the proper paperwork was not there. Emilio Gonzalez was handcuffed and put in Aguiluz's car, while Novoa got into the suspects' car, sitting in the back with the woman, Elena. Aguiluz and I followed behind. I was tail-end Charlie and drove with my mind totally alert. My drug antenna was up – I could smell junk! Aguiluz, like Novoa, could understand and speak Spanish, though, of course, they made no mention of this and hoped to pick up some snippets of whispered conversation. We stopped first at the Toll Gate Motel to ask the manager if the four were residents. He said he thought they had been and that they had checked out earlier. The manager brought Novoa and Aguiluz in to show them the rooms.

Novoa and Aguiluz went into the motel with Emilio Gonzalez, while I sat in the car with the three others, who were very uptight. 'Uno momento, por favor,' was all the Spanish I could manage to say. As the three others came back out of the motel, a bit of an altercation took place. Gonzalez, who was a big, well-built man, became embroiled in an argument with Aguiluz. I quickly jumped out and gave Gonzalez a kick in the groin. As he bent over in sudden pain, I slapped him twice across the face. In the struggle, Gonzalez's gold watch sprung off his wrist. I picked up the watch and gave it back to Gonzalez, who muttered a thanks in Spanish and put it back on his wrist. But when we were back in the car, I noticed it was gone. Aguiluz had taken it off him. Gonzalez was very upset about it. I thought it was a wrong thing to do. If you take money, people don't really mind, but something like a watch is personal. But Aguiluz was like that – he was a cold-hearted bastard. When I thought of it later this was probably what the argument was about.

The three-car convoy drove back to the city, stopping six times when Gonzalez pointed out buildings where his apartment was, then saying he was wrong and confused.

When the cars got to the area of Grove Street and Seventh Avenue in Greenwich Village on the Lower West Side of Manhattan, Aguiluz stopped the car, got out and approached my car. He said we should end the charade, we were back in the city now and we could identify the individuals fully.

We all got out on the street, while Novoa took the keys of the suspects' car. Each of the four suspects was searched and Aguiluz found that Gonzalez had three South American passports with the same photo, but issued in three different names by three different countries. He was arrested for falsifying documents. We then searched the interior of the car where Novoa found a pearl-handled .32 calibre revolver beneath the front seat, where Gonzalez had originally been sitting. This was the reason all four were arrested under the Sullivan Act, the possession of a concealed firearm. All four were presuméd guilty – nobody admitting to ownership of the gun – and were arrested and their car seized.

We took them to the 6th Precinct station house on Charles Street in the Village, but before putting them in the holding cage, all their personal property was taken out and put in separate piles on a table. Male and female prisoners could not be mixed together, so the three men were put in the holding cage, while Elena Risso sat outside on a chair. After a time, Gonzalez asked to use the toilet, but as he was passing the table he grabbed a piece of paper, stuffed it in his mouth and began to chew it. I grabbed him by the throat, and the others rushed over, but despite our efforts to stop him, he managed to swallow the paper. Risso also ran to the table and started to rip up pieces of paper.

Gonzalez was restrained and put back in the holding pen, while Risso was handcuffed and put back on her chair. We sat down and tried to recall what was on this piece of paper and why it was so important. Luckily, we had reviewed the personal effects of the suspects several times, and Aguiluz remembered that the papers were rent receipts and the missing piece of paper had contained an address – 210 West 19th Street. Not surprisingly, he could not recall the apartment number.

It was now about three in the morning. Aguiluz and I took all four sets of keys found on the suspects and went to the address on West 19th Street, an apartment house in the Chelsea area. We couldn't risk ringing a doorbell so late at night, so we tried all the keys until we gained entrance into the building. There were six floors in the building with eight apartments on each floor, so we started at the bottom floor and worked our way up. We examined all the apartment doors for locks similar to the keys we carried – an 'A' lock, which had a special round key. When we got to the fourth floor, we noticed the round lock on the door of apartment 4-F. Aguiluz quietly tried the key. It worked! I rang the bell just in case the apartment was occupied – we did not want to be surprised or surprise anyone inside. No one answered and Aguiluz opened the door.

We went into the apartment with guns drawn. 'Police! Anybody here?' we shouted. There was no one present, but we found what looked like the aftermath of a party, with a number of empty wine bottles and used glasses. We searched the apartment and I found the ID for two of those we had arrested. I also found a South American police ID (which I still have), handcuff keys, which I never handed over, and the passport of a South American, who I later found out was doing time in the US for drug smuggling.

We went through the rest of the apartment and searched the closets, which contained both male and female clothing. There were two locked closets in the foyer that we couldn't open. Assuming there was a good reason for this security, I phoned Novoa who was guarding the prisoners at the station house. I didn't use the phone in the apartment as I suspected other agencies might have it tapped, so I left Aguiluz alone in the apartment and went outside to find a street phone. Talking in code, I advised Novoa that things looked promising and I would call him later. Because of the deep secrecy involved in narcotics cases, nothing was ever said on the telephone – not on any phone, even one in an NYPD precinct house.

Again using the street phone, I contacted Detective John Kidd at his home. Kidd was a locksmith specialist in the Burglary, Safe, Loft and Truck Squad and was known as a 'lock-pick man' because he could get into locks that no one else could. I gave him a street address to meet me at and that was all – I didn't give him any further information.

Kidd met me on the street and I took him to the apartment. As Kidd worked on the closets, Aguiluz lay down on a couch to nap. I checked around for documents and phone bills for any long-distance calls and took down the numbers for further investigation. Then I put all the notes, address books and photos into a large envelope.

Kidd took forty minutes to open the first closet, which contained five large empty suitcases. The first suitcase was put on its end and tapped against the floor, which created a residue of white powder.

I had a small tester kit, something all narcotics detectives were supposed to carry so that if they arrested someone they suspected was carrying drugs, they could test the substance immediately for content and quality. Each kit contained a vial partially filled with Marquis reagent and a plastic spoon. If a small amount of tested powder, mixed with the fluid, turned pink, it was heroin – if it turned bright red, it was high-quality heroin. When I tested the first sample, it turned bright red. Kidd then went to work on the second closet. Aguiluz was still asleep and when Kidd managed to unlock the second closet he opened it slowly.

'Jesus, this has gotta be the biggest haul ever,' he said.

John Kidd and I stood staring in disbelief. I woke Aguiluz. We couldn't believe how much narcotics was there. Dozens of individually wrapped packages, in units of a kilo and a half-kilo, were wrapped in South American newspapers stacked on top of each other. Myself and Aguiluz counted them out; we guessed it must be somewhere between 105 and 110 kilos.

CHAPTER 15
Redux: The 100 Kilo Case

While we were removing the packages from the closet, at a time when Kidd was out of earshot, Aguiluz suggested that we keep some narcotics for our informers' supply – that is, paying off informers with drugs for information on other dealers. I agreed, and we placed several packages of heroin and cocaine in a small suitcase, which I then placed in the trunk of my car. At that time, it was common for cops to pay their informants with a bag or two of heroin taken directly from a bust. Though the practice was plainly illegal and fraught with risk, morally, among cops, it was seen as a necessary evil.

Aguiluz called Novoa and told him we had made a fantastic arrest, that he'd never seen so much narcotics in one place. Novoa did not believe him or thought it was an exaggeration, so Aguiluz told him to come up and see for himself. Novoa broke the news to our four suspects. The woman started crying. The others began cursing in Spanish and shaking their heads in despair. When Novoa did arrive, he couldn't believe it either. Aguiluz told Novoa about the narcotics he had secreted and Joe agreed it was fine.

I called our supervisor, Lieutenant John Egan, who told us he would be straight down, and I also called a friend in the Assistant DA's office and told him to make up search warrants. Outlining the situation, I asked for search warrants that gave the team permission to search the apartment, even though we already had. This was something that had to be overlooked because, technically, we had gained entry illegally. Aguiluz drove to the ADA's office at Centre Street to swear out the warrants before a judge, so the entry and search would be legal. After Aguiluz returned with the search warrants, myself, Novoa, Aguiluz, Lieutenant Egan and others met with the press at the apartment, where we posed for photographs and gave interviews.

The media, always on the lookout for a popular name, called the seizure the '100 Kilo Case', as we had turned over 100 kilos, approximately 40 kilos of heroin and 60 kilos of cocaine, to the police property clerk, at 400 Broome Street. It certainly had a better ring to it than the 105 Kilo Case – but Aguiluz didn't plan on letting those extra packages make the news.

The four South Americans arrested were brought to jail in White Street and formally identified as Elena Aquirre de Risso aged thirty-nine of Montevideo in Uruguay, a dressmaker in whose name the apartment had been leased; Emilio Diaz Gonzalez also known as Alfredo Picardo, a thirty-nine-year-old salesman, also of Montevideo; Jose Luis Mulas, aged forty, a fireman from Madrid in Spain; and Jorge Rodriquez Arraya, aged forty-six, an importer from Santiago in Chile.

Each of them was released on bail of $100,000. This was a lot of money, but it was paid in cash by their lawyer. Jose Luis Mulas and Jorge Arraya fled to Spain, and Elena Risso also skipped the country. After Emilio Gonzalez was released on bail, he was rearrested by the FBI who also had him under surveillance for narcotics trafficking. Another $50,000 was added to his bail. I later found out that all this bail money came from an apartment in New Jersey, and it was probably no coincidence that the suspects were driving to Jersey.

At a later date, Emilio Gonzalez tried to escape from federal prison with six other major South American drug dealers. The exercise yard was on the top of the cell block and the escapees cut the surrounding security wire and tied sheets together to make good their flight. The makeshift ladder was not long enough and Gonzalez jumped to the ground but broke his leg and was recaptured. Six months later he again escaped with the six other South American drug dealers. They again cut the wire and made a makeshift ladder by tying sheets together, but this was just a distraction. A visiting priest had smuggled in a key that opened every door in the prison and the seven top-security prisoners just walked out on a Sunday morning to a fleet of waiting limousines, which drove them away and across the Mexican border. The escape was covered up by the federal authorities, who went with the escape-by-makeshift-ladder story, such was the embarrassment of an inside job. The priest, who had a brother involved with organised crime, was convicted of helping the narcotics traffickers to escape. I later heard Gonzalez was killed in a shootout with police somewhere in South America.

Elena Risso was arrested in South America and taken back to the United States and housed in the Metropolitan Correctional Center. She planned an escape with the help of another inmate, Raoul Martinez, and two prison guards. Martinez was found with $40,000 in his cell, and was moved, ending his involvement. But the two guards were each given $5,000 up front with the promise of another $20,000 each when Risso was free. They got her out to the doctor's office on a ruse that she was sick, where some accomplices picked her up. They had her in a car when FBI agents arrived and arrested Risso's accomplices and later the guards. Risso was returned to the Correctional Center. She had turned informer before the escape and was needed in some big South American drug-dealing cases, so she was going nowhere. She gave up a lot of people, including many already doing time.

There were many unanswered questions relating to our massive drugs seizure. The apartment in New Jersey used by the drug dealers was reputed to have $300,000 hidden there, but no one knows what happened to the money. The suspects' car was parked by Novoa outside the 6th Precinct station house on Charles Street, but when I went outside to get identification marks and the registration of the car, it was no longer there. The team members had vouchered the car but, strangely enough, not even the hire company enquired about it. News of the arrests had got out to someone in the know – good guys or bad guys – and somebody connected to them had picked up the car. Whatever else was in the car remains a mystery to this day.

While the 100 Kilo Case was the pinnacle of my career as an NYPD detective, little did I know at the time that it would also be the worst thing that ever happened to me. The FBI had already become involved in the case as the transportation of narcotics into the United States, or across state borders, was a federal crime. We did not know that the feds had also had the same group of narcotics traffickers under surveillance, which meant they had had us under surveillance.

As for the five kilos or so that Aguiluz had put in the trunk of my car – a week later, he asked me for the suitcase, which I transferred to his car. Aguiluz said he was going to sell the drugs as he needed some cash in a hurry. We didn't talk about it, and I was content to let Aguiluz take care of it. We were just happy to get something out of it. Aguiluz used his brother-in-law, Sal Bouteriera, as the outlet. Sal Bouteriera contacted a friend of his, Frankie Ramos – yes, the very same guy whose restaurant we'd had under surveillance – who found buyers for the drugs.

Left to right: Alfreido Picardo, Jose Aparicio, Elena Aguirre de Risso, Detective Carl Aguiluz and, bent over, Jorge Araya.

The largest seizure of narcotics – 100 kilos – made by the NYPD up to that date, 15 April 1970. Arresting officers Detective Peter Daly, 6th from left; Detective Carl Aguiluz 3rd from right, Detective Joe Novoa, extreme right.

CHAPTER 16
Harlem hit

There was a great deal of competition between the law enforcement agencies, and no love lost between any of them. NYPD investigators resented working with the FBI, as the feds were known to seize the glory in joint investigations. The FBI's use of informants had always been a source of contention between the two agencies as well. The NYPD's informants were kept on an informal basis, while FBI ones were on a retainer. The FBI had substantially more to spend on information. The NYPD was envious of the FBI's tactics and their seemingly unlimited supply of funds. The Drug Enforcement Administration (DEA) was interested in cutting into South American drug dealers and beating the SIU to the arrests, too. They were also interested in arresting some SIU detectives who were engaged in illegal wiretapping and other nefarious activities.

At the time, I was under pressure at home. Most cops' marriages are risky propositions and many end in divorce. The reasons for the break-ups are many – the long and unpredictable hours, as cases often led to weeks and months of long absences. At times I felt like a stranger in my own home. My mind was always elsewhere, planning another case or worrying about the other events I was involved in. I am a natural worrier and even worried when I have nothing to worry about. Like most cops, I was unable to talk to my wife about the stress and trauma of the job.

Stress and strain eventually took its toll on me, mentally and physically, so that by the end of 1970 I was a nervous wreck. My worries became real in November 1970 when our team was broken up and both Joe Novoa and I were transferred out of SIU. I was reassigned to the 32nd Detective Squad in Harlem Central, while Novoa was sent to the 76th Precinct in South Brooklyn. Aguiluz stayed in the SIU for another few months, but he too was eventually transferred to a precinct in South Brooklyn.

Harlem Central at one time was an Irish and then an Italian area, but by 1950 all of the whites had left Harlem. By 1960, much of the black middle class had left too. At the same time, control of organised crime had shifted from Jewish and Italian syndicates to local black and Puerto Rican groups that were somewhat less formally organised. From the mid-1960s to 1970s, the drug addiction rate in Harlem was ten times higher than the NYC average and twelve times higher than the US as a whole. Of the 30,000 drug addicts then estimated to live in NYC, 15,000–20,000 lived in Harlem. Property crime was pervasive, and the murder rate was six times higher than New York's average. Half of the children in Harlem grew up with one parent, or none, and lack of supervision contributed to juvenile delinquency. The 28th and 32nd precincts served the areas of Central Harlem and I was assigned to the 32nd.

From the time I left the SIU in 1970 until my retirement, I worked as a detective investigating murders, assaults and robberies. My days working narcotics were over and I was glad. The SIU really had been my downfall. As a narcotics detective, I had some really brilliant cases and even had the big one. The 100 Kilo Case had brought me to new heights, but also brought me to new depths. Greed had got to me. I sold my honour and my soul for money.

I blamed my surroundings but, in the end, I could only blame myself. Nobody had forced me to do anything. Now I was out. There would be no more big-money cases. Narcotics was behind me and there would be no more temptation – there was no money to be made in the 32nd Detective Squad. It was a weight off my shoulders. It was as simple as that. In the 32nd, I would be catching real crooks – bank robbers, stick-up men, murderers. The robbery squad was a cleansing of the soul. I was a cop again. I had a renewed sense of being a cop, and thought maybe if I caught enough bad guys I could wipe the slate clean. It was my best time as a cop and a time when I had some of my best cases.

I had seen every shade of event that life as a cop could offer. From my years as a patrolman, clearing corners, making car stops, breaking up domestics and checking the doors of taverns and stores against burglaries, to my time as an undercover cop working narcotics in the depths of the city, I knew what it was like to do surveillance, to use and not be used by an informant, to write a coherent search and seizure warrant, and to break a door down and survive. A good detective had to fill his head with enough knowledge of the existing police information database – arrest records, jail records, weapons registration, vehicle information – to qualify for a minor in computer science. But it was more than that. A detective had to think like a cop but also like a criminal to be one step ahead.

In Central Harlem I worked with various different partners, depending on the assignment. My most regular partner was Deke Hawkins, a tall, spare black man with a pencil-thin moustache. Hawkins was a native of Washington Heights, the son of a doctor who was disappointed that his son hadn't followed in his footsteps.

I was in a bad way mentally when I arrived in the 32nd and was having difficulty sleeping. I was suffering from anxiety and stress, and going through a bad time within myself. I used to pray as I drove into work: 'God, just get me through one more day.' Then I used to pray all the way home, to get me through one more night. I was very messed up.

On one graveyard shift I arrived in the squad and realised I had forgotten my revolver. I had to pick up someone in a bad section and asked Deke Hawkins to help me. Deke had been an officer in the air force and he unholstered his .38 Detective Special and handed it to me, but I told him I could not use his revolver. What if I had to discharge it or have to shoot someone! I decided to go and pick the man up alone and pretend to be armed. All I had was my gold detective shield. I made the arrest and sweated the whole way back to the station house.

I also worked with two other detectives, Michael Borelli and Robert Davis – a white and black partnership. In February 1975 Davis was arrested for the murder of Colorado gambler Hal Levine, in Denver, and the serious wounding of Levine's wife. He was a seventeen-year veteran of the force and had partnered Borelli for a long time. Four other men and Michael Borelli, who had recently retired, were also arrested in connection with the crime and Borelli was charged with masterminding the murder. I remember Davis being arrested in the Harlem squad room. Levine had been laundering money for the New York mob, but had siphoned off some of the proceeds for himself. Borelli had moved to Denver after leaving the NYPD and was a major stockholder in Levine's company. Like everyone else, I assumed all this was true, but it turned out Davis and Borelli were innocent and had been set up.

I spent many hours in Harlem Hospital Emergency Room, nicknamed 'MASH' by the cops, after the TV series. Harlem Hospital was a Level 1 trauma centre. When busy, it was like a battlefield casualty area with doctors and nurses running through the corridors with plasma and IVs attached to stretchers. There were bar stick-ups and all kinds of armed robberies and shootouts among drug dealers. As an investigating officer, I had to stand alongside victims wearing a surgical mask, hoping to get first-hand information as a doctor dug around a wound looking for bullet fragments. My job was to find out the where, how and why but, all too often, police department follow-up reports said the complainant advised the detective that he could handle his own business without any police interference. Usually I took the extracted bullets which might match slugs used in other shootings. Sometimes investigating detectives might pick up a shooter with a gun, whose markings or grooves would match bullets and they might solve a few other cases.

One night as Deke Hawkins and I left Harlem Hospital and were sitting at a red light in our unmarked car, our eyes drifted to a line of about fifteen people waiting for a bus. A tall black man in a raincoat and fedora hat with a folded newspaper under his arm casually took two steps on the inside of the queue, raised the newspaper up to the head of the man beside him in the queue and shot him with a concealed pistol. The man fell to the ground as the hitman turned and ran.

Hawkins swung the car around as I hit the siren. He pulled the car to the kerb as I radioed in an ambulance call. He was already out of the car as I put down the receiver. I followed Hawkins and we both ran around the corner, guns drawn in the direction the shooter had gone but he was nowhere to be seen. We searched around garbage cans and found the rolled-up newspaper thrown down steps leading to a tenement basement. Inside the newspaper was a blue towel, wrapped around a plain brown paper bag. There was a smell of cordite from inside the bag. It was returned as evidence as part of the murder investigation for fingerprints and fibres, but anyone that professional would have been wearing gloves. When we got back, other cops were interviewing the witnesses at the scene. The bus was held up until all those in the queue had been questioned. By then, other officers were conducting building and shop searches.

The killer was never found or identified and the murder became another statistic – one of 1,823 killings in NYC in 1971.

CHAPTER 17

Homicide in Spanish Harlem

Because I was a wire-man I was often asked by other detective squad commanders to open up an unofficial area of enquiry into investigations of a serious nature. This was known as a 'steal' assignment. My bosses in the 32nd Squad knew of my experience with wiretaps, legal and illegal, but they turned a blind eye. When big cases needed special information, a specialist who was never mentioned in the case folder, or officially assigned to the squad investigation, was used. The information gained could not be questioned in court and was registered as being from an 'unknown' source.

My work took me to Spanish Harlem, or 'El Barrio', the area on the northeastern side of Manhattan from East 96th Street up to 161st Street and the Harlem River. The drug dealers dressed in the style of old Hollywood gangsters. Their clothes, hats, diamond rings and white cars obliterated the smell of poverty, despair and death. Unlike their Mafia suppliers, whose women were not involved in the 'family business', in Spanish Harlem whole families were involved in the mixing, bagging, copping, delivering and pick-ups.

The 30th Precinct covered the upper portion of El Barrio, and it was from there that a message was sent for me to come, fully equipped. Within an hour I was in the upstairs squad room in a private meeting that I was told never happened, if anything went wrong. In a few hours the case was headlined in all the New York dailies as 'The Jackson Triple Homicide'.

The Jacksons lived in a new high-rise apartment building, one of the best places in El Barrio. Three black male intruders had been waiting for the Jacksons when they returned to their apartment. The father, mother and twenty-six-year-old daughter were taken into the main bedroom. Mother and daughter were made to lie face down on the king-size bed while their hands were tied behind their backs and pillows were placed over the back of their heads. The father, Elmer, was bound hands and feet, brought into another room and sat upright in a leather armchair.

The intruders harassed Elmer Jackson to tell them where a large stash of heroin was concealed. When he did not answer positively, he was punched. While the father was being beaten by two of the intruders, the third went outside and got the elevator up to the landing and waited with the lift door open for the quick exit of the other two. Meanwhile, the two left inside the apartment continued to question Elmer Jackson. One held a gun in his hand, around which he wrapped a pillow to smother the sound, and fired one bullet into the daughter's head, killing her. They questioned Elmer Jackson again and when he did not reveal the whereabouts of the drugs, the same man shot Mrs Jackson in the back of the head. The two men went back into the other room and both fired shots through pillows into Elmer Jackson's head. The trio left the building and fled the area.

However, the two killers had bungled the job. The shots fired into Elmer Jackson's head had not killed him. One bullet had gone through his eye socket and exited an inch or so at his temple on the same side, while the other had glanced into the padding of the armchair back. He managed to get to a phone and call for help. Elmer Jackson was rushed by ambulance to the Harlem Hospital. He was unconscious, but alive and, after three hours of surgery, there was a good prospect of survival. An around-the-clock guard was put on his room.

The Jackson Case stood out in a litany of drug-related murders because Elmer Jackson had heard the shots that killed his wife and daughter. His life had been saved by sheer luck.

Because the murders occurred inside a building rather than on the street where a crowd or prying reporters could gather, the investigators were able to withhold some crucial information. The police decided to say that all three members of the Jackson family had died. Meanwhile, one of the intruders to the apartment was identified by Elmer Jackson as Willie Jones – a six-foot-four-inch black man, know in crime circles as 'Big Moe', who lived in an apartment building on the west side of Amsterdam Avenue on 137th Street.

I accompanied the investigating detectives on a raid to pick up Big Moe and was admitted into his eight-room apartment. Mrs Avril Jones was a supervisor at the New York Telephone Company's downtown offices, and had three different telephone numbers in the house – one was for *her* private life, one for Big Moe's private doings and the other for her teenage daughter's use. There were also two extensions of both his and her phones, in colours to match the bedspreads, curtains and wallpaper of the rooms they were in.

Mrs Jones told the investigators that Moe wasn't in and that she hadn't seen or heard from him in two days, though this was not unusual as he was a salesman for a chain of gas stations that was owned by a Harlem business company. Moe's wife was kept busy answering questions, while I discreetly looked for paid telephone bills to establish a line for court orders and taps, so all would be legal. No information was given to Moe's wife, though she kept asking why the police had this sudden interest in her man. She brought up various neighbourhood crimes that she had knowledge of and while this was noted, it was obvious that she had no intention of giving up anything on Big Moe.

It wasn't long before I found what I wanted – an old itemised telephone bill. I got the telephone numbers to the apartment phone from the top of the bill, which the operator at information advised were unlisted. Then I went to my car and changed into a telephone repairman outfit and got the necessary equipment together. With three different telephones to monitor, I would need a helper and maybe another handset. I contacted a friend and asked him to drop off my handset at a location well away from the area I was actually working in, so as not to give the game away. I prepared my equipment and myself for a long stay. It could be overnight or a few days but, either way, it would mean setting down in a dirty basement.

It was obvious that I could not set up anywhere near Moe Jones's apartment building, so the bugs had to be relocated to house basements away from his home. It took some time to set up bugs on the three phone lines and then set myself in the designated basement where flashlights and small stools were the only comfort for the long night vigil for me and my partner, a black cop named Albert Drucker. We phoned our food order into the 30th Precinct office, they would call on the radio when they were on the block and Drucker would walk west to the end of the street and pick up the food.

A small tape recorder was attached to the daughter's phone as it was in use the most. A call came through on the line from a man. Avril Jones said she could not leave the house. Trouble had come up, she said, and she had to stand by the phone waiting for a call. No other information was given. Half an hour later, Avril Jones picked up the phone and dialled out. It was not a local area number. A woman named Silvia answered. 'Is Moe there yet?'

'No,' was the reply, 'but he may have gone to Elsie's house, he's expected out here later tonight.'

Avril said, 'Just tell him I called and I'm worried. Tell him to call as soon as he gets in.'

I called the 30th Squad and informed them that Moe was out of town but was going to be at this phone number. By taking ten numbers of the regular tape recording and slowing it down on the Sony three-speed recorder, I was able to find that the area code was Philadelphia. I looked at the phone bills and saw there were two different Philly numbers recorded on it. One was the number just dialled.

I made an emergency phone call to telephone security on West Street and gave my police code number so they knew that the party receiving the police-only information was the NYPD. I asked that the information be phoned directly to the telephone number set up for the Jackson Case at the 30th Squad room. The first call was to a Mrs Browne at a Philadelphia address. The other Philadelphia number was listed to Mrs Elsie Moore.

I related all this information to the 30th Squad. Moe was to stay that night as planned at Elsie's address but there had been no call from him to his daughter. The 30th Squad had arrest warrants issued and signed and three NYPD detectives were sent to the Philadelphia police precinct covering Elsie's house. Meanwhile, Moe called Avril and told her he was OK and was at Florie's house, but would be going to Elsie's later, in case she wanted to get in touch with him. She told him that the cops had been up at the house but they may have believed her story, as they were long gone. The kids were out and didn't see any cops on stakeout. Moe signed off in a happier voice. The fact that the kids were looking for stakeout cops was passed along, but the cops were used to this activity in this area.

The house where Big Moe was staying was in a very rough, mainly black area, and the Philadelphia SWAT team was called in to accompany the New York detectives on the arrest. An hour and a half later, the three 30th Squad detectives called back to report that they had picked up Moe at Elsie's house. One New York detective later told me that they had the front and back yard of the house staked out and that Moe pulled into the darkened driveway, quietly went to the back porch of the house and was scratching at the steel screen mesh so as not to make much noise, as if he were the family cat trying to get in, when a detective came up behind him, put a gun to the back of his head and said, 'Don't make a move, Moe, or I'll blow your fucking brains all over the back door.'

Moe thought it was a hit on him and immediately lost all control of his bowels. When he was cuffed and told it was the cops he was somewhat relieved. This relief changed when Big Moe was told that Elmer Jackson was alive and had identified him as one of the men who had killed his wife and daughter and had tried to kill him. He was in shock, confessed that he was a participant, but did not do any of the shooting. Moe was taken through the necessary court proceedings in Philadelphia and then brought back to the Manhattan Criminal Court at 100 Centre Street, and was remanded to Rikers Island without bail.

The other suspect identified was a black male, Richard Stokes, aka 'Snake Eyes'. He lived at State Street in Brooklyn in an old brownstone two-storey building. He shared his second-floor apartment with his common-law wife, a white girl named Lydia. Snake Eyes worked as an enforcer for the Johnson crime mob in Brooklyn. Elmer Jackson identified him positively too, as they were known to each other. An arrest warrant was issued for Stokes, and I accompanied another 30th Squad Detective team to the apartment when Lydia was at home. One of the detectives advised her that Stokes, who was described as armed and dangerous, would be 'hit' first, then questioned later, if there was a later.

When Lydia was convinced that Stokes' only chance was to be arrested quietly without a fight, she agreed to help. She was also advised that her co-operation would not be made known. With Lydia's consent, I hooked up an extra line to her bedroom telephone and also attached a tape recorder, so that a message could be recorded and listened to as it was taking place. Lydia was going to have house company for as long as it would take to get Stokes. If nothing happened, they were going to take her into custody for protection until he was caught. She would be considered a material witness in the case. Lydia knew too much about Stokes for her own safety, not only from him, but also from members of the Johnson mob.

I got hold of Lydia's itemised telephone bills and submitted them to the 30th Squad for the out-of-town addresses and other possible places Stokes may have fled to. It was decided that traffic was best observed from Lydia's protruding front windows, and two cars with stakeout detectives were positioned on side streets up and down State Street. The cops had bulletproof vests, night-sight scopes, shotguns, and radios that were tuned in to the apartment post and each other. In cases like this, uniformed officers were not always advised of what was going on. They might see or make a stakeout car, but it would be a block away from where the actual location would be – this was because some may inadvertently blow a situation and others could have some connection with the criminals and tip them off for money or just to cement friendships.

Stokes rang late that night, saying he was not far away. He wanted to be sure Lydia was not worried and to find out if anyone had been around or phoned. He suggested it would be better if she met him and they went some place, but she would have to take any money he had stashed in the house with her. Lydia coughed and sniffed as planned and said she would feel better and safer at home. Stokes agreed to come, saying he had two friends with him, and for her to put on something to eat as they were all hungry. He said he would ring the phone twice, then hang up, and then ring back again. If everything was OK, Lydia was to answer, but let it ring out if not.

The stakeout cars were told to clear off, but to drop two more men off at the house, with bulletproof vests and shotguns. This had to be accomplished immediately and with as little noise as possible. The cars would have to go a couple of blocks away and look out for a tan Cadillac, with three black males. Then all were told about what exactly was taking place. The best place the trio could be taken down with the least amount of trouble and danger was as they came in the outside entrance doors to the house.

The arrest went off without a hitch. The three criminals were armed but put up no resistance. Stokes was carrying a bag of cocaine. One of the other men arrested, Joe Scaggs, turned out to be the third man involved in the Jackson Case. Scaggs and Stokes were charged with two counts of murder, and possession of weapons and drugs. The third criminal, Tucky Johnson, was charged with weapons and drugs possession.

Moe Jones, Richard Stokes and Joe Scaggs went on trial for the murder of Mrs Jackson and her daughter. Jones copped a plea to manslaughter, saying he was misled by Stokes and that he was the lookout and had not taken part in the shootings. He was given life. Stokes and Scaggs were convicted of first-degree murder and were also given life, though with no possibility of parole. Lydia visited Stokes in Rikers Island when he was on remand; he never knew that she had given him up. Because the cops had so much information on the case Stokes was later killed in Rikers Island by members of the Johnson mob because they thought he was an informer. His killers never realised that all the information came from my phone taps.

CHAPTER 18

The robbery of the Hotel St Pierre

At the end of 1971 I was assigned to Robbery, Homicide and Burglary in the 2nd Robbery Squad, in the 19th Precinct, to begin my new assignment on New Year's Day 1972. The old precinct detective squads had been disbanded and specialised detective squads were being used to investigate major crimes. I was only in my new job a day when the most successful hotel robbery in New York history occurred. A professional gang of burglars and thieves held up the staff at Hotel St Pierre, at East 61st Street near Central Park, and broke into the locked boxes of the residents, escaping with some $10 million in cash and jewels.

The front doorman at the Hotel St Pierre was Vincent Egan, from Pettigo in County Donegal, who had attended the De La Salle Brothers School with me back in Ballyshannon. Another doorman was Mattie Salko, a disbarred lawyer from the New York Criminal Court. He was also a close friend of mine.

Because the 2nd Robbery Squad had caught the case, I was one of the first detectives on the scene and started to help the initial investigation team, filling out the various losses from the boxes broken into. According to a first-hand account given to me, a group of men dressed as musicians carrying their equipment cases had knocked on the main entrance and the two security men – retired detectives from the NYPD – had allowed them into the hotel after hours, as it was assumed that they had been playing at the Copacabana next door.

All the guests who came down to the lobby were held there and the staff had to serve them coffee, tea and sometimes something a little stronger, as they were in shock. These were the cream of American businessmen and women and a big problem in questioning them was that the reporting detectives had to leave the space on the official NYPD form open, as the reported amount of cash changed again and again. The investigating detectives had to allow each complainant time to be sure about how much cash these official forms should read, as it might differ from that declared to the IRS, so it took a long time to get the initial investigation underway and verify just how much was actually taken. The final amount agreed was probably about a quarter of what was actually taken in cash alone.

The team that pulled off the robbery consisted of: Bobby Comfort, Sammy Nalo (known as 'Sammy the Arab'), Bobby Germaine, Ali-Ben, Al Green, Alan Visconti, Tony Frankos and a man known only as 'Petey'. Bobby Comfort and Sammy Nalo were professional burglars and thieves. They had previously stolen $1 million in jewellery and cash from the Sherry-Netherland Hotel and had performed major robberies and burglaries at four of the city's other top hotels – the Regency, Drake, Carlyle and St Regis.

Nalo was the true genius behind all the heists but Comfort, an Irish-Italian from Rochester, was also a major organiser. Bobby Germaine was a stick-up man, drug trafficker, burglar and freelance writer living in New York; Ali-Ben was a Turkish-Albanian contract killer who worked primarily for the New York Turkish mob; Al Green was his brother-in-law; Alan Visconti was a Lucchese crime family associate; Donald 'Tony the Greek' Frankos was a freelance contract killer, who later claimed he killed Jimmy Hoffa; and Petey was a hotel burglar, who was never fully identified.

Sammy Nalo and Bobby Comfort began planning the robbery some weeks before, but it was not until 30 December 1971, in the back room of the Port Said, Nalo's nightclub, that Nalo brought the team together and informed them of their intended target. The group arrived at the entrance of the Hotel St Pierre at 3.50 a.m. on 2 January 1972. Ten minutes later, Al Green, dressed in a chauffeur's uniform, drove a black Cadillac limousine up to the 61st Street entrance. Bobby Germaine, with Petey and Al Visconti, got out and told the security guard, 'Reservations, Dr Foster's party.' The security guard called the registration desk and confirmed that a Dr Foster, who turned out to be Bobby Comfort, had paid for a room, so the guard unlocked the door. They held the guard at gunpoint as they entered the hotel. Al Green remained on watch outside.

Their timing was perfect because most of the hotel's guests were soundly sleeping off their escapades from the previous night's New Year's Eve parties. The idea was that the finest jewels had been worn that night and they would have been kept in safety deposit boxes downstairs until more secure bank vaults reopened at 9 a.m. Also, because of the holiday, the hotel had only a skeleton crew, including guards. Within fifteen minutes, the burglars had taken over the hotel and had rounded up all the staff. Tony Frankos guarded the 61st Street entrance, handcuffing anyone who confronted him and leading them to Al Visconti, who brought the hostages to a large alcove near the registration desk, where he ordered them to lie face down on the floor. The number of hostages grew steadily to nineteen.

The robbers wore gloves and carried guns and were dressed in disguises – wigs, fake noses and eyeglasses. Sammy Nalo forced the hotel auditor to provide the index cards that matched the boxes to depositors. It was Bobby Germaine's job to pry open the steel lock boxes kept for guests in an open vault. He only broke into the boxes of people whose names he, Nalo and Comfort recognised, which included Harold Uris (a real estate entrepreneur), Tom Yawkey (an industrialist and major league baseball executive) and Calliope Kulukundis (the wife of Manuel Kuluk, the Greek-born shipping magnate). The burglars carried handcuffs to use if necessary, but did not handcuff anyone who looked ill or sick. They referred politely to their hostages as 'Sir' and 'Miss', and at no time raised their voices or seemed violent.

The entire robbery took two and a half hours. Within that time, Bobby Comfort and Bobby Germaine managed to break into close on a quarter of the 208 locked boxes in the vault. At 6:15 a.m. Bobby Comfort informed the hostages that they were leaving and warned them not to inform the police if they were able to identify anyone or they would be killed. Before departing, Comfort gave a $20 bill to each hotel employee that they had detained, except for the security guards, and they left at 6.30 a.m., just ahead of the hotel's incoming 7 a.m. shift.

The original police estimates of the losses ranged from between $1.2 million and $4 million, but some reports put the total value of the loot as high as $10 million. In the immediate aftermath of the robbery, the St Pierre's security chief, John Keeney, who was a former NYPD detective and who had been President John F. Kennedy's bodyguard on visits to New York, was summarily fired – even though he had not been on duty that night. He claimed the hotel had the best security in the city, but heads had to roll, and his was one.

My boss – Lieutenant Edward O'Connor – caught the case. Detective George Bermudez, known as 'Georgie B.' to his friends, also worked on the robbery. Bermudez was a lifelong friend of mine and we'd first met when we were in the SIU. Bermudez was a legendary SIU detective. One day he had been driving along when he'd witnessed the stabbing and robbery of a man. Jumping out of his car, Georgie had grappled with the assailant, who had stabbed him in the heart. Despite being severely injured, Georgie had hung on to his attacker until help arrived. Georgie made a complete recovery.

Detectives Bermudez and Ed Fitzgibbon were assigned the task, along with two FBI agents, of locating Sammy Nalo, who they arrested in the Bronx. Nalo was a suspect in several earlier hotel robberies and descriptions had been issued for four of the robbers, including one which fitted Nalo – 'six feet tall with a swarthy complexion'. The stolen jewels had been taken to Detroit to be fenced because Nalo's New York fence had demanded a third of the take as his cut. Another friend of mine, Joe Gannon, was part of the team that picked up Bobby Comfort at the Royal Manhattan Hotel. Joe Gannon was a big, burly Irishman, who I often car-pooled with to work. Joe was known to his friends as 'G-man' because he looked like George Raft, who'd been born in Hell's Kitchen and was one of the most popular and stylish gangster actors in the 1930s and '40s.

While I did not get instructions from the case supervisor, or my own superiors, to put a wire on the case, we were 'advised' that some other source would be needed to get more immediate results. It was known that I had the means and so it was left in the hands of the case supervisor to request me to help, off the record of course. The case detectives called me to see if I was available as a 'steal' and my supervisor allowed me to take time off, but never asked what the task was. I brought my equipment and met with the Hotel St Pierre case detectives to find out what the situation was and what I needed to do. Any information I received would be immediately passed on to the detectives working the case. Most people in the world we were investigating did not have nine-to-five jobs where they could be easily found. So to find someone who knew how to find a source, I would have to backtrack. That was the drudgery of a real investigation, but it was also the part of the job that I enjoyed. I contacted some retired cops who lived or worked in the area. Ex-cops remain 'cops' for most of their lives – it is something that never leaves you.

For several weeks following the robbery I was busy tapping phones, including a row of public phones along the huge lobby of the Waldorf Astoria Hotel, the largest and most expensive hotel in NYC. This was because an informant had arranged to meet another man to buy some of the jewels, which he'd received in the mail from another part of the USA. The man was to bring samples of the jewels. I also tapped phones in rooms where the meet was to take place. Wiretaps were also carried out on Sammy Nalo at his Port Said nightclub. I wired the Plaka Steak House, but I was only able to record pieces of what was going on, so I didn't get to know all the facts.

When the case came to trial, Sammy Nalo and Bobby Comfort received four-year sentences. As the heat was turned up, a nervous fence in Detroit handed over $750,000 in jewellery to police. The other gang members never really got to enjoy their fortune – some of the loot was swindled from them, while three of the gang were later murdered. Bobby Comfort fenced some of his share to organised crime associates, who never paid him. When he attempted to retrieve the money he was nearly killed.

When Ali-Ben and his brother-in-law Al Green read in the newspapers about the stolen property recovered in Detroit, they thought Nalo had tried to swindle them out of their share. They fled to Europe, where they enjoyed their wealth for a time, but

Tony the Greek Frankos, still smarting over what he thought was a rip-off by Nalo and others, killed both Ali-Ben and Al Green in 1981.

An unknown gunman subsequently murdered Nalo in 1988. Bobby Comfort ended up with $1.5 million, but did not live long enough to enjoy it. He died of a heart attack in 1986, aged fifty-three. Tony Frankos later became an informer and went into the Witness Protection Programme. He wrote a book – *Contract Killer: The explosive story of the Mafia's most notorious hitman, Tony 'The Greek' Frankos* – detailing his part in the Hotel St Pierre robbery and other crimes, though much of the stuff he said is very suspect.

George Bermudez, a recipient of the NYPD's highest award, the Medal of Honour, retired from the police department to become a highly regarded private investigator. He died in 2009, aged seventy-five.

In the end, I didn't really contribute much to the case, but this was the way a lot of cases worked out – a lot of work for no foreseeable gain.

CHAPTER 19
The Goodbar Girl

After the Hotel St Pierre Case, I was assigned to the 4th Robbery Squad, in the 20th Precinct on West 82nd Street. My new partner was John Hartigan whose parents had emigrated from Dublin after the death of their first son. John had been born in Brooklyn and his upbringing was typical New York Irish Catholic. He was thirty-two, weighed about 130 pounds and stood five-foot-ten-inches. He was good-looking with dark brown hair, swept back, and reminded me of the singer Bobby Darin. Ours was a good partnership. I was the serious one, while Hartigan was more easy-going. Everything Hartigan said was a joke or a wisecrack, and we soon fell into an easy rhythm. We ribbed each other unmercifully, but never fell out or had a bad day together. Hartigan had joined the NYPD in 1964 and had been a patrolman in the 7th precinct at the same time as me, but we had never worked together until we were assigned to the robbery squad.

There were two shifts in the robbery squad – from 8 a.m. to 4 p.m. and 4 p.m. to 1 a.m. – and we dealt with all types of robberies – bank, store and other stick-ups as well as street robberies, purse snatches and guys ripped off by flim-flam gangs. The *modus operandi* of a flim-flam gang was when a john picked up a prostitute and engaged in sex, her accomplices jumped him. This could lead to blackmail if the john was married or had a business. Victims made up stories to cover what happened, but I always said, 'You can tell your wife what you like, but I need the truth on the police report.'

One day in early July 1972 I was 'catching', meaning I was the detective assigned to any arrests brought in by the patrol force or citizen complaints, when two young women came into the station house. The desk officer was busy answering the switchboard, but he took time out to give the two women a polite, enquiring eyeball. They were white and dressed in hippy-style outfits. One of them said she had been raped, robbed and beaten up. 'Robbery squad,' the desk officer said, and gave them a half-sympathetic smile and a look of *What's new?*

They took the elevator to the second floor and a detective was consulted about who the proper officer was. I was catching up on overdue paperwork when my concentration was distracted by the words: 'Daly, two coming your way!'

I rose to greet the two girls with a smile, and a 'Ladies, how can I be of service?' Joanne Quinn said she had been robbed, beaten and raped in her hotel room about 2 a.m. that morning by a black man who had broken in, taken her wallet and, after taking some money from it, had thrown it back at her. Then he'd beaten her about the face and body and raped her on the bed.

'How much money was taken?'

'A hundred dollars,' she replied.

I asked the age, height and description of the attacker and, finally, asked her to go over the crimes again in more detail. A squad number was printed on the DD5 form and the case became official. Quinn was given the robbery squad telephone number and my name. Anything further she had to add could be done at another time, but I had to be the detective consulted.

Often, there were extenuating circumstances that would evolve over time through slow, polite and clever questioning. A good investigator never asked questions straight out. He usually beat around the bush and found out a lot more in extended conversations.

I accompanied the women out of the office and we took the elevator to the ground floor. 'There are a few things I would like to have cleared up,' I said, 'if you can take a moment to answer some more questions.'

I took Joanne Quinn aside and said, 'For someone who was just raped, you are quite calm and relaxed. We get many victims in here who are hysterical and it strikes me that you are so calm. Why did you not report the rape immediately after it happened?'

'It was much too late to call and disturb the police,' Quinn said.

'I don't think so,' I said. 'If you were being murdered would it be the same? I hope you realise there is a law where you can be arrested for filing a false report with the police. Do you understand this?' I decided to give it to her straight and hard. 'I have to tell you that I don't believe one word of what you just said. You're mad at someone and want him arrested and put in jail. You've set the case out just as you've seen it on TV. A rape case wasn't enough, so you added the robbery and assault to really throw away the key. You thought it would get more attention with all three ingredients. So tell me what really happened.'

The woman didn't answer. I said, 'Remember, I have to go out and find this person, arrest him on your signed complaint. He'll be prosecuted by the Manhattan DA's office before an open court and found guilty.'

Quinn moved about nervously. She looked like she was about to say it was all a mistake, but then she said that she intended to go through with it, as it was the truth.

I asked her again why she hadn't reported the rape earlier as the prosecution would be almost impossible because the law requires that certain facts are present, so questions had to be answered – Was there penetration of the vagina by the attacker's penis? Was there ejaculation? – and these could only be properly put in evidence if a doctor took samples immediately following the attack. That was the rape! The assault was much the same. Were there any doctor's reports of injuries? I told her that I had to go on what she told me, but that did not include me believing it. Finally, I told her that if there was any more information at a further date, she was to tell me. I let this advice hang for a few moments, but saw that I was getting nowhere. Joanne Quinn left the station house with a friendly 'thank you', a warm handshake and a vacant smile.

Two days later Joanne Quinn returned to the robbery squad room, but this time she invited me to join her for a drink and some food. I declined, saying I didn't drink alcohol and, besides, I felt it best if complainant and investigator did not become too close. She said that she usually hung out at a certain bar and grill and that, if I happened to have a change of heart, I would be very welcome anytime.

I reminded her that if she saw the man she'd said had attacked her, she was to call the precinct and advise any officer of the case, who could then contact me. She then produced a New York State driver's licence, which carried a photo of its owner, and handed this to me, saying she had found it under the bed and that her attacker must have dropped it. I asked her to sit down in front of my typewriter while I added this new information to the case. This would make things easier. The attacker's name, date of birth, address and other relevant information was put into the Bureau of Criminal Identification (BCI) system. However, he had no record and seemingly had never been arrested for anything that required photos and fingerprints.

The attacker's name was Leroy Gibson and his home address was in Greenwich Village. A check of his address revealed there was no telephone, so I picked a reasonable time to go there but found no one at the apartment. I did not visit the building superintendent or alert anyone, as I was not satisfied that Gibson was guilty of anything. All along, I felt there was another side to the story, which was yet to be revealed. I left a note under the door for Gibson to contact the detectives via telephone, but did not state the reason.

On two further occasions I was contacted by Quinn and advised that Leroy Gibson was in different bars in the 72nd Street area and, when I got there, Quinn was already waiting to advise me that Gibson had just gone. She said she had told Gibson of the charges facing him.

Near the end of September, nearly three months after the alleged attack, John Hartigan and I were cruising around the road through Central Park when John calmly said, 'Hey, ain't that Leroy Gibson on the bike?'

I saw a black man dressed in athletic gear riding a ten-speed sports bicycle heading east on the roadway to the left of our unmarked detective's car. The man was asked to stop and pull over, and I asked him quickly if he was Leroy Gibson. He said he was. I advised him that he was being arrested on the complaint of Joanne Quinn and that there was no need to say anything, that he could make his telephone call from the precinct. Gibson was put in the back seat of the car and his bicycle placed in the trunk with the front wheel sticking out. Hartigan drove to the precinct station house, where Gibson was advised in detail of the charges and fingerprinted.

Joanne Quinn was told about the arrest and that she had to be in court that night to sign the charges. I asked Leroy Gibson about his opinion of the charges; this wasn't necessary but I wanted to know – off the record – what he thought. Gibson appeared to be a clean, neatly dressed person. His bicycle was also well cared for and nothing seemed to be out of the ordinary. While he was unemployed, he spoke politely and clearly, with no use of street slang. He wanted to give his explanation of what this was all about if I would listen. Out of habit, I never showed excitement – never wanting to give away the edge. I said it was not necessary and possibly counter-productive and could be used against him. However, Gibson insisted on being heard, though he felt it useless because no one would believe him, given that he was black and the victim was a white woman. I agreed that even if I did believe him, the court probably would not.

Gibson had met Quinn at a bar on West 72nd Street. He was out for a good time and, after a good few drinks, they went back to her hotel room. He wasn't inside the door when she was all over him and using dirty words, as though that was how she got her kicks. Gibson said he screwed her a number of times that first night. The next morning when the alarm went off, she awoke and they did a half-hour of screwing before she got up, showered and got dressed. Quinn told him to stay on and she left him a set of keys for the room. She taught in a school for deaf children in the Bronx and would be back in the evening, hoping he would still be there. She said there was food in the corner fridge and a small stove for coffee. She left the telephone number of the school in case anything came up. She kissed him and then took off. She forgot to give Gibson her full name and all he knew her by was Joanne.

This went on for the next three days and then Gibson decided to leave. Quinn did not want him to go, so she took his wallet and money and hid it in the room. He left for his own apartment and returned later that night to retrieve his wallet and cash. Quinn admitted to having them, but wouldn't give them back as she wanted him to stay. Gibson said he would do anything she liked, but he had to get out at some point and go to his own apartment. He had other commitments in his life and she should understand. Quinn still wouldn't give him the wallet and his money, so he lost his head and hit her. There was a bit of a struggle – he thought she seemed to like a fight and this worked her up until she wanted sex. Gibson got the $100 that was his, but couldn't get his wallet. He finally left about 2 a.m. with his money, but still no wallet.

While Gibson's story was probably the truth, he was nevertheless arraigned by the Assistant DA at Manhattan Criminal Court and held on $1,000 bail for a hearing in two weeks. Joanne Quinn stuck to the statement she had signed. Gibson was represented by a free legal aid attorney, who argued with the court that the high bail was unattainable for his client and, seeing that it was only to insure the defendant's reappearance on the two-week date, it was excessive. His client, he argued, could not afford that amount. Leroy Gibson was of good character, did not give the arresting detective a hard time and had never been arrested in the past.

The prosecuting female ADA said that the charges were of a serious nature – rape, assault and robbery – and that if the defendant was freed on bail, he could do bodily harm or worse to the complainant and, with that in mind, she requested that the bail be set at $1,000 in cash.

The judge took a minute as he read the charges to himself, then fixed the bail at $500 cash and put the case over for two weeks. Leroy Gibson went back into the court holding pens and, from there, to a cell in the overcrowded Tombs Prison, adjoining the Criminal Court Building.

Later I met Joanne Quinn at a Chinese restaurant. Over a meal, tea and coffee, I advised her that Gibson had confessed his part of the story and, unusual as it seemed, I told her I believed him. I was still uncertain about what she had told me. Quinn was upset that anyone would doubt her word and, after lunch, invited me back to her hotel room for refreshments and anything else I felt would satisfy me. I politely declined. I was aware that all this would have to be decided in court.

When the date arrived, the court pushed on the case for two weeks because that day's calendar was overcrowded. So one month from the day that Gibson had been arraigned, the case was called. The ADA asked for ten minutes to discuss the facts with the arresting detective. I was asked what I felt about the case and I told the ADA that I felt the defendant had spent enough time in prison and that his story was more believable than the plaintiff's. However, I was aware that Gibson had two strikes against him – being black and unemployed – while Quinn was white and a teacher.

Joanne Quinn then went into the witness box and was sworn in. The ADA asked her to recall the facts of that day in July as best she could. After she had finished, the legal aid attorney then cross-examined her. 'Did the man stay in your hotel room for two or three nights before all this took place?'

'No!'

'Did you return the defendant's wallet?'

'No! I mean I never had it!'

'Your Honour,' the attorney said, 'I now offer Exhibit A.' He produced a hotel key with a number on it.

The judge asked Joanne if that was the key to her hotel room.

'Yes! But he could have paid someone to get it at the hotel desk. My name is on the room.'

The district attorney agreed with this. The judge then turned to the legal aid attorney and asked him if he had anything further to add.

'Yes, Your Honour, I do, a lot in fact. My client Leroy Gibson does not know the surname of the plaintiff and after listening to his story, I found out what actually did take place. This key was not picked up by anyone at the hotel desk. It was the key given to him by Joanne Quinn on the Thursday morning before she left for work. To add more, I myself got a signed form filled out by my client while he was incarcerated in the Tombs Prison to release his apartment keys to me. I then went to his apartment, at McDougall Street in the Village, and opened the apartment door with the key Mr Gibson had in his pocket when he was arrested a month earlier and as per Mr Gibson's instructions, I went into the bedroom and found the hotel key that I first put before the court today as Exhibit A. Your Honour, I now move that this case be dismissed and that my client, Leroy Gibson, be exonerated and freed from custody.'

The ADA asked for a five-minute recess so she could confer with the arresting officer and Joanne Quinn. The ADA then stepped out into a small corridor with me. I had more experience in street matters than she had and she was unassuming enough to admit it to me. She asked, 'What can be done next for the best of all concerned?'

I asked her if she remembered the story that I had told her as it was told to me on the night of the Gibson arrest, and I again said that I felt Gibson had been telling the truth all along, but that she must now decide in her own mind where the truth lies and, if she believed me, she should return to the court and move that the case be dismissed.

Back in the courtroom, the ADA said there was no medical evidence available before the court and that should have been taken immediately following the rape, which was not reported until some hours after it may have occurred. There was also no medical evidence before the court documenting the injuries incurred by the complainant. She was dismissing the case for lack of evidence and because the charges could not be proved beyond any doubt. She asked that the defendant make a statement whereas he did not hold the court, the City of New York, the arresting officer or any employee of the city responsible for his arrest or subject to any future suit for false arrest. Gibson stood up and after the legal aid attorney explained what was said to him, he said loudly, 'I do not hold anyone responsible for my arrest except Miss Quinn.'

The judge hit his gavel on the benchtop loudly and said, 'The case against Leroy Gibson and all the charges contained therein are dismissed.'

I felt Joanne Quinn was dangerous and fond of pushing buttons, and warned her that if she continued to do this, somebody would do something to her. But she said this wasn't true and that things really had happened the way she'd said. She had a lot of issues. She had a short leg or high hip or something of that nature but, even though it was not easily noticeable, she was very conscious of it, to the point that she felt inferior to most girls.

I also talked to Leroy Gibson and told him he was arrested on the foot of a complaint, but that I believed him. He thanked me. I warned him not to contact Joanne Quinn or go near her again, and that if he did, I would personally see to it that he did time, but he said he would not go near her.

One night in early January 1973 the phone rang at my home. The call was from the 4th District Homicide Squad and I was asked to come in right away, there was an incident that I might be able to help with. The detective said it was a young female schoolteacher who had been murdered in her hotel room and someone had mentioned that Pete Daly might know who did it. As I drove the fifty miles to the city from my upstate home in Rockland County, the only schoolteacher I could remember from the past few months was Joanne Quinn. Could it be that Gibson had got his revenge for the month he'd spent in prison and the embarrassment that would follow him throughout his life having an arrest record? That would be too obvious. Only a fool would retaliate so soon and it would just be a beating rather than a murder. Gibson did not strike me as being that stupid. On the contrary, he was a smart, sharp man.

I went to the hotel room. The detectives from 4th Homicide and the fingerprint guys, photographers and spectrograph specialists were there. Joanne Quinn had been dead for two days. My job was to find Leroy Gibson and talk to the other girl who had been with Quinn on the night she'd first come in to report Gibson for rape and robbery. Quinn's friend might know who would harm her or who she might be in fear of. It was probably someone Quinn had taken back to her hotel room, as there was no forced entry.

I was put on special assignment off the regular chart and working on this case only, by orders of the police commissioner. Gibson's pictures were printed and given out to the investigating detectives, who were told he was a suspect and was wanted for questioning only. I pushed a note under Gibson's apartment door and pushed a match down near the floor in the doorjamb, which would tell me if anyone came in or out. When the door opened the match, unseen, would drop to the floor.

The next day, I was back to check the door – nothing. On the third day, the match was on the floor. This meant Gibson was around town, or someone was using his key and apartment. I called the office on a hunch that maybe someone may have left a message for me. After all, Gibson had been treated fairly by me in the original case. Usually, no matter how much of a prison sentence a man got, if he received fair treatment by the arresting detective, then it was accepted in good faith. I was in luck. A message had been left – someone would call back in time, but would only speak to me. The message was recorded, as were all messages to do with cases of a serious nature.

Two hours later, Gibson rang and said he wanted to speak to me. He seemed to be far away, his voice barely audible. Gibson would not say where he was, but he stressed that he had nothing to do with Joanne Quinn's death. I said he should put in a personal appearance and make such a statement for the record. I also told him that he could appear with his attorney and make such a statement, but until such time as he did, or in the event that another person was charged with Joanne Quinn's murder, he would still be considered a suspect. It wasn't just enough to say it over the phone, he would have to prove where he was at the time and answer any questions put to him.

I offered to meet privately with him and discuss the case and then escort him to the squad room and stay with him until his questioning was over. I told him a priest, minister or anyone else of such social standing could stay with him for further assurances. Gibson was probably afraid of being framed for something he hadn't done, so he said he would think about what I had said and would call back the following day at 2 p.m. – again, he would only speak to me.

The next day the call came in on time and Gibson told me that he was just around the corner with a legal aid attorney and that they would be right in.

Gibson made a full account of his time for the period Joanne Quinn was killed and was told he was free to go, but he was asked not to leave the city limits without first letting me know where to reach him if anything came up. I took Gibson aside before he left and said that I appreciated him making himself available and asked if he would do one further thing. When he was in his usual haunts on West 72nd or anywhere else, he should keep his ears open and if he heard anything whatsoever that might cast some light on who Quinn was with before her death, I would appreciate the call; nothing would be said to its source. Nothing became of this and, a short time later, the murder was solved.

The NYPD released a police sketch of the last man seen with Joanne Quinn, an accountant named Geary Guest. A friend of his, John Wayne Wilson, had confessed to the murder of Quinn and Guest had given him money to leave the city. Frightened that he was now the murder suspect, Guest contacted the police and gave them the details and Wilson's whereabouts.

Detectives Patrick Toomey and John Lafferty of the 4th District Homicide Squad flew to Indiana and picked up the perpetrator, John Wayne Wilson. Wilson was a homosexual who had been picked up by Quinn in her regular West 72nd Street bar and had gone back to her hotel room. In the room, Quinn had undressed him and found he was wearing women's panties. Wilson claimed he couldn't get an erection and Quinn continued to mock him, saying that as he wasn't a real man, he couldn't perform like one with her. Wilson finally lost control and, in a rage, picked up a bronze statue and smashed Quinn about the head with the heavy base. Then he stabbed her eighteen times. Four months later while on remand, Wilson hanged himself in his cell in the Tombs.

In 1975 Judith Rossner wrote a book about the whole case, though the victim's name was changed. A movie followed. Both were called *Looking for Mr Goodbar*.

CHAPTER 20
Almost the end

On 10 January 1973, a couple of days after the Joanne Quinn murder, I was assigned to the 20th Precinct Investigating Unit, Detective Division. It was to be my final police posting. The Robbery Squad had thirty-odd men assigned from a number of citywide squads to the 1st Precinct Squad, which was responsible for the protection of the biggest financial district in the world – Wall Street – and also the Federal Gold Depository, the New York and World Stock Exchanges, and bank headquarters from all over the world. It would be a near-impossible task to protect the total area. Most banks had their own security with all the most modern electronic protection equipment.

An inside informant had supplied the NYPD with information that the Black Liberation Army (BLA) planned to make a big impression on the public imagination with a number of simultaneous, armed daytime stick-ups on Wall Street banks. Several police teams were placed in banks throughout the financial district in the hope of catching the BLA in action. I was partnered with John Hartigan and Joe Gannon and we spent two weeks in one bank building in an open public area.

The three of us sat at separate office desks with piles of papers and boxes around us in different parts of the area. To make it look good, the phones rang occasionally, though it was mostly us talking with each other to relieve the boredom. We were armed with shotguns (usually broken and under the desk) and a collection of revolvers and automatics. I had a Smith and Wesson .38 Detective Special service revolver, plus a .22 Beretta in an ankle holster. The shotguns fired single-shot cartridges for use in crowded areas, for fear of innocent civilians getting caught in shooting. Each of us was in a good position with a wide field of fire and observation. There were a few scary moments when three black men, dressed like business executives – which they actually turned out to be – got together for a meeting. To us, these meetings took on the appearance of what could be a BLA stick-up team disguised. However, the meetings turned out to be regular business get-togethers. We spent two weeks on the job and were bored, tired and fearful that action would come when we were on edge or that it would happen a day or two after we were pulled out.

On 1 February 1973, Hartigan, Gannon and I went to the 20th Precinct squad room where we picked up our pay cheques and continued on our way home. All three of us lived upstate in Rockland County where many cops and firemen lived. We car-pooled to save expenses and I had brought my large Chevy that day. It was a clear but very cold evening, as we drove to the West Side Highway, then up to the George Washington Bridge, over into New Jersey. Traffic was in full rush-hour, bumper to bumper conditions. We got through the toll banks, and went forward to the Palisades Parkway and drove in the left lane of traffic, again bumper to bumper. There were two lanes going north and two going south, with about thirty feet of an open grass area separating the roads. The car was stuck in one spot for quite a few minutes as the traffic ahead was backed-up about a mile or more. We sat there, discussing the assignment and how pissed off and tired we were about it, saying we were glad it was over and that we could get down to all the robbery cases we had started.

Suddenly, Hartigan shouted, 'Look out!'

I quickly looked to my left, as Hartigan ducked down under the dashboard, on the passenger's side. All I could see were two headlights coming at the car. There was no place to drive as the car in front was only about three feet away, so I pulled the steering wheel to the right and tried to squeeze my car in. At that moment, the rear of my Chevy was hit by the rear of the oncoming car, which spun my car around. I was knocked unconscious from the impact. The Chevy was still in gear and ran out of control across the grassy area and onto the southbound traffic lanes. My car was hit again by two fast-moving oncoming vehicles and totally written off.

We learned later that there was a light coat of ice on the road that caused the driver of the southbound car to lose control and run across the grassy divide into the northbound lanes and into my Chevy. Fire trucks and ambulances from nearby Fort Lee quickly arrived at the scene. We were taken to Englewood Cliffs Hospital in New Jersey. Hartigan had escaped injury when he hit the floor and just had a black eye, and Gannon received dozens of stitches to the v-shaped gash in the middle of his forehead. John told me later that he'd had to hold down the crown of Joe's head, which had peeled back like a banana skin when his head hit the doorjamb.

I was X-rayed and was found to have a fractured skull. The doctors said I was talking and making sense, and Hartigan joked that that should have been their first clue – everyone agreed I'd never made sense before!

I had amnesia and could not remember anything for the first four days after my hospitalisation. Rita was rushed to the hospital and I told her that my pay cheque was in my wallet, under my pillow, which she took. However, I don't remember this. It was four days before I regained consciousness. I was hospitalised for three weeks with a Lenoir fracture of the skull, three fractured ribs on my left side, probable loss of memory (including no recollection of the accident), severe cerebral concussion, abdominal trauma and multiple bruising.

On 22 February 1973 I was discharged, though I still complained of headaches and dizziness, double vision in my left eye, loss of hearing, ringing and popping in the left ear, and insomnia. I had frequent nausea, tired easily, was nervous and irritable, apprehensive and had difficulty concentrating and memory loss. I complained of persistent pain in the back of my neck, numbness in the small and ring fingers of my left hand, restriction in motion of my neck and pain in the left rib cage. Despite this, I was helped into a wheelchair, and waited to be taken home. I started to hook a yellow and red flowery throw over myself as an exercise to get my eyes and hands co-ordinated.

When John Hartigan and another cop, Brendan Tumulty, came to collect me, they found me sitting in the wheelchair struggling with my knit and stitch exercise.

'Hey,' Hartigan said. 'It looks like Daly's all washed up!'

'Why?' asked Tumulty. 'What do you mean?'

'Look, they have him in there, doing some basket weaving or something!'

The two laughed and wheeled me out to their parked car.

Back at home in Rockland County, Hartigan and Tumulty carried me into my own bed. Rita had laid the pillows down flat, and I passed out with pain when I was put down. That night, I couldn't sleep because of the severe pain in the lower left rib cage area. Tears rolled down my cheeks, but Rita assured me that the hospital had discharged me so I must be all right.

I tried to sleep, but the pain was unbearable and I again woke Rita and asked her to call the local doctor, as I thought something was seriously wrong. She told me all the children were sleeping and calling the doctor would wake them. I had no choice but to suffer in agony as the phone extension was on her side of the bed.

Some sleepless and agony-filled hours later, I struggled out of the bed and crawled around on the floor out to the kitchen telephone. I dialled the local police station and was lucky enough that a friend, Joe Morano, answered. Morano knew about my accident and immediately came out in his radio car, with the siren off and the lights flashing, so as not to wake the neighbourhood, but also to let me know he had arrived.

Morano found me sitting against the kitchen cabinets behind the back door. He was a big man and physically lifted me out to his squad car and drove me to the emergency room of Ramapo Hospital in Spring Valley. I was given a shot to deaden the pain and put into an elastic bandage that covered my chest area, which almost immediately relieved the discomfort. It took the rest of that year before I could walk unaided around the house.

As I convalesced, I received a visit from my old partner Carl Aguiluz, who wanted to write a book about our exploits as SIU detectives, including the 100 Kilo Case. I had my suspicions of Aguiluz and was afraid that he might be trying to entrap me.

Joe Novoa was equally suspicious of Aguiluz's motives and intentions. Aguiluz drove Novoa and me to the home of the writer Hank Whittemore, author of *The Super Cops*. Despite our misgivings, we went to see Whittemore to find out what Aguiluz's angle was. But as soon as he introduced us to Whittemore, he excused himself and took the writer into another room to talk privately.

We could overhear Aguiluz telling Whittemore of his early life in South America, flying planes and working undercover in New York against Cuban communists, and agreed that we did not want any part of Aguiluz's venture. We told Aguiluz we wouldn't discuss anything with Whittemore or agree to write a book with him. Whittemore twice arrived at my home uninvited and brought a tape recorder to get statements from me to help him in his research for the book. Rita let him in, but I ordered him out of the house and advised him strongly not to return.

Aguiluz even took me to Detective Joe Nunziata's wake. He lived at Comack on Long Island, and so Aguiluz had to go out of his way to pick me up. We attended the wake in Queens and I said a few prayers for my old friend. The death was labelled a suicide, but mob sources said that Nunziata's death was a hit, ordered by the Gambinos because they feared the detective might talk about the heroin thefts at the police evidence lockup at Broome Street and other things.

The author Robin Moore wrote that, as far back as 1967, he, Nunziata, Eddie Egan and Sonny Grosso had joked about stealing the French Connection heroin haul, and that Nunziata had even asked Moore to write a fictitious book about it. However, many cops believe that Nunziata did kill himself because he left a long, rambling suicide note.

Nunziata was laid out in his full uniform in a funeral home in Queens packed with hundreds of cops. SIU detective Jack McClean handled the wake for Ann Nunziata. All the old SIU detectives were there – it was like an old family reunion, even Bob Leuci went. However, Nunziata's death shocked everyone.

At that time, the SIU was falling apart. There were only two ways out, it seemed – jail or death – and it looked like Joe Nunziata had chosen the latter. He wasn't the only one. Dave Cody, another SIU detective and ex-partner of Leuci, was also brought in by investigators. There were three choices given to detectives caught in a bind – inform, jail or shoot yourself. Cody – an old-style cop and Second World War veteran – went on a drink bender and shot himself dead in a public park.

The SIU had begun to crumple about a year earlier with the revelations that the unit's best-looking detective had been arrested as a serial rapist. James Farley had raped several women by posing as an insurance salesman. While working with the robbery squad, John Hartigan and I had actually investigated some of these cases. During a follow-up search of Farley's home by Nassau County detectives, they found police department property-clerk envelopes containing narcotics evidence scattered about. Farley said that the SIU was a citywide unit and he sometimes worked in one borough and attended court in another and, as he lived on Long Island, it was easier to hold on to the evidence until he was in Manhattan where he could return it to the Property Clerk's Office on Broome Street. The Nassau County detectives thought this was a violation of rules and procedures, but Farley assured them that everyone in the SIU did it. The Nassau County police notified the NYPD, who in turn notified William Bonacum, the commanding officer of the Narcotics Bureau.

Bonacum, a meticulous cop, didn't like the sound of narcotics evidence lying around one of his detective's houses. His 'cop's intuition' thought there was something seriously wrong. Bonacum called for an inspection of the property clerk's inventory book. He told them to check all the narcotics evidence that had been signed out and not returned in a timely fashion. Clerks checked out the evidence of the large seizures and discovered that, three years earlier, a 'Detective Nuzziato' had signed out 50 kilos of the French Connection haul, but that there was no return signature. There was also no 'Detective Nuzziatio'.

Further investigations followed and what they revealed was staggering. In six separate withdrawals between 1969 and 1972, 261 pounds of heroin and 137 pounds of cocaine had been replaced with flour and cornstarch. This quantity represented one-fifth of all the narcotics seized by the police department since 1961. Among the narcotics stolen and replaced were the Taft Hotel and 100 Kilo Case seizures made by me, Joe Novoa and Carl Aguiluz.

Everyone in the NYPD was in shock – this was the biggest drugs robbery in history and it was stolen from the cops and it looked like cops did it. I had heard bits and pieces of what was happening with SIU but now a feeling of doom came over me. All the old anxieties came rushing back. I was waiting for a knock on the door, but fate had something else in store.

CHAPTER 21

A canary in a pear tree

Following the Knapp Commission hearings of 1970–72, which investigated police corruption within the force, the NYPD adopted a new policy of offering immunity in certain cases to police officers caught in illegal activities if they co-operated in uncovering more corruption. Fifty-one SIU detectives, including the commander of the unit, co-operated with prosecutors: fifteen were put on trial, eight were convicted and served time, and seven were found not guilty. A number committed suicide before their cases came to trial.

In a moment of true irony, several SIU detectives were fingered in the theft of 398 pounds of heroin and cocaine from the police evidence lockup at Broome Street.

Early in 1971, Detective Bob Leuci had been chosen by federal prosecutors Rudy Giuliani, Maurice Nadjari and Tom Puccio to probe this world of corruption as an undercover agent. Leuci had enjoyed a swift rise from patrolman to the rank of detective in the SIU. His boyish looks gave rise to his street nickname 'Babyface' and part of his success as a cop had been due to his innocent appearance. As an SIU team leader Leuci had access to all of the players in criminal justice from judges down. (Leuci retired from the NYPD in 1981 and became a crime writer, lecturer and teacher.

He was interviewed by the author for this book. Bob Leuci died on 12 October 2015, aged seventy-five.)

I knew Bob Leuci from our time in SIU, but we had never worked together. I had heard rumours that he was working for the government. He once asked me to set up a wire in a Pleasant Avenue restaurant, which was a mob hangout. I told him the chances of getting a wire in there was nil – I'd visited the restaurant and it was too dangerous, and noisy, to even try to put a wire in.

Leuci said in a 2013 interview with an Irish journalist, 'I love this guy,' meaning me, and I can say the same about Bob. We had not met since 1974 but, in 2013, we contacted each other for the first time in thirty-nine years and had a few conversations after that.

The night before his story hit the headlines, in August 1972, Novoa and I met Bob Leuci in a restaurant in Chinatown where SIU detectives often congregated. Leuci seemed to be under a lot of stress. We had a few drinks – tea for me – and Leuci began to unwind. He talked of the old days. Leuci spoke to Aguiluz alone and told him the rumours were true but that he would not hurt his friends. He told us 'to read the papers tomorrow' but not to worry, that we were 'in the clear'.

The following day, the New York *Daily News* printed a story outlining each and every case Leuci had been involved in. He was taken into protective custody, along with his wife and children. He would be testifying for the next two years or more. Sometime later, Carl Aguiluz was called in on an old perjury case. He was accused of tipping off Frankie Ramos to stay away from the restaurant where he was working because the FBI were about to raid it for a narcotics shipment. Aguiluz was arrested and brought to an undercover office where federal prosecutors interrogated him. He was terrified. After several hours of interrogation, Bob Leuci was brought in to help persuade Aguiluz to co-operate, though he never told him to implicate either me or Novoa. Aguiluz told prosecutors that they should investigate Leuci too.

Aguiluz decided to save his own skin. I wouldn't think prison or suicide was even contemplated. His debriefing lasted three days, and the prosecutors were amazed by it. He hung everyone out to dry – no one was spared.

He implicated Joe Novoa and me in the 100 Kilo Case. He said that we had not seized 100 kilos of heroin and cocaine, but 105 kilos. Aguiluz had held five kilos back and sold it. He said he had stolen tens of thousands of dollars from drug dealers and sold prisoners their freedom in exchange for tens of thousands of dollars. Aguiluz admitted that he had perjured himself in court at least twenty times. He had given narcotics to informants hundreds of times and had planted dozens of illegal wiretaps. He argued this was nothing out of the ordinary.

At times, he tried to justify his conduct. Every narcotics detective he had ever known gave junk to informants. It was the way things worked. Perjury in court was necessary to put drug dealers in jail because of the search and seizure laws. Wiretap laws were impossible to work with so without illegal wiretaps, most cases could never be made. Stealing money from drug dealers was justifiable because most would be out on the street and back dealing again before the arresting detective had left the court building. Drug dealers would pay off bondsmen, district attorneys and judges. Money was no object. In fact, the only way to stop their drug dealing was to seize their cash at the moment of arrest. As for selling them their freedom, this was only done when, because of scarcity of evidence, a legal arrest could not be made.

Aguiluz said the reason he held back the five kilos was that he was so excited over such a large seizure that he hardly knew what he was doing. He had done it instinctively, but then he didn't know what to do with it. He couldn't turn it in, because there would be too many questions asked, and he couldn't flush it down the toilet because it was worth too much money. He said we'd known he had the drugs and wouldn't have believed he'd flushed them away, but would think he sold them for himself. For weeks after, he'd driven around with five kilos of narcotics stashed in the trunk of his car. Finally, he'd begun disposing of the drugs. He sold them in instalments for safety's sake. He didn't think another five kilos on the New York drugs market would make any difference. Aguiluz had South American friends and relatives who bought the drugs from him at a price where they would be able to make a tidy profit for themselves. Frankie Ramos was a relative of Aguiluz's and he ran a South American soccer club and owned a bar where South American drug dealers met and sold large amounts of drugs.

Not one to stand on scruples and principles, Aguiluz turned out to be a very cold individual. I knew this, of course, but he still surprised me. Even the prosecutors were shocked as Aguiluz gave up cops without a thought. He told them not to be so shocked because their star witness Bob Leuci was just as dirty, but when the prosecutors asked for concrete proof Aguiluz could not provide any.

Aguiluz blamed Leuci for provoking the entire investigation into the SIU and for having persuaded him to roll over. The prosecutors arrested Aguiluz's brother-in-law, Sal Buteria, a former SIU detective, and two other cops who had worked with Aguiluz. All three quickly cracked and corroborated Aguiluz's stories of drug dealing. Using dates Aguiluz had provided, the prosecutors subpoenaed the bank records of our old supervisor, Lieutenant John Egan, which showed that on the day following virtually every arrest, Egan made substantial deposits to one or another of his many savings accounts. Mine and Novoa's bank records were next to be assessed, but I never made bank deposits. Aguiluz said one score had been divided up in a room in the Taft Hotel, so the hotel's records were subpoenaed. These showed that the room in question had been registered in the name of Detective Peter Daly, but this room had been used by the team to make the big arrest in the 100 Kilo Case. The witch-hunt went on and on and more SIU detectives were implicated and, in turn, implicated others. Very few against whom charges were brought were acquitted.

As Christmas 1973 approached, the word on the grapevine was that indictments for corruption were about to be handed down on former members of the SIU. I was subpoenaed along with Novoa and Aguiluz to give evidence on an investigation into the Taft Hotel narcotics seizure, but my lawyer, Jack Field*, argued that this case was still in progression and I could not give evidence. We were allowed to go without having to give substantiation, but I knew it was only a matter of time before we would be called again.

I put a wiretap on my home phone so the relevant investigating authorities would not officially entrap me in a conversation that would put me in jeopardy. As a wireman, I knew all the hiding places and removed the sockets from the wall, so I could see whether they had been fitted with bugs. During my recovery from the car accident, I couldn't drive and also had difficulty walking. Because of the impending indictments, I received phone calls from friends who asked that I call them back at certain specified times on a phone number supplied. I had to get someone to drive me to a public telephone so I could make the calls.

On one of the outside calls a friend on the inside told me about certain named police friends who had met in a hotel room for several hours with members of a specific organised crime family. They were to be called to a grand jury at a date that had not yet been set. It was then up to me to tell these friends about this secret information from the grand jury sitting, and let them know exactly who was named on both sides.

One man named in the indictments was Lieutenant John Egan, my old SIU commander. I telephoned Egan and complained to him about not 'visiting his sick friend'. Egan knew this was a coded message and immediately drove to my home in his big Cadillac, puffing on a large cigar and looking like a well-heeled mobster rather than a police lieutenant. I did not openly display any signs of wealth and frowned on cops who did. Egan parked his car on the road and I walked out and told him of what I had heard and that he would soon to be called to testify. Egan was shocked and became visibly upset, but I told him to calm down and face up to the realities. I also disclosed who had mentioned his name and related the exact circumstances word for word. Egan left, warning me not to talk to anyone else, as this would severely affect many others.

Some weeks later, Egan was subpoenaed to appear before the Nadjari grand jury investigations of the NYPD. Nadjari's office and his grand jury were in Tower Two of the World Trade Center. Under questioning by the grand jury, Egan described dozens of corrupt acts, ranging from the ordering of illegal wiretaps to the stealing of hundreds of thousands of dollars; from suborning perjury of search warrants to confiscated drugs being sold. When Egan had finished giving his evidence, he was asked one further question:

'Did anyone advise you that you were to be called to testify at the grand jury?'

'Yes,' Egan replied, 'Detective Pete Daly!'

There was no reason for my name to be mentioned. I had nothing to do with the case being investigated – it was a State of New York investigation and was separate from the federal investigation that Carl Aguiluz had given information to, so Egan was obviously trying to curry favour with the grand jury by naming me.

Before a criminal case could be brought to trial, an indictment by a grand jury had to be obtained. A grand jury was made up of twenty-three citizens – twenty-two jurors and a foreman, all volunteers, most of them professional or retired people of relative affluence. In New York State, a witness was required to answer questions before the grand jury when summoned. What they said before the grand jury could not later be used against them since the United States Constitution protects a witness against self-incrimination.

A grand jury meets in secret and the proceedings remain private – no public record is kept of what happened in the grand jury room. I was summoned at short notice to appear before the Nadjari grand jury on 26 December, for the purpose of finding out how I knew about the secret minutes of the grand jury that I had revealed to John Egan. Former detective Jack Field, my regular attorney, was advised that he could not represent me as Nadjari also wanted to indict him, as it was alleged that I was paying Field and his office a yearly fee in case I was indicted on any charges. Field's law partner, Richard Ernst*, was then appointed to represent me.

Because of my injuries, I needed someone outside my house to drive me to visit seven other NYPD detectives, who resided in the area. They were in my confidence as I was in theirs. I was to telephone them the night before I was to appear at the grand jury and request each one in turn to drive me to the hearing the following day. It was arranged that they were to refuse me a lift for a variety of personal reasons. My detective friends were made aware that all these conversations were to be taped by me. In this way, I could prove that I had made a serious, albeit unsuccessful, effort to get transportation to appear before the grand jury.

I knew that Egan and any others under investigation could not find any means to alert me and they likewise understood that if I thought I was under surveillance I also could not communicate with them.

When the day came that I was to make my series of phone calls I was very apprehensive. These calls would decide my future. I had a new tape reel in the telephone machine ready to go. It was Christmas Day and I had been up early. I spent time with my children, playing with their new toys and watching Christmas movies, and the hours ticked slowly by. My mind was elsewhere, though, as I waited to make my calls. Suddenly, it began to snow heavily.

It was every child's dream – snow at Christmas. On this occasion, it was also my Christmas wish come true. What better reason to refuse to drive into NYC than snow? By 7 p.m. that evening, there were fourteen inches of snow on the ground in the city and also in upstate regions. I was saved by snow. I started my series of phone calls, but to a man all of the friends I rang replied, 'Are you mad? Drive to New York City in fourteen inches of snow? Not on your life!'

I phoned my appearing lawyer – Richard Ernst – to advise him that I could not be in attendance, as I had no transport, or anybody willing to drive me to New York City because of the inclement weather. Ernst said that he would advise the jury of my failed efforts, but he would be there as he lived in New Jersey, and it was just a short trip through the Holland Tunnel directly into the underground train station of the Twin Towers.

On the evening of 26 December, Ernst phoned me to tell me that there were not enough people at the hearing to convene a jury and that I would be informed of a future date to appear. I was delighted and could not have planned it any better.

Because of my accident, I decided to retire from the NYPD if I could secure a disability pension. As a result of the injuries I sustained, my left arm and fingers went numb constantly. I had persistent pains in my head, suffered memory loss and found it hard to walk at times without stumbling and felt that I could not return to duty and perform the responsibilities of a street cop and I definitely did not want to end up behind a desk. Since I had sustained an on-duty injury, I was eligible to retire on a disability pension. This pension would be tax-free, equivalent to three-quarters of my final year's pay, as a cop's pension was based on total earnings in the final year of service. I appeared before a Police Department medical board, which reviewed my medical history and decided that I was, in fact, disabled and not fit to work full duty. Because of my head injury, I was deemed a danger to myself and others. If at some future date I shot, injured or killed someone, the City would be responsible for my actions and could be sued for permitting an injured policeman back on the street.

The NYPD also conducted a 'round robin' investigation on me to make sure that I did not have any case pending against me anywhere – by city or state prosecutors. If I was facing any charges, I would not qualify for a pension, but as my former partner Carl Aguiluz was an informant for the federal authorities, their information was secret from city and state investigators.

I was called before the Police Pension Board, which included representatives from the city's various police unions. Four personal friends were part of the seven-man pension board. I had known them for many years and asked them to bring my pension before the 26 December grand jury hearing date, so I could be retired in January 1974, one month earlier than expected. The City and State of New York had no knowledge of the federal investigation and my application for a disability pension was approved. I retired as of midnight on 24 January 1974, but I had to wait a month to get the first pension cheque.

I then decided to return to Ireland for recovery treatment and to spend time with my father, who was terminally ill with cancer. In February 1974 I was helped to my aeroplane seat by a police friend to make the flight home to Ireland. I landed at Shannon airport and was met by my ailing father and brother. A medical examination in Bundoran in County Donegal revealed that I had patchy loss of memory for recent and more distant events. I suffered from constant headaches and double vision following any prolonged period of concentration reading or watching TV, and was also very nervous and agitated and found it hard to sleep unless with heavy sedation. The examining doctor concluded that these symptoms would be expected to continue for some time.

In my absence, on 8 March 1974 I was indicted along with Joe Novoa, Frankie Ramos, Demetrios Papadakis (aka Jimmy the Greek), Joaquin Nieves and Elissa Possas by a grand jury on six counts of narcotics violations. Both myself and Novoa were charged with conspiracy to defraud the United States and its departments and agencies in investigating and prosecuting violations of the narcotics laws. The grand jury stated that after arresting Emilio Diaz Gonzales, Elena Risso, Jose Luis Mulas and Jorge Rodriguez Araya, we seized approximately $1,200 from them in the 6th Precinct station house, which we divided among ourselves and 'others' (namely Carl Aguiluz), and which we did not report to law enforcement authorities. We also retained possession of five kilos of heroin and cocaine seized with a further 100 kilos from Apartment 4F, 210 West 19th Street, New York City. While it is generally agreed that the three of us held back five kilos, it is thought by some that Aguiluz kept a further five kilos for himself. Aguiluz had his own motives for this.

The trial by jury, before Judge Inzer B. Wyatt, against Joe Novoa, Jimmy Papadakis and Joaquin Nieves began on 15 May 1974. It ended thirteen days later in convictions for Novoa and Papadakis. Novoa was offered a chance to co-operate, but said he would not turn on his former partners and friends. He was found guilty of conspiracy to obstruct justice and received a five-year sentence. He was also given a ten-year sentence, to run concurrently, for the sale of the five kilos. He appealed his conviction some months later, but it was upheld.

Papadakis was sentenced to five years for conspiracy to obstruct justice, to run concurrently with consecutive five-year terms he was then serving for prior violations of federal narcotics laws. Frankie Ramos pleaded guilty to conspiracy to purchase and sell narcotics, for which he was sentenced to ten years' imprisonment. He had co-operated with the prosecution – in this and other cases – and was granted immunity and his sentence suspended. Joaquin Nieves was acquitted by the jury on a charge that he bought a kilo of heroin.

Carl Aguiluz, after testifying in eight trials and pleading guilty to felony tax fraud both in the Southern (Manhattan) and Eastern (Brooklyn) Districts, received a suspended sentence and was relocated to an unknown destination. His wife once appeared on a television chat show, in silhouette, but I never found out where Aguiluz disappeared to.

It grieved me to see my friends going to prison. The whole system was corrupt and now the higher-ups were using other cops who were just as guilty to gain convictions against those who were just following the system that had been in place since the foundation of the NYPD. The guilty, like Aguiluz, were being let off because they co-operated. It didn't erase their guilt, it just got them out of going to jail.

Myself and Elissa Possas were considered fugitives as we were not within the jurisdiction. It was known that I was living in Donegal and I had learned that I could not be extradited as no extradition treaty existed between the Republic of Ireland and the United States. A letter to the US Embassy in Dublin from the Secretary of State in Washington revealed that even if minor changes in the text of an extradition treaty between the two countries were resolved immediately and a treaty was placed in a final form for signature, the US ratification process would involve submission to the Senate through the president, Senate foreign relations committee hearings and report, and full Senate action. This process would, at the best of times, take months, and the Secretary of State believed it 'impractical to try to rush treaty through all above steps for Daly case'.

I was advised of the indictment in my absence on twelve counts arising out of information given to a Federal Grand Jury by Aguiluz. According to Robert Daley in his book *Prince of the City*, I sent a picture of myself to Aguiluz. The photograph showed me sitting by a lake in Donegal, wearing a crew-neck sweater and waving. There was a pier nearby surrounded by beautiful scenery. However, because of my skull fracture, I had various continuing side-effects, including loss of memory, and now I have no recollection of this.

It would take three years before I was totally back to myself. In the meantime, I would experience some traumatic problems with law enforcement in England and the United States.

PART II
FALL

*It took many years for me to go from an arresting officer to friend and
that is the true joy of this strange life we all share.*
Mike Levine, former DEA agent

CHAPTER 1

Guest of the Queen

It was known that I had entered Britain in late 1974 and British police began enquiries in an effort to locate and arrest me. My sister, Maeve, was living in London and I had called to see an old family friend, Fr Herbie Bromley in Bristol, on my way to visit her. My US passport had expired in August 1974 and I had made no application for a new one. The Special Consular Services Branch at the US Embassy made a written request to the British Home Office for the extradition of me under the 1931 Extradition Treaty. The British police also received a passport photograph of me and information of my arrival flight to Britain. A warrant for my arrest was issued, to be used if I re-entered Britain. During my first visit, Scotland Yard detectives missed me. The second time I was not so lucky.

Because I had been living in the US, I was unaware that my sister Maeve had fallen out with the family. It was only when I returned to Ireland that I heard about this. Word had come back that Maeve was not in her usual haunts and because of my police background I thought I would be able to find her and possibly heal the rift. I flew to Cardiff airport and took the train to Bristol to see Fr Bromley. Many people from Ballyshannon, living or visiting

England, would come down to Bristol to attend parish dances organised by Fr Bromley; it gave them a chance to meet friends.

I returned to Britain a few weeks later, in December, flying in to Newport in Wales and staying in a bed and breakfast before I got the train to London. Again I called on Fr Bromley. Years later, when I was in Lewisburg Penitentiary, I found out that Fr Bromley had informed on me. I was devastated, as I had grown up with Fr Bromley and we had been school-going friends. It was only when I was looking for my trial documents that I received an unclassified US Embassy document dated 20 November 1974, which stated:

> *Embassy informed that British police inquiries at Bristol indicate Daly departed UK for Ireland some 14 days ago after visiting Father Bromley who has offered police full co-operation in apprehension of fugitive. Warrant for his arrest remains outstanding to be used should Daly re-enter UK.*

I don't know why Fr Bromley informed on me. It could have been because my brother, Anthony, was a prominent Irish republican, and he possibly thought I was involved with the republican movement. Anthony served twenty years as a Sinn Féin councillor on Ballyshannon Town Commission and twice held the position of chairman, the only Sinn Féin member ever to do so. I had picked the worst time to travel to England. The Irish Republican Army had initiated a bombing campaign on mainland Britain that left hundreds dead and injured.

The British Special Branch was responsible for matters of national security and, because of the nature of my arrest, handled the investigation on me. I was arrested in a hotel as I sat down for breakfast with a cousin. Another hour or so and I probably would have been flying home, but the day before, a police detective had asked me for identification on the stairwell of the hotel, so the Special Branch were obviously on my trail. Special Branch Detective Inspector Michael Atkins and Detective Constable John Bennie visited me at Huyton Police Station outside Liverpool. Atkins asked if I was Peter Daly, to which I said I was, and he told me he was in possession of a warrant issued on behalf of the US authorities in connection with narcotics offences in New York. He then read the warrant and cautioned me that I was not obligated to say anything unless I wished to do so, but what I said might be used in evidence against me. I read the warrant and said I had nothing to say. Atkins and Bennie left but returned the next morning, took me from my cell and brought me to Liverpool Railway Station where we boarded a train to London.

During the train ride I asked about my legal representation and extradition procedures. The officers told me legal aid was available, depending on my financial condition, upon application to a magistrate. After asking about my legal status regarding extradition I told them that I received an NYPD pension.

Detective Bennie asked me if I knew Gabriel Stefania, Carl Aguiluz, Joe Novoa, Charles Wooster and John Egan. I answered that I did and that all were members of the Narcotics Bureau of the NYPD. I also said that Joe was in jail as I had received a letter from his wife. I said that I knew Carl Aguiluz had turned informant. During the conversation, I admitted that I knew the American authorities were after me, but only after I had flown home to Ireland. I told the detectives I had come to England to visit my sister as I hadn't seen her in seventeen years (when I had been home for my brother's wedding). When I asked the detectives how much they knew about the charges pending against me, Bennie answered by reading a copy of the indictment.

When the train reached London, the two detectives brought me to Bow Street Police Station where I was formally charged. Later I was brought to Bow Street Magistrates Court to be remanded.

Inspector Atkins outlined the case to the magistrate. Under cross-examination, he clarified that he had made the notes in Bow Street Station and not on the train and that they were from memory and not of the actual conversation.

Detective Bennie said he had cautioned me on what I was saying in the first interview in Huyton Police Station and that I had handed him my handwritten resumé and that he had also taken notes of the conversation he'd had with me. The notes, however, were taken after the conversation. He said both he and Inspector Atkins had had general conversations with me about the legal aid system, solicitors and extradition procedures. Bennie clarified that he had never shown me the notes or asked me if I wanted to see them. He also mentioned that I had said 105 kilos, not 100 kilos, in the conversation about the famous narcotics seizure.

Next, I was called to the stand. When the magistrate asked if I was applying for bail I said that I was. Inspector Atkins opposed the granting of bail, saying that because of the seriousness of the charges, he thought I might leave the jurisdiction. When asked if I would go back to Ireland if I was granted bail, I said that I'd like to. Bail was refused. A hearing was set for 30 December, at which the Director of Public Prosecutions was to represent the United States.

I was remanded in custody to C Wing in Pentonville Prison, which was used for prisoners on remand. The Irish police considered me a republican supporter and sympathiser and told the British authorities as much. I was segregated for the first nine days in Pentonville on twenty-three-hour lock-up, with just one hour's exercise, which I took separately from other prisoners. I found this very traumatic – I was the one who put people behind bars, not the one to be behind bars. It was a shock to my system and coupled with my memory loss and more importantly, the absence of my children from my life, it took a huge toll on my mental stability. I was lucky that I had at least one book, Elvis Presley's biography, to read, which had to last me from 23 December 1974 to 3 January 1975. A prison guard came to bring me to mass on Christmas Day. He said he was to take me to visit my God, but I told him that my God was here in my cell with me. I had no need to be escorted to visit Him, so the guard left.

A stricter level of security was imposed on Irish political prisoners than the ordinary criminals. I was entitled to one-hour's exercise – by law – each day. I was guarded by three officers and a dog as I walked around a yard in uniform known in prison garb as 'patches' – consisting of a brown jacket with a football-sized yellow ball on the front and the back, and trousers with a two-to-three-inch-thick yellow stripe running down both outer legs. This uniform was reserved only for IRA prisoners.

My brother was an active republican and I knew many people who were involved in the IRA because we lived on the border with Northern Ireland. It was not a big thing at home in Donegal where there was a lot of IRA activity. I could have told my captors that I was not involved with the IRA, but that would have been against my principles. I did not, or could not, ask for different or more lenient treatment. It was not in my nature. My decision of non-co-operation extended to the British police.

During the day, my bed was taken out of my cell, and I was left with a wooden table and chair, a plastic water bottle and a white plastic pot, in which I was to urinate and defecate. There was an extra set of bars on my cell window and all the cells around mine had to be occupied, above, below and each side. I was checked regularly during each twenty-four-hour period. A prison officer would peep into my cell through the spyhole and, as petty harassment, pull the door lock back and forth often throughout my sleeping hours. One particular officer would shout, 'Hey, Irish, what are you doing?'

I would reply, 'I'm trying to remember how to swim.'

The prison officer would remind me that you never forgot how to swim or how to have sex.

The small cell had two lights – a white light for daytime and a red light at night. Often during the night, my cell door would crash open, usually at 2 a.m. or 4 a.m. I would be woken by the shouts of up to three prison officers, ordered to strip naked and stand on the balcony outside my cell. One officer would stand guard over me while another would beat the bars of the window with a rubber hammer and the third officer tore my bedclothes apart and searched under and over the bed and through my prison uniform. My legal papers, family pictures and incoming post and outgoing letters were thrown all around the cell, while I stood naked with my back to the wall and my arms outstretched. I was then ordered to bend over and grab my ankles, exposing my rear end. In the final act of degradation one of the officers inserted a rubber-gloved finger into my rectum. It was their way of saying to me, the alleged IRA member, 'Fuck you!' Sometimes, they just said it, 'Fuck you, you Fenian bastard!'

I would then be ordered back into my cell. The heavy cell door was shut loudly and the big bolt banged sharply into the locked position. With my night light on, I could see all my papers, clothes and bed sheets thrown from one corner to the other. Sometimes I cried tears of anger, but I was determined not to allow these actions to discourage or demoralise me. Often I would return to a makeshift bed and clean up the following day.

Because of the shock of my sudden incarceration, I often had panic attacks and used to pace up and down the small cell like a caged lion. I worked myself into a state to the point of not being able to breathe and I would pass out. I was allowed extra plastic containers filled with water for when I was like this, and I would drink and drink the water and urinate almost immediately. I would press the bell – a small metal dial inside my cell – indicating that I needed help. It was often ignored but, depending on the prison officer on duty, I would get a sleeping tablet, which knocked me out until the next morning when I would wake up, fresh and full of vigour.

The funny thing was that the many nights when the screws (which is what we called the guards) did their late-night searching were the ones when I never got a panic attack.

Unlike the American system of having toilet facilities in a cell, the British prison system had a process called 'slopping out'. British prisons date from the Victorian era and were never originally designed to have toilets in the cells. Urinating was done into a plastic chamber pot with a holding handle on its side and a lid over the top. This would be stored in the cell until the next morning. The prison officers went to one cell at a time. An officer released the large outside bolt pin, which let the occupant know that release was at hand. When the door swung inwards the inmate rushed out, pot extended to the open toilet area at the end of the block and quickly emptied the contents into a large open bin where a tap was continuously running cold water. The pot was held under the flow of water, emptied, and rinsed quickly.

If I needed to defecate, I would spread a newspaper sheet out over the top to catch the waste. The newspaper was neatly folded up, as the smell would infect the cell all night, and was then thrown out into the yard below. The cell windows were so high that I had to stand on my bed to reach them. Sometimes the waste hit a patrolling prison officer below. Direct hits were planned by listening to the noise of an officer walking his dog, and brought shouts of delight from other prisoners.

In the mornings, the screws would leave the door open and an officer would appear with a canvas pouch, from which he took paper-enclosed razor blades inserted in small pockets with each cell number inscribed on it. I would take out the one with my cell number on it. The officer would then leave and the cell door would be slammed shut again, and I had ten minutes to put the blade in my safety razor, soap my face and shave, then replace the blade into its paper cover and wait for the return of the screw. I would then hand it to him and he would check it to be sure the blade was in there and then put it back into the same numbered position in the canvas holder.

These were the daily routines in Pentonville Prison for the five long months I was there. This was at a time when the IRA was conducting a bombing campaign and was engaged in prison riots, protests and prison breaks. I got lucky some time into my Pentonville stay as a prison officer supervisor, whose name was Daniel Goan, arrived. He was a native of Ballyshannon and, along with his sisters and brothers, had been brought into the world by my father, Dr Patrick Daly. Dan may have told the screws that I'd been in America for the past thirty years and that I was not a member of the IRA because although the cell searches continued, the brutality and animosity disappeared. However, I still remained a security risk and a Category A prisoner.

My sister Maeve visited and brought cooked food packages. Every visit, she brought me in a box of matches, even though I didn't smoke. I gave them out as favours. A match for smoking could be split in four to make four cigarette lights. In return, I often got some decent food, stolen from the prison kitchen. The visiting room was large, with a separate table for each family, with one prison officer sitting at a desk at the top of the room and another walking around. I, however, had one screw handcuffed to me, sitting with me at my table.

A family friend, Fr Ambrose O'Gorman, who was in Ilford in London, visited me five or six times and brought me in my local newspaper, the *Donegal Democrat*. Fr O'Gorman had survived several bombing raids during the Blitz while serving in London parishes and as a chaplain to the RAF. At one stage he was president of the Donegal Association in London. When he heard I was in prison, he did not hesitate in visiting me. Fr O'Gorman retired to Ballyshannon and died in 2014, aged 102, being at the time Ireland's oldest priest.

People in prison have a lot of time to think. These thoughts can be put to constructive use. I, like most prisoners, thought that my mail was being read for ulterior purposes and so devised my own way of preventing this. As a cautionary measure, I always put a strand of my hair in the folded letter I was sending out and if the hair was not in the letter it meant the envelope had been interfered with. A check mark was put on the letter, which meant the reader was to check for the hair strand in the folded paper.

On 30 December 1974 I was further remanded for appearance on 6 January 1975. Following the hearing, I was asked if I had any objections to speaking with US federal agents. I didn't, and agreed to meet them.

Two Drug Enforcement Administration (DEA) agents had travelled from Paris to London on 29 December to interview me. Arrangements were made for the agents to do so at London's Bow Street Court the following morning when I appeared for a bail hearing. I was escorted to an empty cell adjacent to Bow Street courtroom. The DEA agents told me that it would be in my best interests to waive extradition and return to the US. I told them that I felt it best to consult an attorney before making any decision. I was asked why I'd left the safety of Ireland, knowing that the US authorities were looking to extradite me. I told them that I had received information that my sister had got into trouble and I had travelled to England in an attempt to find her.

I was informed by the DEA agents that they had raided my home and found confiscated South American federal police ID cards belonging to police involved in the transportation, shipping and conveying of people who were carrying narcotics over various state and country boundaries. The agents stressed they were interested in my co-operation on the matter and also on records of telephone numbers and names that were listed to other parts of the US and South America, which they had found in my home. In return for my co-operation, the federal agents offered to escort me to Ballyshannon, where my father was dying of cancer. I would later travel on to New York, where I would enter the Federal Witness Protection Programme and testify in a grand jury hearing about other police officers and members of organised crime. I was told I would be held in a special correctional prison in an unnamed location. This would all be agreed with my lawyer present, and worked out to my satisfaction. I would get a change of identity and physical features, if required. My social security number would also be changed and my home and property sold with my agreement so that I could be set up in a new location. However, after my initial visit home, I would never again be able to return to my hometown or country.

The interview ended after about half an hour when I said, 'I respectfully decline your kind offer.'

The agents told me that I had three choices: co-operate, take my own life or go to prison. I chose to go to prison rather than testify and, in so doing, knew I risked losing my family because they could not understand why I would take such a course of action.

As bad as my situation was, I could see clearly. There was no such thing as conditional or limited co-operation: it was all you knew or no deal. I knew if I turned informant, I would have to implicate everyone, and the remorse I would feel would be too much to bear. I would have to betray men I had worked with for many years. Whatever way I thought of it, I could not bring myself to turn on my friends and colleagues. In my world, I would be the most hated of creatures, a rat, a snitch, an informer. My friends would never forgive me. The old saying is not true, there *is* honour among thieves, and the thought of giving up my honour was more unbearable to me than the prospect of going to prison for a long time.

I was determined to remain true to my personal code, which told me that an honourable man never informs on another, regardless of the consequences. You make a choice somewhere along the way and then you live with it. There's no turning back.

So I decided not to co-operate. That meant giving them no information whatsoever. You cannot co-operate a little or on one particular thing or circumstance. If you co-operate at all you are trapped, and it escalates. What would start out as one small piece of information would snowball to become an avalanche and include all my friends. All these people had pensions and families, and when they were faced with going to prison, they'd reveal other information, which would include their friends, and on and on it would go. If I gave information on one person, in the end, dozens of other lives and futures would be lost and destroyed. In the process one, or more, finding that they are going to be destroyed and their families disgraced, may decide to end his or her life rather than make their family victims of this situation. Then I would have to accept that because I saved myself, I destroyed others. So I accepted responsibility for my actions, alone. That is what Joe Novoa and I did.

In total, about twelve detectives refused to co-operate with the authorities.

At my 6 January hearing I was further remanded until 27 January, with the Home Office urgently telephoning the US Embassy that if the minimum documents – actual request for extradition, certified copies of original warrants, a statement from US government authority about the law in the US, a statement of facts relating to the offences alleged to have taken place and evidence of identity – were not received by that date, I would be released. A time limitation of two months in which to provide sufficient evidence to justify committal would run out on 27 February 1975 and, at the hearing, the US authorities were admonished by the court for not submitting the necessary documentation in a timely fashion.

The problem was that although Carl Aguiluz had said in his affidavit that a subsequent test by a chemist revealed that the narcotics they had seized in the 100 Kilo Case were heroin and cocaine, this was only hearsay and was not admissible in the British court. Sworn evidence from the chemist who analysed the drugs haul was needed and, without this, the British DPP felt the case for extradition would fail. While British law allowed the jury to convict on the uncorroborated evidence of an accomplice, in practice this was extremely rare. Further evidence was needed. The DPP was also worried about the analysis of the narcotics seized – the heroin and cocaine needed to be clearly distinguished, with the heroin defined as diamorphine, for the corresponding English dangerous drugs legislation.

On 27 January 1975, at Bow Street Court, the DPP informed the US Embassy that the British Home Secretary had signed the order to proceed and further remanded me in custody. My American passport had expired in August 1974, but because I was listed as an Irish republican and a Special Category A prisoner, the British authorities wouldn't allow me to be taken to the US Embassy in London, so an American representative came to Pentonville Prison. I was taken to a small private room, photographed, and issued with a visa to return to the US if the extradition case was successful.

My next hearing was scheduled for 27 February, with the US government granted one month's extension – until 20 March – to furnish the DPP with all the necessary documentation requested in order to make a decision on my extradition. Following the hearing on 27 February the DPP, on advice from counsel, said that while the certified court transcript and related affidavits were sufficient, the evidence covering the identification of the narcotics was not adequate and would cause them a lot of concern. An unclassified letter from the DPP to the US Embassy dated that day said:

> *We have already stressed to you that we consider this evidence to be vital to the case in our courts … I cannot over-emphasize the very great risk of failure that will arise when the case is heard at Bow Street if this evidence is not properly dealt with …*
>
> *The further affidavit of [Gene] Ferrar therein does not assist us in any way other than proving that heroin is diamorphine. In the circumstances it is therefore of the utmost importance that you should once again refer back to America as a matter of extreme urgency. As you are aware, we must present our case at Bow Street before 20 March, and accordingly, time is very much of the essence. In view of this I now suggest various ways in which this defect might be cured and*

leave it to the local authorities to choose which is most appropriate to what in fact occurred.

Method 1: Ideally, Aguiluz should swear an affidavit covering the handing in of the suitcases and drugs at the police station and especially indicating to whom he gave them. Affidavits should then be obtained from the persons who handled the suitcases and drugs between that time and the time Ferrar examined them and record, if it be the case, the facts of their having handled them. Ferrar, preferably, should swear a completely new affidavit saying from whom he seized the suitcases and drugs and setting out his findings. He should also say the heroin is diamorphine.

Method 2: Alternatively, it may be simpler if Aguiluz were to identify the suitcases and drugs in the presence of Ferrar who should then confirm that they were the ones that he examined. Suggested forms of affidavits to cover this method would be subject to the true details as follows: Ferrar: 'On the 18th day of April, 1970 I examined four suitcases at the police laboratory of the City of New York and found them to contain {specify drugs}. On the {blank} day of {blank}, 1975 I identified the same suitcases and drugs in the presence of Carl Aguiluz.'

The affidavit of Aguiluz: 'On the {blank} day of {blank} I was present when Gene L. Ferrar identified four suitcases containing drugs. These were suitcases and drugs I seized from Apartment

4F at 210 West 19th Street, New York City on the 14th day of April, 1970. At {name of place} I handed in the said suitcases and drugs at blank {or other method of disposal}.'

Method 3: Whether in the last resort Aguiluz can identify from his own knowledge the suitcases and drugs referred to in Ferrar's report {Exhibit D-1} by any of the references and numbers therein as being the suitcases and drugs he seized, if so he should set this out in an affidavit.

You will observe that we require evidence to prove that the drugs examined by Ferrar were in fact those seized during the raid and handed in to police headquarters by Aguiluz. Our courts would then be asked to draw an inference that the material retained by Aguiluz and disposed by him to Bouteriera was also cocaine and heroin.

Counsel has again confirmed that he is anxious to receive the evidence of Ramos which I mentioned in my letter of 5th February and I shall be grateful if you would be good enough to stress this to Washington.

Daly was today remanded in custody until 6 March. Sir Frank Milton indicated that he would wish to consider on the day possible arrangements for the hearing so it is essential that I have the above evidence by 6 March or at least a firm indication as to its arrival here. Sir Frank again made the point of reminding us that any further extension of time would not be favourable.

Because of court calendar problems, the hearing set for 6 March was postponed until 17 March, giving the US authorities some leeway on sending evidence. The new evidence – that the drugs were exactly confirmed as the British system requested – arrived by special courier in time for the DPP to successfully present its case for my extradition. I was indicted on nine counts of criminal narcotics conspiracy. Counts 1 to 4 were: conspiracy, obstruction, misprision and narcotics conspiracy. Count 5 was the five kilos of heroin and cocaine, and counts 6, 7, and 8 were the three heroin transfer counts. However, I was to be extradited on counts 5 to 8 only. In a letter dated 17 March 1975, the US Embassy stated it wished to commend the British DPP for its outstanding performance in representing the US government in this case.

Sir Frank Milton, London's Chief Metropolitan Magistrate, who was described as the epitome of wisdom and common sense and who was known to tolerate no action viewed as deceiving, misleading, disingenuous or false, ruled that there was sufficient evidence for me to be extradited to the United States to stand trial. I was remanded in court to await extradition on an order that was to be signed by the Home Secretary, with fifteen days' notice to lodge an appeal.

I had the right to apply for a writ of habeas corpus within fifteen days, on the basis that the British police had no reason to arrest me. Under advice from my initial solicitor – Paddy Madigan, my cousin who had flown over from Dublin – I then applied for legal aid in connection with my proposed appeal for a writ of habeas corpus. The London Legal Aid Office turned it down. While I could then appeal to the Area Office to further delay my departure from London, the decision was not likely to be overruled. The British Home Secretary, Roy Jenkins, signed my surrender order and set my extradition to New York for 12 May 1975.

I could not help but feel angry that, in order to succeed with my extradition, both the British and American judicial systems had manipulated evidence – one of the crimes they were charging me with.

CHAPTER 2
The West Street Zoo

After a six-month legal battle, I was going back to the USA.

On 12 May 1975 I was brought under heavy police escort to London's Heathrow airport and handed over to two American DEA agents, Mike Levine and Danny Martin. Our small party boarded TWA Flight 701 to New York, which left Heathrow at 6 p.m. Agent Martin read me my rights from a small printed card. I responded to each separate question and then, at the end, said to both agents that I was remaining silent and wanted an attorney present for any questions about the actual case, or anything that could be considered in any remote way as relating to the overall affair. I asked to be made aware of my right to silence and a right to a lawyer over international waters.

All the comforts of first class, including hot dinner, music, a mini bottle of wine – which I refused as I don't drink – were available to me on the 747 jumbo jet.

When Agent Martin went to the toilet, I said to Agent Levine, 'Mike, people told me it would be you coming. I hear that you're a good guy. Let's talk about anything but the case. Sports, whatever, anything but the case.'

He said, 'Sure thing,' and that's what we did all the way back to the US, talked about everything in the world but my case.

What I meant by 'I hear you're a good guy' was essentially this. Mike Levine had worked with dozens of informers who had betrayed their old friendships to save themselves from doing prison time. Mike had respect for me, regardless of the fact that I had done wrong. A man prepared to take his punishment and not turn on his own was deserving of his respect. Mike was not about to judge me. That was not his job. His assignment was to bring me back to New York.

The flight arrived at New York JFK at 8.30 p.m. local time. At the airport, I was met by three more DEA agents and transported by car to the DEA headquarters at 59th Street on the West Side for fingerprinting, photographing and other particulars.

There were other ex-SIU detectives present and I thought that the DEA was trying to fool me by their presence in the building, hoping that I would think the SIU men were under arrest and I would talk to them. Their job was to prise out any information on whether my memory was impaired, which I had told the police and courts in London it was. The SIU men were testifying against their fellow officers and were supposed to be in the same boat as me, but I smelled a rat and didn't even bid them the time of day.

I was then brought by car to my new destination, the West Street Federal Detention Center, and was stripped of the little I had from Pentonville Prison – a Timex watch. This was my last valuable possession, but I cared little for it. I had been shut off from daylight for so long that there was no need to know the time of day. My legal papers were returned with me, including several letters I had written to the US ambassador in London, to which I had never received a reply. As a US army veteran and a naturalised citizen, I found this very hurtful. There had been other foreign nationals in jail with me in England whose embassies and ambassadors had had no problem corresponding with them, and, in some cases, visiting them.

The West Street Detention Center was a huge warehouse four storeys high, where federal prisoners were kept while awaiting trial. It was sectioned off into large cages, called tanks, where iron bars ran from floor to ceiling, and then across the top and down the other side. There was a three-solid-iron-bar cage with a crawl space above for lighting, plumbing and where correctional officers crept along and struck each bar with a rubber mallet to make sure they were not false or hadn't been cut away to the last millimetre for a planned breakout. The bunks were one above the other in a smaller inner cage. The street name for this prison was 'the Zoo'. I could imagine my children being taunted by their pals that 'their dad was in the West Street Zoo'.

I had to have a medical examination before I was admitted, which I thought was laughable, that I had to pass a physical to get into this hell-hole. A night-shift medical attendant, a friendly, concerned young man, examined me and gave me a sleeping pill. When I was being taken to my cell, at around 3 a.m., one prison guard whispered to another, loud enough for me to hear, 'The Old Man wants him in his cell.' It meant nothing to me. I was so jetlagged and tired that I did not give much thought to what was happening. I was put in the top bunk of a darkened cell and slept until the doors were opened at 6 a.m.

I climbed down from my bunk, still groggy from the sleeping pill, and sat at the only table. An elderly man was sitting on the opposite side. He had a white plastic knife and a grapefruit. He cut the grapefruit in half and pushed me over one half. 'My name is Tom,' he said. 'That's yours. Eat it.' I didn't tell him my name, but he obviously knew it. I later found out who Tom actually was. He was Thomas Di Bella, the acting head of the Colombo crime family.

Some person, or persons, unknown to me had arranged my protection. To this day, these protectors are still a mystery to me. Tom Di Bella ran the prison, and he took me under his protection because he knew I was a man of my word and that I had not testified against my colleagues. If he hadn't, my life would have been in danger. He did not want the others in the cage to know who I was because, he said, some were rats testifying against others. Di Bella was serving two six-month sentences for refusing to identify himself before two federal grand juries by pleading the Fifth Amendment.

Di Bella was doing his time at the West Street jail comfortably. He was easily the most eminent figure in the prison. The guards gave him special respect, acknowledging his unique status as a boss of a crime family. The Old Man was allowed extra time with his lawyers, and had a 'special' contact to the outside. The guards liked him and Di Bella was always respectful to them. He was never bothered by the usual problems of prison life: harassment from the guards, petty punishments or vendettas with other prisoners. In prison, the real currency was status. If an inmate was not the big fish or connected to the big fish, they were in trouble. Tom Di Bella was the big fish and somehow I was considered his friend. I would have no trouble in the West Street Prison.

The following day I was brought from the jail to the Federal Court at Foley Square, where I was arraigned before Judge Inzer B. Wyatt and held in lieu of $100,000 bail. Wyatt was familiar with my case as he had tried Joe Novoa, Frankie Ramos and others connected with the 100 Kilo Case. Defending attorney Jack Field stressed that I would not get the proper medical care I needed in the West Street jail. However, Judge Wyatt was not to be swayed, citing me as a very poor bail risk. He felt that if he granted bail, I would again flee the country, maintaining that I had not returned voluntarily. The prosecutor asked for no bail to be fixed and Judge

Wyatt set bail at $100,000 – an impossible sum for me – so, in fact, there was no bail. After further discussion with my defence lawyer about my medical condition, Judge Wyatt set a trial date of 2 June 1975.

On my return to prison, I found there were two others in the tank, or cage. Dr George was accused of selling prescription drugs from his premises, while Dr Jackson was selling medical draft exemptions from the military. They were both informing on each other. Both were on green grog medication, which kept highly stressed and depressed people in a twilight state twenty-four hours a day, with the result that the two slept most of the time. Di Bella became aware of a plot by other inmates to kill Dr Jackson, who was known to be co-operating with the authorities. He passed the word that nothing was to happen Jackson while he was in the jail, as he wanted nothing to occur that would upset his time there.

Dr Jackson tried to take an overdose, but was saved by my intervention. I called the guards more out of fear that I might be accused of killing him, given my distaste for informers. Dr George also took an overdose and survived.

Another inmate of the West Side jail was Jerry 'The Jew' Rosenberg. I knew Jerry well. He had shot two cops dead – Detectives John Finnegan and Luke Fallon – just a few blocks from where I was living in Brooklyn in May 1962 in a botched robbery. Jerry was in the West Side jail as a witness for another inmate from Attica Prison, who was in federal court in Brooklyn, accused of killing a fellow inmate alleged to be a prison rat. This was in 1975 after the Attica riots.

At first, Jerry didn't know I was an ex-cop. Joe Novoa was asked to testify against me and was returned to the West Street jail. We were talking one day when Jerry saw us and told Tom Di Bella that I was talking to an ex-cop. After our chat, I returned to the table where Jerry and Tom were sitting. Tom smirked and said, 'Pete, we better tell him.' I turned to Jerry and said, 'OK. Joe Novoa was my partner and I am an ex-cop too.' Jerry nearly shit himself. He was shocked, but we still remained friends.

Jerry was addicted to Valium and concealed a few hundred pills in a carton of cigarettes he wanted to take back to Dannemora Prison. I felt the weight of the cigarettes and told Rosenberg that it was like a loaded dice – no matter what way you put it down it would roll over to where the weight of the hidden pills were. Rosenberg was wary as the prison guards at Dannemora were notorious for brutality and if he got caught trying to smuggle in drugs, he'd expect a severe beating. I got a large bar of Irish Spring soap, and with the aid of some cell-made tweezers, cut out a plug of soap big enough to conceal the pills. The soap plug was scaled down until it was small enough to go back into the bar and was then smoothed over, concealing the hidden pills. Word was later sent back through the prison communication network that the smuggling operation had been successful.

After cash, cigarettes and tobacco, pills were the next best currency. Their value depended on their type, strength and purity, as well as demand, need and supply. Almost every man was schooled in what to say and how to act to get a doctor's prescription. Those skilled in this deception had honed it to where they could give certain symptoms to get required 'script', as it was called in prison slang. Most big-time gangsters, rather than ask a doctor or disclose to anyone their need for some Valium support, used others to get their pills.

While confined in the West Side jail, I received a number of telephone calls from ex-SIU members, including Jack McClean, recalling circumstances of old cases. I replied to McClean that he must have a wrong number, that I never heard of him. But I knew

McClean well, and thought it was suspicious to receive a call in, as inmates usually got a ten-minute call going out but never one coming in. McClean was an informer trying to set me up and the call was probably recorded. He had been convicted of depriving narcotics dealers of their civil rights and illegal wiretapping and had received a nine-year sentence. Before long, he began to co-operate with the government in order to reduce his sentence. He helped convict his old partner, Frank King, but still served time in prison. When he was released, McClean was given a new identity and resettled in the southwest.

On at least five occasions I was taken out of the West Side jail at 6 a.m. and brought to the New York Federal Prosecutors Offices in Foley Square, where Assistant US Attorney Joseph Jaffe interviewed me. As soon as I was taken out of the cell for my visit to the prosecutor, Tom Di Bella would jump into action. At this early hour, the inmates were locked down, sleeping, and I was moved without any notice. By some unknown means, Di Bella would have someone contact my trial lawyer's home in Rockland County. Jack Field would then drive the one and a half hours into the city and make his way over to the prosecutors' office and demand immediate access to me. I still don't know what action Di Bella took on my behalf – who made the telephone calls to my attorney and got him to drive through the early morning darkness to get to the interview rooms in the Federal Courthouse in Foley Square.

In the prosecutors' office, I would sit in silence, as I'd been instructed to do by my lawyer, and listen to what was being offered. Jaffe asked me to listen to his offer, and then take time to think it over before responding in any form. So I did a lot of listening, but very little talking.

The only feature of interest to me was the plastic surgery offer to change my appearance, as I had a broken nose from an old football injury. At the end of each sitting, Jack Field would arrive and we would then be escorted to an empty interrogation room to decide if I would take the agreement and testify. Being a former wireman and aware of bugging methods, I never spoke, but answered, 'No!' in sign language. Then we would be escorted back into the main room where Jaffe would advise my attorney that I must vocally express the answer, at which time I would say, 'I respectfully decline your kind offer.' My reply was always the same. I was never offensive, but always polite. I was then taken back to the prison.

The prosecution moved to disqualify Jack Field from representing me because of a conflict of interest as he had represented the main witness, Carl Aguiluz, in previous criminal and civil matters. Jaffe asked that Field be relieved from the case so that I could get a fair trial. The motion was denied, but Judge Wyatt advised Field that the defence should consider getting another attorney to cross-examine the main witness.

In July 1975, the West Street Zoo was closed down and the inmates were transferred to the newly built federal detention facility in downtown Manhattan, the Metropolitan Correctional Center. I went to trial from both the West Street Prison and the MCC.

CHAPTER 3

Trial

Throughout my life, I've always been aware that every one of my choices and acts had a potential consequence – good or bad – somewhere down the line. I knew that somewhere along the road I travelled, there would be the devil to pay. This I could accept. Twelve years in the service of the NYPD meant everything to me and I could not betray my friendships lightly. My main loyalties were to my friends in the police department and those I met on life's travels, on both sides of the law. Both Novoa and I were convicted on the testimony of Carl Aguiluz, his brother-in-law Sal Bouteriera, and known drug dealer Frankie Ramos.

Carl Aguiluz saved himself from going to prison by making us and others the guilty parties. Knowing that in order to disprove his allegations Joe and I would have to further implicate many others – people we loved and cared for, and their families – we decided to stop the rot and knew what the final outcome would be. The federal prosecutors were not happy. They wanted to know every item deemed 'corruption', right back to when we were appointed to the NYPD.

Aguiluz lied in every case he had ever brought to court. He had lied in every affidavit he had ever made up in all the boroughs of New York City. Carl's co-operation, however, came only after his arrest for perjury and believing the authorities had knowledge of his corrupt narcotics role. He suddenly became a man of good conscience. This was particularly hard to swallow because I knew the real Aguiluz.

He testified in federal court and put fellow officers in prison. Their families were destroyed as he went free. I saw his wife when she was interviewed on TV, where her features were only a dark silhouetted outline. I was in Minneapolis at the time. She was asked what name would go on his headstone – the old or the new name?

Aguiluz made shocking admissions, which were not doubted by the prosecution or defence – he said that on nine separate investigations, he and his partners had received over $400,000 cash, stolen from drug dealers they had apprehended or arrested. However, in some cases his testimony was not sufficient to gain a conviction. Despite this, he was the main prosecution witness at my trial which began on 2 June 1975 in the Federal Criminal Court in downtown Manhattan.

I had no family or friends present in the courtroom, only my defence attorney. After the motion to disqualify Jack Field on the grounds that he had previously represented a government witness, namely Carl Aguiluz, was denied, Field withdrew from active participation and brought in Victor J. Herwitz as my defence attorney. The prosecuting judge was Inzer B. Wyatt, who had also tried me in absence at my original trial when Joe Novoa was convicted.

Because I'd been extradited on four counts, Judge Wyatt reminded the court that I could only be tried on these four counts. Count 5 was the charge dealing with five kilograms of heroin and cocaine, and counts 6, 7 and 8 were the three heroin sale counts. I was charged with four counts of obtaining and selling narcotics, to which I pleaded not guilty. The indictment charged me with receiving, selling and sharing in the proceeds of five kilos of heroin and cocaine obtained on or about 15 April 1970. I was also charged with participating in the subsequent sale of three kilos of heroin and charged that, with my partners Aguiluz and Novoa, I sold these quantities of narcotics through Frankie Ramos from which we received more than $50,000 and shared the money among ourselves.

In his opening statement to the jury, Assistant US Attorney Joe Jaffe described the case as one that involved the theft and distribution of enormous amounts of heroin and cocaine by corrupt police officers. The prosecution outlined its case against me, the only one on trial, as the others had already been convicted. The details of the 100 Kilo Case were revealed – the surveillance and arrest of four suspects, the seizure of 105 kilos and our confiscation of five kilos. The prosecution also alleged that we took a total of $1,200 from the four drug dealers, which we divided among ourselves. Jaffe outlined how Aguiluz's brother-in-law, Salvador Bouteriera, was chosen as the go-between to sell the five kilos. Bouteriera met Frankie Ramos, owner or part-owner of the Café Madrid, and between the two they fixed the price at $12,500 per kilo of heroin and $9,500 for a kilo of cocaine. Ramos was to get $500 commission. All the sales of narcotics took place either in the area of the Café Madrid or some place nearby.

The prosecutor touched on all the essentials of the case, namely how we followed Bouteriera from the Café Madrid to the Taft Hotel to witness the first sale to Jimmy Papadakis and Elena Possas, where the $12,000 handed over for the kilo of heroin was put on a bed in a rented room and counted. Bouteriera was allegedly to be given a quarter share of $3,000 for helping with the sale.

The next two sales were also brokered at the Café Madrid – the first to Papadakis and Possas, the second to Joaquin Nieves. We allegedly listened to its progress on a wiretap. This time, Bouteriera kept the money from both transactions and divided it up into four envelopes of $6,000, one each for himself, Novoa, Aguiluz and me. A meeting was arranged with us and the money was handed over.

Bouteriera then sold the remaining two kilos to an individual named Lorenzo Cansio for $18,000, after Ramos's commission. This was divided up and handed over to us. The prosecution alleged that, in total, Aguiluz, Novoa and I each received $17,000 in cash. It was also presented that we had located an apartment, which belonged to one of the drug dealers, Elena Risso, and found $5,000 there, which we divided among ourselves. The prosecution said we offered to 'sell' the case to the four defendants in order to change our testimony so that the traffickers could go free. The asking price was $100,000. The prosecution stated that Carl Aguiluz was arrested on 14 February 1974 and alleged that, on hearing of this, I fled to Ireland two days later. By the time the case was outlined, it was lunch-time and the court adjourned until 2 p.m.

The court reconvened after lunch and began with the opening statement on my behalf by Victor Herwitz. He outlined my defence, that there was no dispute in the arrests of the four drug dealers in the 100 Kilo Case, but that it was Aguiluz who planted the gun in the car – not me, as Aguiluz had alleged. Herwitz said that I did not take the drugs, but that Aguiluz did, he was the only one to leave the apartment on a ruse to get a search warrant from the district attorney's office. Herwitz asked that the jury only convict me if they believed I was guilty beyond a reasonable doubt.

The first witness was Carl Aguiluz. He was called and began to repeat the testimony he had given in previous cases, recounting in great detail the story of corruption and greed among members of the SIU. Aguiluz claimed to be still employed in the NYPD as a patrolman. He testified that he had never signed a completely true affidavit in a court proceeding and that he had lied, also under oath, to the Knapp Commission and to the State of New York Investigative Commission.

He testified that on 14 April 1970 he, Novoa and I were watching the Café Madrid in Manhattan when a car drove up containing three men and a woman, later identified as Emilio Diaz Gonzalez, Jose Luis Mulas, Jorge Rodriquez Arraya and Elena Risso. Two of the men approached the café and tapped on a window. A person 'vaguely known' to Aguiluz as a narcotics dealer spoke to the men, who then got back into the car and drove away. We followed in two separate cars all the way to New Jersey, finally stopping the suspects' car to ask for identification and in order to search the trunk. Speaking in Spanish, the four occupants of the car stated they were respectable people and would show us where they lived.

All seven of us then returned to New York, where Aguiluz decided to arrest the four based on possession by one of them, Emilio Gonzalez, of apparently forged passports. Aguiluz testified that he had expressed to Novoa and me his apprehension, lest the arrests be deemed illegal. At this point, according to Aguiluz, I winked and told him that I thought they had a gun in the car. A gun was 'found' by Novoa under Gonzalez's seat and the four were arrested and brought to the 6th Precinct on a gun possession charge. The three men were put in the holding pen, while Risso was seated outside as men and women could not be held together. The three of us examined the personal effects of the prisoners, which included various pieces of paper and between fifteen and thirty keys.

In Spanish, Gonzalez shouted to Aguiluz that he had been robbed of $100. The money had, in fact, been taken by Aguiluz, but he became indignant at the accusation and allowed Gonzalez to come out of the cell to locate the money. Gonzalez ran to the table where the papers were placed and swallowed a piece of paper.

Aguiluz said Novoa grabbed Gonzalez and tried to force his mouth open, even though it was I who did this. He withdrew his fingers in fear of being bitten. Meanwhile, Risso also ran to the table and ripped up some papers.

Order was quickly restored and Gonzalez was placed back in the cage, while Risso was put back on the chair outside, but handcuffed to the bars. Aguiluz said he overhead Gonzalez say in Spanish, 'The cargo is safe. We will not suffer any loss.' Novoa and Aguiluz were able to ascertain that the destroyed papers were rent receipts from an apartment. Aguiluz testified that he and I took the keys and went to the apartment in my car. We were able to gain admittance, but were unable to open two closets in the room. A locksmith friend of mine, Detective John Kidd, arrived and was able to open the two locked closets, in which we found packages of heroin and cocaine stacked from the floor to the ceiling.

Aguiluz said we began to remove the packages from the closet and then stacked, counted and placed them in suitcases also found in the apartment. He said that I put five one-kilo packages in a brown suitcase, telling him I wanted to keep it for 'flaking' purposes, which is the planting of drugs on a potential defendant in order to tighten up an arrest. He said he agreed to this, and I left to put the suitcase in my car. When Novoa arrived, after congratulations, Aguiluz and I told him that we had secreted five kilos in my car, to which, according to Aguiluz, Novoa replied, 'It is fine with me.'

Then Lieutenant Egan arrived and we advised him of our entrance into the apartment, which could be deemed illegal. Aguiluz said he needed a warrant and was going to get one from a detective who was in charge of issuing warrants at the DA's office. Egan agreed and a call was placed to the DA's office, though Aguiluz did not mention that we were already in the apartment. Aguiluz drove to the DA's office on Centre Street in Egan's car, where he obtained a warrant to search the apartment. He went back to the apartment where the media and several superior officers were by then congregating. Aguiluz stated that, back at the 6th Precinct, Sergeant Stefania asked for a cut of $1,200 taken from the four drug dealers. Aguiluz told the court that we gave Stefania a share of the confiscated money. The four defendants were transported to Manhattan Night Court and each was arraigned on a bail of $100,000.

Aguiluz testified that a week later, he asked me for the suitcase, which was then transferred to his car. It remained in the trunk of Aguiluz's car for about a month, when Aguiluz, Novoa and I met to decide what to do with the drugs. We met at the Club Espagna on 14th Street and, according to Aguiluz, Novoa wanted to dump the drugs in the river, while I said to think things over. By the time the meeting ended, we had agreed to sell the drugs, using Aguiluz's brother-in-law Sal Bouteriera as our conduit. Aguiluz contacted Bouteriera, who agreed to sell the drugs, even though he allegedly had never even seen drugs before. The suitcase was brought to Bouteriera's home.

Bouteriera contacted Frankie Ramos, who agreed to find buyers for the drugs. Ramos sold a kilo of cocaine to Jimmy Papadakis. The proceeds of this sale and two others were allegedly divided among Aguiluz, Novoa and me. We were still working the 14th Street area and, according to Aguiluz, were able to keep an eye on the sale of the five kilos. Using our surveillance techniques, we observed the delivery of the money and the collection of the drugs. Aguiluz concluded his testimony and was excused.

The trial was adjourned until the next day, 3 June, and I was taken back to the MCC. When my trial resuméd, Aguiluz took the stand to be questioned by Jaffe. He stated that after the sale of the first kilo we had tried to follow the individual, who was on a motorcycle. He had picked up the package in a parking lot and dropped it into a waiting cab, which took off at speed. We tried to initiate a pursuit, but the motorcycle and the cab left the scene so fast that we couldn't catch them.

Aguiluz said the three of us met Bouteriera at 14th Street and proceeded to the Taft Hotel where I booked a room. Bouteriera had $12,000 inside his shirt from the sale, so we split it four ways as agreed. However, Bouteriera stressed that he did not want us watching him making the sale because he felt that, if people found out we were involved, it could lead to repercussions for him. Aguiluz said we agreed to let Bouteriera handle the sales without our help. However, we could still monitor what was going on, as, according to Aguiluz, we had an illegal wiretap on a phone at the Café Madrid. Unknown to Bouteriera, we were able to hear him making another deal to sell more of the narcotics. But all was not well, Aguiluz said, as Novoa and I were 'very mad that Sal would be so stupid as to talk on the phone' about his narcotics deal.

Aguiluz claimed that he met Bouteriera and told him we were aware of his next sale and that he should be careful. However, he did not reveal anything about the wiretap or how he knew. Later, he said he met Bouteriera, Novoa and me in front of the Maritime Building on Seventh Avenue and 13th Street where we each received $6,000 from the sale of more narcotics. Aguiluz went to Mexico City on holiday on 19 June and, when he returned three weeks later, he met with Novoa and me, when he received more money from the sale of the remaining narcotics.

Aguiluz told the court that the sale of the five kilos was between $53,000 and $56,000 and that we all received $13,000–$14,000 each in total. He also claimed that Novoa and I told him we'd entered the Brooklyn apartment of Risso, the woman involved in the 100 Kilo Case, and confiscated $5,000. Novoa gave him one third of this. Aguiluz went on to relate that an attorney asked the three of us if we would be willing to 'fix' the case for approximately $100,000. The deal fell through when the drug dealers' attorney allegedly rejected the price as being too high.

Herwitz attacked the credibility of Aguiluz, charging that he was the only one to connect me to the theft and sale of the drugs. Herwitz disputed most of Aguiluz's testimony, saying that I had never, in fact, met Bouteriera at any time in my life. He pointed out that Aguiluz had been arrested on 14 February 1974 for perjury and had admitted to illegal wiretapping, the theft and sale of narcotics with others, perjury, sharing of $80,000–$100,000 taken from narcotics dealers with others and planting narcotics on defendants. Herwitz pointed out that although Aguiluz was not granted immunity, he would have to plead guilty to two felony counts – theft of money and sale of narcotics – but that, at the time of sentence, the judge would be made aware of his co-operation in other cases. Aguiluz had been told that his family would be protected by the US Marshals Service and that, ultimately, he would be relocated outside the United States for his own protection. Aguiluz was demoted from detective and paid as a patrolman and was told the government would intervene on his behalf on his application for a disability pension because of a heart problem.

Aguiluz claimed he 'never took a dime until he went into that den of iniquity – the SIU'. However, he denied that Novoa and I corrupted him, saying that it was a collective decision to sell the narcotics. Aguiluz said he previously took money on two occasions with Novoa as his partner, prior to the 100 Kilo Case. He claimed that myself, Novoa and other members of the SIU shared money seized in the course of various narcotics investigations. Herwitz asked Aguiluz if he had tipped off Frankie Ramos about an impending investigation. He said he hadn't, claiming that Ramos was an informer working for him. He said that he was on a crusade against corruption, and that it was not the fear of going to prison that made him agree to testify against his former partners. Aguiluz admitted that he had flaked suspects, shaken down drug dealers and tried to sell his story to the writer Hank Whittemore.

Ramos was called as a witness on behalf of the government, and his testimony was given on Tuesday evening and Wednesday morning. He spoke of his dealings with Aguiluz and Bouteriera and the buyers of their illicit haul of narcotics. He'd been arrested in 1973 and convicted on a tax count of conspiracy involving narcotics. Sentenced to two years, Ramos only served four months. He also testified in several other narcotics cases after being sentenced to a further ten years for narcotics trafficking. His sentence was suspended and he was granted immunity for his co-operation, even after he admitted to perjury and helping to sell narcotics on behalf of Aguiluz and Bouteriera. He claimed he needed the money because he had to pay debts and taxes. Ramos said he thought Aguiluz was a corrupt cop and that he was in it for the money. He also said that even though he was a confidential informant for Aguiluz, he did not trust him.

Bouteriera was called next as a government witness. At the time of the 100 Kilo Case, Bouteriera was working for a shipping company undertaking ship maintenance, which was not steady work. He was married to Aguiluz's only sister, had four children and claimed he was close to his brother-in-law, who had once given him a car.

Bouteriera described how, accompanied by the three detectives, he passed over the first kilo of narcotics for sale. He said he'd stored a kilo of narcotics in the pay lockers at the Eighth Avenue, 14th Street subway station. The money was exchanged for the locker key in the Café Madrid and the narcotics were then taken by one of the buyers. Bouteriera brought the money – $11,000 – to an apartment at 509 East Fifth Avenue and left it under the bed.

After the sale of the next kilo, Bouteriera met us at the Taft Hotel and divided the money from the further sales with us outside the Maritime Union building on 13th Street. He claimed at the time that we were not impressed that he had organised the sales without our participation and told him not to make any more deals until we came back from vacation. After the next sale, Bouteriera told the court, he'd divided the money for us into three envelopes, which he gave to Novoa and Aguiluz. He said I was not there when the money was handed over. Again Bouteriera said he was chastised for not having involved us in the sale.

The defence again disputed this version of events, pointing out that the stories were all made up by Aguiluz, Bouteriera and Ramos to save themselves from prison. The prosecution called several other witnesses: John Kidd gave evidence of how he went to the apartment on 19th Street and opened the closets. Kidd, while present at all times, saw nothing out of the ordinary and did not see either Aguiluz or me leave the apartment with a suitcase. He did not think a suitcase was missing and did not see any packages being placed in a separate suitcase.

The superintendent of the building, James Sheridan, revealed that the newspaper reports had said that he had let the detectives in, but he said that was not so. He identified me as having said that I'd taken keys from the suspects.

Gerard Hall, an accounting clerk in the Taft Hotel, testified that there was a registration card in the name of 'Peter Daly', and this placed me at that hotel at the time of the division of the proceeds from the sale of one of the kilos, as stated by Aguiluz and Bouteriera. A laboratory chemist, Gene Ferrar, was called and testified as to the quality of the heroin and cocaine seized in the 100 Kilo Case.

Gabriel Stefania was then called. Stefania had been convicted of income tax evasion after being charged with conspiracy as an accessory and with obstruction of justice arising out of the keeping of certain money seized by him and other detectives. Stefania pleaded guilty to income tax evasion and co-operated with the authorities, making known all illegal acts in which he had been involved. He was given two years and six months, of which he served only four and a half months. Stefania also retained his full police pension rights.

Stefania denied that Novoa had given him any money at the 6th Precinct station house.

Stefania continued with his evidence. My memorandum book was produced to prove that the signature in the Taft Hotel record books was mine. Stefania admitted that while he'd been my supervisor, the supervision he'd exercised had been limited. He claimed that the team had not trusted him because he was too honest and that they had not always informed him of all the money they'd seized. Stefania claimed that he was not caught in any wrongdoing and had, on his own admission, volunteered to help the authorities in weeding out and getting rid of corrupt cops in the NYPD. However, Herwitz told the court that when Stefania had been sentenced, his trial judge had imposed a stiffer sentence on him because he was 'older and should have known better' than his two accomplices. Stefania was then dismissed.

The last two witnesses called were the detectives from Britain. The court had earlier ruled that the testimony that I would have returned to Ireland to resist extradition be deleted, as I had merely said that if I was granted bail I would return to Ireland.

Detective Inspector Michael Atkins was the first of the two British detectives to be called. Atkins said he'd first met me at Huyton Police Station outside Liverpool in England. He gave details of my arrest and explained how he and Detective Constable Bennie collected me at the police station and escorted me by train to London. Atkins made notes of the conversation he'd had with me on the train journey, which he kept as evidence.

According to Atkins, I'd outlined the seizure of 105 kilos of narcotics and said that the trial of Joe Novoa was a 'farce and a circus'. I admitted to Atkins that I'd known the American authorities were after me, but that I had come to England to see my sister, who I hadn't seen in eighteen years, and told him that I should have stayed in Ireland. Atkins outlined how they brought me to Bow Street Police Station, where I was formally charged, and Bow Street Magistrates Court in order to be remanded. Under cross-examination by the defence, Atkins clarified that he'd made the notes in Bow Street station and not on the train and that they were from memory.

Detective Constable John Bennie was then sworn in. Bennie outlined how I had handed him my handwritten resumé, which I'd kept to remind me of events because of my memory loss, and that he'd also taken notes of the conversation he'd had with me, though they were taken ten minutes after the actual conversation. He said we had general conversations about the legal aid system, solicitors and extradition procedures. Bennie clarified that he had never shown me the notes or asked if I'd wanted to see them. He also mentioned that I had said '105 kilos', not '100 kilos', in my conversation about the famous seizure.

With all the evidence summed up, I was then called to the stand. I explained my family situation, my health status and my work as a patrolman and detective. I also said that because of my car accident, I had trouble remembering exact dates. I was cautioned by the judge that if I understood the question I was to answer either 'yes' or 'no' or 'I can't remember', and not to give any further explanations. I said I did not recall any past transactions – the taking of narcotics or the receiving of money for illegal ventures or making any agreements with Aguiluz and Novoa. I'd had a lot of memory loss and the only reason I remembered the 100 Kilo Case so vividly was that I had newspaper cuttings of the event and I agreed that there were a lot of things that could have happened but I just couldn't recall them.

I admitted that I had gone to Ireland but for medical reasons only. Aguiluz had been arrested on 14 February 1974, two days after I had flown to Ireland, so that I would not have known that Aguiluz had been arrested or that indictments were proceeding. I did not know Ramos had been arrested but the prosecution alleged that I'd known an investigation was going on and that I had tipped off Lieutenant Egan and warned him to be careful.

I had not been indicted until 8 March 1974, and, a month later, I'd been indicted again on an income tax evasion charge which was, at the time of my trial, still open and pending. In order for there to be flight, ideally there should be knowledge that I was being looked for. The ruling on my reply – that if I knew I could be extradited from England I would never have left Ireland – was given by the judge, that I had a right to resist extradition by any means possible, that it was just like pleading the Fifth Amendment, which was my constitutional right. I also pointed out that I never, at any stage in my life, met Sal Bouteriera.

As the state neared the end of its presentation, the prosecutor produced my passport and a .32 calibre revolver. Jaffe claimed I had planted the revolver in the car belonging to the four suspects in the 100 Kilo Case. It was alleged by the prosecution that I had brought large amounts of cash to Ireland when I'd returned there for holidays on several occasions, despite admitting that my tax return for the year 1970 reflected an NYPD salary of about $15,000. The prosecution claimed that two weeks before I had travelled to Ireland, I had phoned both Aguiluz and Novoa and said, 'There are indictments coming down; you better be careful.' I told the court that I did not recall this.

The evidence ran into the next day, 6 June, the final day of the trial. Prosecutor Jaffe began proceedings by addressing the jury, summing up all the evidence and witness statements. He pointed out that the gun found in the car of the suspects in the 100 Kilo Case was a small calibre .32 that would probably have blown up if fired, not something major drug dealers carrying millions of dollars worth of narcotics would arm themselves with. He said that if the suspects were smart enough to hide their narcotics, they were not going to be stupid enough to be carrying a gun so they could be stopped and arrested, and claimed that the detectives had planted the gun in the car. Jaffe said the arrests had been illegal, the entrance to the apartment where the narcotics were found had been illegal, the confiscation of the narcotics had been illegal and lastly, the stealing of five kilos by myself and my partners had been illegal. Jaffe said I was claiming amnesia incurred through my car accident in order to avoid having to answer incriminating questions.

Jaffe said, obviously, the government's problem in this case was to make the jury believe the confessed perjurers were, in this instance, telling the truth. The prosecution attempted to solve this problem by telling the jurors that they needn't decide if these people were lying, because the government and a United States judge had vouched for them. Their duty was reduced to a mere rubber-stamp of the implied prior findings of the government and federal judge. 'Don't worry about these people who have been known to lie,' the prosecutor argued. 'I believe them, the United States government believes them, and a judge believes them.' Jaffe argued that, 'If any one of you thinks that this government and this court participated with any one of these people in a frame job … sit there and acquit him.'

My defence counsel, Herwitz, then addressed the jury. He said that the issue in this trial was not whether or not I was a dishonest cop, but whether or not I committed the crimes I'd been charged with. The trial was essentially whether the four indictments were what I was to be convicted of in court.

In order to convict me, the jury had to believe the testimony of Carl Aguiluz, his brother-in-law Sal Bouteriera, Frankie Ramos, Gabriel Stefania and other government witnesses, all of whom were in court because they had been found guilty of crimes, including perjury, corruption and the sale of narcotics. They had a lot to gain by my conviction, Herwitz said. When they came up for sentencing, it would be pointed out that they had co-operated with the government.

Herwitz argued that the testimony of the two British detectives was from memory, not actual notes taken during their conversations with me, so it was unreliable. He pointed out that the government's star witness, Aguiluz, had planted narcotics on other suspects and sent men to jail on fabricated evidence. Aguiluz had admitted lying in every case he'd ever prosecuted. 'How can he be believed now?' Herwitz asked.

The court was adjourned until Monday morning, 9 June. Judge Wyatt addressed the jury, outlining the case, and asked them to consider all the evidence. The indictments were read out and explained again, after which the jury retired to the jury room.

The jury asked to see the police lab report, along with my written statement and those of the British detectives. They deliberated for less than two hours before reaching their verdict.

The clerk asked the foreman of the jury to stand. 'How do you find the defendant Peter Daly in indictment number 5?' the clerk asked.

'Guilty.'

I felt my head swim.

The foreman was asked about each separate indictment. I was found guilty of four narcotics charges on counts 5, 6, 7 and 8. All four counts of the indictment carried a mandatory minimum sentence of five years.

Jaffe asked Judge Wyatt to revoke the $100,000 bail he had set for me at my arraignment. My bail was revoked and I was remanded to jail for sentencing pending completion of a probation report. I was very nervous of what lay ahead. I was now going where I had sent many people – prison. I was destined for a federal prison, Lewisburg, from where I launched my appeal against my sentence.

CHAPTER 4
Sentence and appeal

Sentencing is the most upsetting moment in a criminal prosecution. One human being punishes another by putting him in a cage.

It requires a lot to be a judge, to try to show fairness and compassion to both victim and criminal. In most sentencing hearings, the defendant does not speak for himself. His lawyer addresses the judge and, although he knows that the judge has decided on a sentence before coming into the courtroom, he tries to persuade the judge not to impose a prison term, or at least to keep the sentence as light as possible. A good lawyer will use whatever he can – emotion, logic, a plea for human compassion and sympathy – to help his client. There is always the chance that, with the defendant and his family and friends in the courtroom, he can make the judge change his mind. To the defendant, even a year less in jail is a great deal.

In most criminal cases, the verdict is not the end – it's the beginning of the next phase, the sometimes endless series of legal manoeuvrings.

I returned to the Federal Criminal Court on 22 August 1975, my forty-first birthday, to be sentenced by Judge Wyatt. My defence attorney Victor Herwitz and the prosecutors Joseph Jaffe and Thomas Cahill were present. Herwitz asked for a dismissal of the indictment and an acquittal.

Judge Wyatt refused the motion, saying, 'Our position is that Peter Daly ought to be viewed as perhaps one of the worst narcotics offenders who has been prosecuted by our office in the area of police corruption. This is a man who took an oath to enforce the narcotics laws, and the jury, after the evidence was presented to it, found him guilty of seizing and stealing more than five kilograms and putting the money in his own pocket … This man and his partners, in addition to taking vast quantities of narcotics, took huge sums of money from narcotics offenders and let those offenders go free in some instances; in other instances flaked some of the defendants in order to make cases. The type of conduct that Mr Daly engaged in is the type of conduct that only brings disrepute to the police department and to law enforcement in general, and encourages people to engage in narcotics sale and distribution, and in general makes respect for law enforcement something that is unachievable. The government's position is that this man not only engaged in these acts, as the jury found, he fled the country in order to avoid prosecution, and when he was returned to the United States before the court and the jury, he took the stand, and we believe that the evidence shows beyond a reasonable doubt that he perjured himself.'

Herwitz argued that I was not a bad man, that I had set out for a new life in America with good moral standards. I had presented a large number of letters, mostly from Ireland, attesting to my good qualities. These letters included testaments from my father and mother, written some weeks before. Herwitz maintained that there was a general breakdown in the SIU and that the government's witnesses had testified before Judge Wyatt in other cases that everybody was corrupt in that unit.

'I don't mean to suggest that because everybody was corrupt or apparently corrupt or allegedly corrupt that Mr Daly should be given any commendation because he also was. But I would suggest, Your Honour, that there is something definitely wrong with a system where all of a group of seemingly previously incorruptible officers become corrupt. Perhaps it is part of the narcotics sickness. It is this great amount of money which this nefarious trade generates which apparently made it virtually impossible for a whole group of men to withstand the degree of temptation. As I say, that does not call for a medal to be given to any who did succumb, but I feel that it has to be taken into consideration where there is seemingly such unanimity. It is true that Mr Daly did not take the route that some of the other corrupters or corrupted officers did. He did not take the offer to come in and earn points for himself by testifying against his colleagues, and I am realistic enough to know, and Your Honour is experienced enough to know, that if he had done that we would be in a much better position. However, it speaks for a different kind of character that he would not do that.'

Herwitz asked that the judge take into consideration my difficult family life, my car accident and my nine-month incarceration. He then said that I wanted to address the court. I took the stand and began:

'I'd like to say that this is the first time I have found myself in this position, as Your Honour well knows. It is quite difficult for me to put words together. I have been up since 6 o'clock this morning, unfortunately, and I am not always in the best of health.

'I can only say that I would like to be in Ireland with my father for the last days of his life. I would like Your Honour to take that into consideration. I'd like Your Honour to take into consideration my ill health. I'd like Your Honour to take into consideration the fact that, in the past couple of years since the accident, I have lost my family, I may be losing my father. I am retired.

'I have served nine months in jail so far. I feel that if I was released in the future due to my past record, I wouldn't be a burden on any community. Nevertheless, this community wouldn't have the burden of me because I would wish to reside in Ireland. If the court stipulated that I return to Ireland, other than losing my citizenship, I would gladly do so for an exile period, whatever the court determines. Anything that would form a structure that would bring me closer to my father in his last years. I don't know that I … I cannot say that … I don't recall the facts of the case that did happen, but I was before this court in 1970. I don't recall a lot of the past, unfortunately. It is part of the injury. I am sorry that I … I feel very weak now.'

I got very emotional and Judge Wyatt asked me if I would rather sit down while addressing him and I agreed. I then continued, 'I'd just like to make the court aware of the fact that if and when I am released from prison, that I would not be a burden on this community or any other community, but that I would wish to return to my native land and my father. That's about all, Your Honour. Thank you very much. I know that you have taken this into consideration already, I know you have my father's letter at hand, I read it myself, and I was personally very touched by it because I know my father and it must have taken an awful lot for him to sit down and structure that letter himself. If you knew the man, he himself, he is not the type to put words on paper like that. I am sorry for my family, my own personal family, my children, my wife, and for my father and mother, for the discredit I brought on them. That's all I want to say, Your Honour.'

Judge Wyatt then addressed the court. 'Mr Daly, my mother is Irish, I am half Irish. I understand a good deal about these matters and if I were free to follow my personal sympathies and emotions, I would send you back to your parents in Ireland, but I cannot do that. I am not free to do it. I am a public servant. I have a responsibility to the community. The jury verdict which for present purposes I have to take as correct, is that you are guilty of most serious offences; and also at an earlier trial others were convicted for the same offences, including notably Joseph Novoa, who was sentenced by me to ten years' imprisonment. I feel that you, Mr Daly, were at least as involved as Novoa, and there are reasons to suggest that you should receive a heavier sentence.

'However, bearing in mind all of the circumstances, I feel able to exercise leniency as to you, Mr Daly, to the extent that I can justify giving you the same term of imprisonment as Novoa, but I cannot justify giving you a lesser term. The counts on which you were convicted are counts 5, 6, 7 and 8 and, on those counts, the defendant is committed to the custody of the Attorney General for ten years, the sentence on each count to run concurrently with the others.'

Judge Wyatt dismissed the other counts and gave me credit for my time spent in England and on remand in New York. I was also given leave to appeal. An appeal was immediately lodged and the case was adjourned.

During my sentencing, my lawyer informed the judge that the day in question, 22 August, was my forty-second birthday.

'So?' was Wyatt's curt answer.

It was an open court and people regularly came in to listen to the cases. At recess, I was in the corridor standing against the cold marble courthouse wall talking to Herwitz when an old woman who had been in the courtroom came over to me and said softly, as if in a confidential whisper, 'Are you really only forty-two?'

I smiled at this old woman, whose obvious daily interests and entertainment in New York City was attending trials. A soft, sweet female voice was one of the many things I'd missed when I'd been in prison, and I replied in an equally soft tone, 'Yes, dear, I am really only forty-two years old.' It was a touching moment in a somewhat unsavoury atmosphere and something that has remained with me since.

On 30 January 1976, Judge Wyatt denied a motion to reduce my sentence. I had appealed for a reduction under Rule 35, and had asked that Jack Field represent me, which was also denied. Medical reports from five doctors – two in the US, two in Ireland and one from Dr Maxwell Carter in London – accompanied the appeal. I was not eligible for parole until at least 1981, and I asked if the court would at least permit me to be considered for parole or release some time within the next five years of my sentence.

Victor Herwitz withdrew as my appeal counsel in February and I withdrew my appeal on his advice. I then requested that my appeal be reinstated, but this was dismissed because I had failed to take the steps required to lodge my appeal in a timely fashion. On 28 April 1976, on motion of Ira Leitel, my new counsel, that dismissal was vacated and the appeal was reinstated.

My new appeal was heard on 19 July 1976 at the US District Court for the Southern District in New York. This appeal was based on prosecutorial misconduct because the judicial system had giving the impression that it was vouching for the perjured witnesses presented by the prosecution, thus denying me a fair trial. There were other instances of prosecutorial misconduct, the defence argued – the admissibility of other alleged acts, the Airport Case, and theft of money from drug dealers and extortion, which allegedly proved I was in possession of illegal drugs. This evidence, corroborated by Aguiluz and Stefania, had been deemed admissible.

After their testimonies had been given, they had been stricken from the record, but the defence argued that the damage had already been done. Deliberate failure to abide by the instructions of the trial court as to the admissibility of evidence proved a prejudicial error according to the defence. Other evidence had also been ruled inadmissible but had led the jury to believe that I was a bad person who took bribes. The defence also claimed that I was not competent to stand trial and the court should have ascertained this. While I was well-versed in courtroom procedure, my answers under cross-examination obviously showed I was not competent enough to be on the stand. When brought before the English magistrate, I casually replied that if released I would immediately return to Ireland, not something a man in his full senses would do. Even my own defence counsel expressed annoyance with my apparent inability to answer his questions. The decision to continue proceedings without affording me a hearing on my competency had deprived me of due process. The attorney of my choice, Jack Field, had not defended me because Aguiluz claimed to have been previously represented by him. Instead, I went to trial with another attorney, resulting in an 'inadequate and ineffective representation'. The attorney failed to consider that his knowledge of the defendant is an important component of a proper defence of the case. Herwitz committed a more grievous injustice to me by chiding me for not answering questions and disassociating himself from me in front of the jury.

My testimony was basically that I could not remember whether or not the things testified by the government's witnesses had actually occurred. At the end of my testimony, my defence counsel, Herwitz, had apologised to the court for having put me on the witness stand, claiming a lack of knowledge about the extent of my memory failure. Ira Leitel argued that I had been denied a fair trial and that my conviction should be withdrawn and a new trial instigated.

However, after listening to all the arguments by the defence, the appeal judges ruled that my conviction should be affirmed on all counts. The appeal judges ruled that I was competent to stand trial and that I had received a fair trial.

I had exhausted all legal avenues to stay out of prison; now I would have to face the next several years behind bars.

CHAPTER 5

The new guy

Federal crimes are generally more serious than crimes tried in state courts, and so the penalties in federal cases are generally harsher. Federal prisons are also tougher places, and I was to serve my time in a federal penitentiary.

After I was originally sentenced, I looked out through the grimy barred window of the prison bus returning me to Lewisburg Federal Penitentiary in Pennsylvania. I stared at the world passing by, knowing that it would be a very long time before I would be on a bus going the other way. I had already served nearly five months in Pentonville Prison, then another three months between the West Street Federal Detention Prison and the Metropolitan Correctional Center. But now I was looking at possibly the next nine years in Lewisburg, one of America's most notorious prisons. Lewisburg had been opened in 1932 and had a population of about 1,500 men, including around 600 on the prison farm.

Despite the fact that I had friends serving time there, I was still apprehensive. Lewisburg was a tough place to spend the next few years and I was quite fearful of what the future might bring. My main concern was whether or not I could survive mentally. I had a much greater fear of going insane than of physical violence. I would rather be knifed to death in Lewisburg than to come out a blubbering wreck, fit for nothing but the asylum.

I knew a number of my fellow passengers on the four-hour drive to Lewisburg but there was no conversation and no introductions. I had heard through the grapevine from organised crime figures in New York, and word of mouth from their attorneys, that I had nothing to fear from any of their people. In fact, word had been sent ahead to Charles Di Palermo, aka 'Charlie Brody', and he would be responsible for my safety. I had never met Brody before, but he was to be my main protector.

Ultimately, I would serve five years in Lewisburg alongside some of the toughest gangsters in America – killers, enforcers and drug dealers like Charlie Brody, Butchie Mamone, Jimmy 'The Gent' Burke, Joe Di Napoli, Bobby Maher, Paul Vario, Johnny Dio, Benny Ong and Vinnie Aloi. But I always believed in the good of people. To be honest, there isn't a man I couldn't find some good in, even in there.

Lewisburg was known for its 'Mafia Row' – or G Block – a maximum-security wing that housed many gangsters. Some of America's most prominent criminals have resided at Lewisburg: Al Capone, Whitey Bulger, John Gotti, Carmine Galente and Jimmy Hoffa.

In addition to the forty-foot-high wall around the prison, there was an electric trip wire running along the top. Eight bulletproof glass watch towers with armed guards extended some twelve to fifteen feet above the high wall. The rear entrance gate for trucks and prison buses had a huge double iron-gated holding port. Prisoners arriving were cuffed and shackled at the ankles, the cuffs in front, attached to a waist belt. Like all new inmates, I went through processing – got my mugshot taken, was fingerprinted and filled out forms. I was stripped, searched and given a complete cavity exam. Butchie Mamone, a major mafia drugs dealer, took my prison photo in a separate room away from the prison guards. He introduced himself in a casual manner.

'You're Pete Daly,' Butchie said. 'I want you to know you're welcome here. That comes from me and I talk for a number of others you will meet as time goes along. When you walk through that gate, you're going to do time. Nothing can stop that. So do good time. Learn how to relax. Forget your family, forget your friends on the outside. Pretend they don't exist. Don't count the days, throw out the calendar. Just play it cool. Don't get pushy or be in anyone's way. Keep your nose clean, but don't take no shit from nobody. Anyone fucks with you, grab something and break their head, that way nobody will fuck with you. Everyone here knows you don't have to be here. Charlie Brothers will meet you upstairs later. He wants to be helpful, says he owes you a favour. He will get you settled into the reception block, as you will have nothing for maybe two weeks or so.'

Butchie continued talking as he went about his work. 'Your partner, Joe Novoa, is delighted you're here. We would all want to be anywhere else but in the can, regardless of friendship or good company, but he is trying to get you in to share his cell. I live two slammers away from Joe. If there is something you need – like soap, coffee, cigarettes or just any questions that may be on your mind, let me know. I will be delighted to help. These first few weeks are the worst, then things start to make a little sense and you can get settled.

'At present you face doing six years and ten months on the ten you got, so make each day count. The hardest part is knowing that you can't do all the things you used to take for granted, and, of course, no broads. The richest and the scum of the earth are all reduced to less than human in here. They all start through this processing centre with the same wrinkled khakis – three T-shirts, three underpants and five pairs of white socks – a so-called toothbrush and a bar of what some people call soap, but what my mother used to do the stoop steps with. Anyway, see you later.'

I thanked my one-man welcoming committee and Mamone, having taken my photo, turned and left.

Later, I was transferred to the reception unit. The long, grey, stone-walled corridors and red-tile floors smelled of cleaning and disinfecting fluids mingled with the odour of dirty socks and sweat. New inmates spent roughly two weeks in the reception area and were not allowed out of their cells until they'd been assessed.

During that time I was given shots, shown the rules and regulations, was issued my clothing and told how to get by and be a good inmate. The new prisoners were not allowed to mix with the general population or go out into the exercise area because some were known informers and would be killed immediately. In reception, or the beginner's block, most inmates did not talk to other prisoners. Nobody could be trusted, as any inmate could be an informer or a co-operating witness. An Irishman named Jimmy Dooley* from County Clare tormented me with mundane conversation, but he was rushed out of the reception area after a few days. Dooley had 'ratted' someone out and received some friendly 'advice' not to talk to me. He was moved on for fear of his safety.

During this period I was brought before a classification committee of prison officials – the associate warden, the chaplain and others involved in prison work programmes. My background was read out and I was asked what I'd like to do. The committee described the prison industries and the work and education available to inmates. New inmates had to wait for an opening in the industries, so it generally took time before a job became available. I asked to see my case worker as I wanted to be assigned a job as soon as possible.

Each new inmate had to have a case worker assigned before being introduced into the general prison population. Some days after my arrival, I met my council of case workers, who would intercede for me with the outside world, and who would manage my other affairs – bank account, family problems, etc. At my interview, the case workers asked me if I had any fears from any of the inmates, to which I replied my only fear was from some nut, some prison Jesse James, who would want to make a name for himself by killing an ex-cop. The case workers all burst out laughing, much to my shock and annoyance.

'What the hell is so funny about that!'

They then introduced me to the man assigned as my personal case worker. His name was Jesse James!

———————

Two weeks after arriving in Lewisburg, I was processed from reception into the main prison to G Block – Mafia Row – to share a cell with my old partner, Joe Novoa. He had already served nearly a year of his ten-year sentence. We had both taken our separate courses of non-cooperation with the authorities. It was not a mutual agreement. I had always replied politely, 'I respectfully decline your kind offer.' Novoa's reply was always more aggressive, 'Go fuck yourself.' This earned him no favours with the parole board and prison committees. He was bitter at his detention and had taken his incarceration hard, and was often depressed and irritable. That said, he was delighted to see me, and he gave me a present of shower slippers. He had also stocked up on teabags because he knew well I didn't drink coffee.

I met Butchie Mamone again, who shared a neighbouring cell with his narcotics partner, Joe Di Napoli, who had been caught with $1 million in cash, the proceeds of narcotics deals, allegedly some of the Broome Street French Connection theft.

Charlie Brothers, who I had collared on two occasions for narcotics possession, also came to my cell with a 'Not you, here?' smile on his face. Through the prison grapevine, Charlie Brothers had heard that I had been arrested in England. Brothers and other organised crime figures knew me and my 'code' on the street. He had respect for me because I had let his accomplice, Tommy Marchione, walk free from a gun and drug bust. It was good to know. Besides, most anybody of consequence in Lewisburg knew I had spent the last five months sharing the cell of mafia boss Tom Di Bella.

Brothers brought mild, sweet-smelling soap, cocoa, chocolate bars, toothpaste and other toiletries. I had collared Brothers twice on the outside, but now he came as a friend. He offered me advice, echoing Butchie, that would keep me going for the next few years.

'You gotta take it one day at a time. Keep away from the freaks. There's nothing they can do for you that you can't do with your right hand. Get involved in prison activities. Go to school. Get involved in team sports. Don't talk to the hacks (prison officers), you've got nothing to say to them. They have got nothing to do with what happens to you in here. It's the cons who run the prison. They're the clerks. They do all the paperwork, keep the files, assign the good jobs, the good cell blocks. They see that you get extra privileges. The hacks do nothing but watch. In time, you'll get a good job. This is a hard place and it has killed a lot of good men, young and old, but it can't kill somebody who wants to survive. Do good time. That's the secret of surviving in the joint. Do one day at a time and let the outside world go fuck itself!'

The Catholic chaplain at Lewisburg, I soon discovered, was Fr Pat Duggan from Moville in County Donegal. I went to mass once a week and sometimes had a private conversation with Fr Pat in his office.

During his time as chaplain, he got to know me very well and I appealed for his help to allow my children to visit. Fr Duggan allowed me to call Rita and the children numerous times, but the visits never materialised. Fr Duggan even got in touch with Fr Gallagher, a priest in Rita's parish. Fr Gallagher promised to bring the children to Lewisburg himself, but that also failed to materialise for whatever reason. I tried everything in my power to encourage and motivate my family to visit, but it was no use. I felt they held the fact that I did not co-operate with the authorities against me. To them, I could have avoided going to prison. My children were too young to understand why I couldn't co-operate. I had very few visitors during my time in Lewisburg and it hurt me to see other families visiting the prison. I had two sisters living in Canada – one in Vancouver and one in Edmonton – and I later learned that my mother and one of my sisters, with her husband and family, drove from Canada to Florida and passed within sixteen miles of Lewisburg but never stopped to visit me.

The majority of inmates in Lewisburg were not organised criminals and were distinct from them. The ordinary inmates looked normal – even the crazy ones. Many were highly intelligent but, at the same time, they usually showed poor judgement and lack of control. Most of them were self-centred. They rarely found fault with their actions and felt victimised, always blaming someone else for their incarceration. It was never their fault, never their actions that had led them to prison.

The organised crime inmates were different – people who with full knowledge and forethought had broken the rules that society had created. They found a method that, when properly executed, would allow them to benefit financially by widening the boundary lines, and they did so with impunity until caught. But they suffered the penalties with no regrets, as it was a venture that reaped a generous bounty, even if a personal price may be expected in confinement. While doing time, they knew that their families would be cared for and that, when released, a position would be made available to them in the mob's structure.

Prison could be a state of mind. I, for the most part, was strong in body, but weak in mind. At times, I was close to despair and plummeted into the depths of depression. But for my friends, I might have had a major nervous breakdown. Lewisburg was a world of cement walls, cold floors and iron bars. The walls closed in, the day was regimented and, in such an environment, dreams withered and died. An inmate could be crushed by the institutionalised monotony, whether it was one year or ten. I learned that I had to live from one experience to the next – no matter how trivial they were. I would look for one little pleasure in everything. Meal times, despite been repetitious, became a contentment, as was conversation with new friends. The few with the intelligence to be business people on the outside were the most understanding, as were the ones who worked hard at trying to be helpful, and alert in terms of security at the same time.

There were some inmates who functioned expressionlessly with no emotion or willingness to appear human. The rules guided their computerised, mechanical actions. Some inmates deserved to be there, while others seemed to enjoy this home away from home. There were many who were happy to be in prison and almost enjoyed the solidity of an institutionalised world.

As in any group of people, there were a few sadists. They made the weak, sick, lonely and degenerate the willing victims of their own depraved pleasures. These unfortunates suffered an unending life of horror until they were released or died, sometimes at their own hands. The sadists lived off the misery of the weak and those who had no friends. I knew that without friends, I could not survive in prison.

Inmates mixed with their own: whites with whites, blacks with blacks, Hispanics with Hispanics, Asians with Asians. Within each ethnic group, inmates again mixed with their own clique: organised criminals stayed together, as did hillbillies, white-collar criminals, drug users, homosexuals. Everyone had their own area, separate table and yard space. A new prisoner soon found friends, who he looked to for protection. It was important to know that you would be safe from being raped, beaten up or shaken down. Your friends provided this safety, and I soon realised that I had a certain amount of protection. I was told in no uncertain terms that both Joe Novoa and I were looked up to and admired by what we called the 'OCs' – the organised criminals. That meant a lot, because it meant nobody would dare to bother us. We could sleep soundly, safe in the knowledge we had protection against the dangers of prison life.

After meal times, prisoners had plenty of spare time on their hands – time to deal drugs, rape one another and, at times, murder each other. So it was important to have a job during the day and to keep out of the way of the real crazies. Most connected prisoners were able to secure a job – cooking, cleaning, sweeping the floor, anything which helped to pass the monotony. Prisoners were locked in at 5.30 p.m. and if a prisoner couldn't read, he was in trouble because that was the main occupation until lights went out four hours later at 9.30 p.m. This was when prisoners would start flipping out because they had nothing to occupy their minds. The prison had a limited library and inmates would fill out chits to order books, which were delivered by orderlies who worked in the library. Books (often outdated), and the weekly movie, which could not contain any crime, violence or sex, were the only escape from the prison monotony. The library was stocked with mostly classics and plenty of law books, because everyone was trying to prove they should not be in prison, while the movies were dramas and the odd comedy. I did not go to the weekly movies and read very little. Newspapers were not allowed and only a limited number of magazines found their way to inmates. I was extremely lucky that I shared a cell with my former police partner, who I knew and respected.

CHAPTER 6

Hail, hail, the gang's all here

During the time I spent in Lewisburg, I was befriended by many people I had met on the outside, which included Irish and Italian political bosses from New Jersey: Hugh Addonizio, the former mayor of Newark, who was jailed for taking bribes for construction contracts; Tom Wheeler*, another former mayor, and Tom Flannery*, a city council president, who were jailed for corruption; and Eddie Rosner and Robert Schultz, criminal lawyers, who were jailed for bribery and corruption. I was also taken under the wing of Irish, Italian, Hispanic and black gangsters from New York. However, these friendships were unspoken and no one ever explicitly guaranteed my personal safety in words.

There were a number of murders within the prison, and I could have become a statistic only for the protection of the mob bosses who were friends of friends on the outside. Police and organised criminals shared a respect for each other. This was not the petty pickpocket or junkie or rapist, but the gangster whose daily existence was governed by a crime structure with bosses, etc. There was a huge difference between these people, especially in prison. Gangsters and their families would have nothing to do with street trash criminals. I could easily have been killed inside, but mutual respect goes a long way.

Though there were people from my former life in prison, I also got to know new people. I'd always been an outgoing, friendly person and a good listener – I listened to people's problems and offered my advice, good, bad or indifferent. In prison, time is not in short supply, so many inmates sought out the well-connected ex-cop just to talk and to hear what he had to say. I made friends this way. I exercised a little: running, which I had practised in my youth and in the military, and soccer with South American inmates, a number of whom I had investigated while with the SIU.

One of the South Americans, named Tony T., who looked Italian to me, insisted I read his trial minutes as he wanted to get my advice. I reluctantly agreed but, while I was reading, I realised that Tony T. was, in fact, Tony Torres, the owner of the 100-kilo haul that I had confiscated in April 1970. Torres was amazed when I told him. We thought it funny that the actual detective who had made the seizure and its owner were in prison together! Torres told me that he and his partner, Luis Romano*, were watching TV when it was broadcast that police had seized their narcotics shipment. For some time after the bust, we had been on the lookout for Tony T., who we knew was connected to the huge haul. Now I had found him. The irony was not lost on either of us.

While I was in the main prison, many people were good to me. A New York wiseguy, Bobbie Maher, was one. Bobbie's father was an Irish cop and his mother was Italian. He smoked those little stogie cigars just like the Italian mob guys, which was very unusual for an Irishman. He used to take up my call time on the telephone – because I had no one to call, I would arrange my phone time and let Bobbie use it. He called home and always paid me back with little presents. I went to see Bobbie when I was released and had dinner with him and his wife. He did not look like a gangster. Bobbie looked like any ordinary businessman, but he was a well-connected organised crime figure, a stone killer and a very dangerous person to cross. We never spoke about 'business'. Bobbie knew who I was and I knew who he was. There was a mutual understanding, we did not talk about street stuff. I didn't know what he was in for, but it was a short sentence.

Another friend was a Jewish bank robber, Mark Lippstein. He was known as '30 Mark' because he used to give a note to the bank teller that read: 'This is a stick-up. I have a gun in the bag and will use it if you don't do what I ask. Put all your 10s, 20s and 30s in this paper bag.' Lippstein had held up about ten banks with the same note and this led to his eventual conviction. He passed it to all the frightened tellers, who didn't see the humour in it. Of course, when he was caught in the act, the frightened bank tellers could remember the wording of the notes because of the reference to thirty-dollar bills.

Lippstein was arrested for all of the jobs he had pulled. The judge was Jewish, as was his lawyer, so Lippstein got out on bail pending his pleading guilty at the trial. He made all kinds of promises not to go into another bank, even to open an account. But Lippstein was a degenerate gambler and was soon broke, so he went out and bought an actor's make-up kit. At home, he darkened his pale face to a deep tan, darkened his red hair and moustache and made an imitation scar down one cheek, adding a mole to his nose. Then he got a colourful silk scarf and made a big knot where his tie usually was and left the top two buttons of his shirt open. He looked a completely different man and headed to a bank where he passed a better-worded threatening note. It worked beautifully, with no hitches.

Lippstein was so impressed with his new disguise that he decided to stop off for a drink in a local bar on his way home. It was the middle of the afternoon and the inside of the bar and grill was dark. He walked in and went to the farthest end of the long bar, his confidence rising as nobody said hello. Lippstein felt fantastic. If his disguise worked in his own neighbourhood local, he would never be caught. Then the bartender called down to him, 'A regular for you, Mark?' He was disgusted, drank down his beer quickly and walked casually, when he really wanted to run, out of the bar. As he left, he could hear the laughs of the regulars and the bartender saying, 'I wonder what he's getting up to in all that make-up? Is he gone gay or what? Ha, ha!'

When Lippstein went back to court on his original charges, the investigating detectives had his latest bank robbery to add to the list. His disguise hadn't worked there either. The tellers had identified him from photos. One detective said to him, 'Hey, Mark, how many copies of the photos would you like sent to you?' Lippstein was sentenced to ten years for armed robbery.

I met other Irishmen jailed in Lewisburg. Five Irish republicans had been caught in Baltimore in a sting operation with a consignment of guns and ammunition that were to be shipped to Ireland to the IRA. Four were convicted and became known as 'The Baltimore Four'. Three of them – James Conlon, Michael Larkin and Harry Hillick – were in Lewisburg Penitentiary at various times. All three were jailed for six years.

I became very friendly with James Conlon. We talked almost every day, just small talk about nothing in particular. Conlon gave up smoking in prison. He bought a dozen packs of cigarettes and stuck them at various points about his prison cell, so if he wanted one, it was there for the taking. That was the way he gave them up. Conlon died in Belfast a few months after being released.

Harry Hillick defeated an attempt to deport him to Belfast and died in New York in 2005 of lung cancer.

I also met so-called 'Goodfella' Henry Hill (played by Ray Liotta in the movie *Goodfellas*) in the main prison and later when we were transferred to 'the farm'. Henry was always up to some scheme. He was what we called a 'loob'. Despite what he has said and written, Hill was not known as a big-time gangster, but a 'go-for' – a loob – 'Go get me a match … make my bed … steal some steaks … cook this spaghetti and meatballs for us …' He only made his name when he became an informer and created his own prestige. When he broke his arm playing softball, I used to write Hill's letters to his wife Karen, who was not as beautiful as depicted in *Goodfellas*. Henry was not a bit like his character, either – he was short and tubby.

Loobs were the ones who made kings out of gangsters and became their footmen, waiters, chambermaids and all-round handymen. This was what Henry Hill did, although the FBI advertised him as an inside informer for the fixing of basketball games and other sports. Hill also claimed to have information on Jimmy Burke and other high-ranking mobsters. But he was just a loob for the New York Mafiosi, especially Paul Vario and Johnny Dio, whose meals he cooked. Both Vario and Dio were good friends to me. It was a big laugh to underworld figures and others who knew him to see the feds take information and advice from the lying lips of Henry Hill, who had flipped when he'd been arrested on a narcotics charge. Henry made great talk about being a partner and confidant of Jimmy Burke, but Jimmy would never have confided in the likes of Henry. They were just not in the same league.

I also knew Jimmy 'The Gent' Burke, who was played by Robert De Niro in *Goodfellas*, just as I knew many other gangsters from New York, New Jersey and Canada. He became a friend of mine in Lewisburg and also in the halfway house, the Bryant Hotel. Jimmy the Gent was a mentor to Tommy DeSimone, whose sister, Phyllis, was Burke's mistress. According to Henry Hill, when Burke hijacked lorries, he would usually take a truck driver's licence. He would warn the driver that they knew his address if he went to the cops. But he would also give the driver $50, as if he were tipping him for the inconvenience – this is how he was supposed to have got his nickname Jimmy the Gent. The reality was that Burke would rather give you two bullets behind the ear than two dollars in your hand. But Jimmy was an absolute gent to me while I was in prison. We were released around the same time.

I remember one small incident from my time with Jimmy. Ex-cop Pat Intrieri was housed in segregation on his way to another prison. When he'd retired from the NYPD, Intrieri had worked for New York gangster Vinnie Papa as a bodyguard. Intrieri had been convicted of income tax evasion, for which he received a short jail term. All of those convicted with him were sent to separate jails in an effort to get one to turn against the others for a reduced sentence. Jimmy, who was at the tennis courts, told me that Pat was waving and calling out to me from his third-storey cell window. I took a list of what he wanted, coffee and cigars – which are forbidden in segregation – which he shouted down from his cell window. Because I worked as a supply manager in the commissary store, I got my supervisors to allow my personal prison account to pay for the items as he had no jail account in Lewisburg. Things like this can be passed over by the unknowledgeable as a simple act between friends, but it is much more.

The mob guys in G Block received alcohol, cigarettes and the best of food smuggled in by either warders or their family. I was able to avail of the good food, but I was not interested in anything else. In our cell, Joe was the coffee freak and my indulgence was tea. In G Block, days were spent on work detail, going to rehabilitation programmes and school. Nearly everybody had a job, as it counted a lot with the parole board. Johnny Dio didn't work, because he was old and frail and was never going to get released, but he spent all his time filing appeals and chatting with the priest. Dio was a 'labour relations expert', but had been jailed for fifteen years when he'd branched out into stock fraud. He died in Lewisburg in 1979, aged sixty-four.

Another friend I made was Benny Ong, a prominent Asian figure in the Hip Sing Association, a Chinese-American criminal organisation based in New York's Chinatown. Benny Ong was a pleasant, well-preserved elder, known as 'Small Benny' and 'Benny of the Seven Sons, from Pell Street'. He was born the son of a peasant farmer in Harbin in China and had arrived in New York in 1923, when he was sixteen. He was a soldier in the 1920s Tong Wars, where the weapon of choice led to the term 'hatchet man'. Also known as 'Uncle Seven' because he was the seventh child in his family, Benny had the formal title of adviser-in-chief-for-life of the Hip Sing Association, the largest of the seventy tongs that dominated life for over a century in Chinatown in Lower Manhattan.

Benny had been convicted of second-degree murder in 1935 and had gone to prison for seventeen years. The word in Chinatown was that he allowed himself to be framed to protect someone higher in the organisation. After emerging from prison in 1952, Benny resuméd his activities in Hip Sing, which by then was under the presidency of his brother, Sam. It was when he went to jail for bribery in 1977 – for only one year – that I met him. As it happened, I would see him again on the outside.

The convicted spy Robert Thompson was also someone I befriended while at Lewisburg. He claimed that Robert Thompson was not his real name, although US investigators maintained that he was a Detroit-born American. But Thompson maintained that he'd actually been born in Leipzig of a Russian father and German mother. Thompson had been a US Air Force clerk and he confessed to passing hundreds of photos of secret documents to the Soviets when he'd been based in West Berlin. He'd received a thirty-year sentence but was released after thirteen years. In Lewisburg he used to paint landscapes and, on his release, he brought about 400 paintings back to East Germany with him. Thompson's release came in a three-way spy swap. As part of the deal, an American student held by the East Germans and an Israeli pilot imprisoned by the Marxist regime in Mozambique were released.

John Wojtowicz, the bank robber who inspired the movie *Dog Day Afternoon*, was serving a twenty-year sentence for armed robbery when I arrived at Lewisburg. He fancied himself as a jailhouse lawyer and would drop down to my cell during recreation time to chat about his case. Wojtowicz was bisexual and had robbed banks to pay for his lover's sex-change operation. I always left the door of our cell open when he visited in case anyone thought there was something going on.

The majority of people I met in prison were genuinely nice to me. Nobody ever threatened me or made my life miserable in any way. I found that most prisoners were there because of circumstance. I'm not saying they should not have been there – they were all there for a reason, but that one reason seemed to be the same, a criminal enterprise involving money.

It is said that the love of money is the root of all evil and, as any of the inmates would testify, if you want to see how people really are, wait until there is money involved.

CHAPTER 7

Button man for the mob

Lewisburg was a massive federal prison, with walls fashioned of heavy stone and cement, set in the hills of central Pennsylvania. The majority of inmates were black and Hispanic. Whites prisoners were in the minority, but the guards and prison authorities were exclusively white.

Inmates were housed in seven separate cell houses and four dormitories. The cell houses (A–G) looked like high-rise zoos with single and double cells. The dormitories (K1, K2, J1 and J2) were reserved for inmates who maintained good behaviour or who paid cash for one. The elite of organised crime, of course, were only a small part of the prison population in the 1970s. However, I was among this most influential percentage.

Murders and mutilating assaults were commonplace in the prison, but sex was one of the biggest problems. The absence of female company was one of the worst aspects of prison life, so – for a certain class of people – a substitute for sexual gratification had to be found. Love affairs blossomed in the prison and 'lovers' met in areas of the prison considered 'hot spots', like the laundry and kitchen, where prisoners could conceal themselves – at least for short periods – in nooks and crannies. However, not all the sex was voluntary. Most was performed for money or drugs, while the most sadistic and brutal inmates sodomised and raped one another in the cells, in the showers, in the bathrooms and behind the baseball bleachers. If an inmate was not a 'connected' prisoner, he was at risk from the many sexual predators inside Lewisburg.

Prisoners witnessed beatings and murders, which they did not want to see, in case it put their own lives at risk. Lewisburg was a place accustomed to physical violence and pain, and many of the inmates were not repelled by the suffering and anguish of others but enjoyed it.

The periods of restraint were from 7.30 p.m. (an hour earlier in the winter) until 6 a.m., and a brief lock-up in the late afternoon for a head count. There was supervision of recreation or work areas but inmates with time to think were always a step ahead of the prison officers. Many inmates spent their time trying to get high on narcotics or on alcohol that was brewed daily. Yeast and sugar were stolen from the kitchen, while fruit was bought at the commissary. Sugar and fruit were fermented in yeast and water, which made a type of 'hooch'. Inmates self-medicated with drugs or alcohol to ease the pain of confinement and to try and forget where they were. Most of the big gangsters were taking Valium on a daily basis, smuggled in by staff members to loobs – never directly to them.

Narcotics of every kind poured into the prison – smuggled in by corrupt guards or carried into the visitors' room by the friends, wives and children of the inmates. Sophisticated drug-dealing organisations made distributions up and down the cell blocks. Dealers were generous with credit. There was no interest on the loans, but there were no defaults either, at least none that the debtor survived.

Even though an inmate earned money in the prison industries, he was not allowed to receive that money until his release (the money was paid into his account in the commissary department for his use within the prison), so other means were found to generate cash. Tens of thousands of dollars circulated in the prison. Inmates had other ways to earn money to buy narcotics and liquor in the prison's hidden economy. Some inmates barbered for the big-time gangsters, ran their errands, cleaned their cells or washed their clothes. Some hired themselves out as bodyguards. A well-connected inmate in Lewisburg could have everything he wanted, except a woman. A murder contract started as low as a carton of cigarettes but progressed according to the prestige of the victim. A third party on the outside, having payment posted to the assassin's commissary account, could even arrange a murder inside the prison walls.

Except for religious service and a movie shown once a week on Saturday, every day was the same. Whatever the season, prison routine varied little. Inmates were usually well-behaved when a movie was playing because other prisoners would get angry if the movie was stopped. Inmates with disabilities were given the seats up front. Many gangsters pretended they had disabilities and picked their prime seats first. Eventually, even Joe Novoa got in on it, but I never went to the weekly movie. I stayed in my cell, washing and cleaning my clothes in a makeshift washing machine – fashioned from a plunger and a bucket. I used a metal bucket and a toilet plunger with holes cut out of its rubber cup base that allowed the soapy water to gush through it while its main body pressed and squeezed the cotton whites until clean. I did these on a weekly basis for myself rather than use the prison laundry. Through my various connections, I had ten to twelve sets of everything that was allowed. Of course, all inmates had to wear prison coveralls, but mine were always impeccable, with my chambray shirt perfectly creased.

There were three head counts daily: before breakfast; before night-time lockdown and lights out; inmates were also locked in their cells at 4 p.m. for a count. These lasted twenty to twenty-five minutes. Meals were served after the morning and evening counts, with each block going separately. The first to eat was A Block, then B Block, C, D, E, F, G and then the dormitories. The tables accommodated six to eight people and I always sat with Novoa. Inmates were not allowed to bring any food out of the dining room, and every piece of food on their trays had to be eaten. Depending on the quality of the food – the good meals took the longest to finish – 1,500 inmates ate their dinner in an hour and a half. This left inmates with plenty of time on their hands – for some, time to plot murder, mayhem and rape, for others, time to plot how to get out. One prisoner, Tyrone Nobleman, a hardened killer, walked out during prison visiting time dressed as a woman. He had spent his time well, looking at how and where the hacks were lax in security.

The winters in prison were hard to bear. No one was allowed outside after dusk because the darkness presented a security nightmare. So we went to the second-floor gym for sit-ups, push-ups and pumping iron.

The cell block noises were no replacement for the sound of city traffic, blowing horns, children laughing, even the barking of a dog, and these were the commonplace sounds I missed, along with the lack of a toilet seat or just the smiling face of a woman or having children sit on your knee. Prison smelled of slowly decaying human flesh and disinfectant. At Christmas and New Year, everyone felt like they were climbing a mountain of emotional snow and ice, for three or four weeks up to and after the holiday season.

Even hardened criminals found it hard to adapt to Lewisburg, including ones who had been in prison before. Nobody wanted trouble in prison – black or white – everyone just wanted to get along and do their time. I wasn't bothered by any of the inmates. The guards left me alone too. There were guards who were sadistic in nature, who took sexual advantage of feeble-minded, easily impressed young prisoners. Sometimes they goaded them into violence for their own ends.

After many long hours pent up in five-by-nine-foot cells, frustration was high and violence common. Emotions intensified; frustration quickly turned to fury, anxiety became terror, and dislike changed overnight to absolute hatred. On the outside, an argument could be quickly solved; in prison, it was completely different. A person could not walk away from an argument. It was kill or be killed. If an inmate lost face, he lost everything and became prey to the bullies and the sick and twisted. One of my main fears was killing another inmate in self-defence and then being sentenced to a life inside for murder. Alliances formed quickly against real and imagined threats and could lead to multiple murders. But even in this feverish atmosphere, there was one matter that broke all taboos – informing. Many of the killings in Lewisburg were of informers – real or imagined. They were usually killed with prison-made weapons.

Over long periods of time, inmates could build up animosity towards each other, animosity that sooner or later was acted out, usually by stabbing. Apart from the items the prison industry produced, like lockers and mailboxes, the machine shop fashioned illegal weapons for inmates. (There was also a dental school making false teeth.) Every kind of material was available and used – metal, wood and plastic. Hand-fashioned knives, called 'shanks', were tempered and honed in forges and grinders. Some were up to fourteen inches long, basically middle-sized swords. Head knockers – iron pipes or heavy wooden clubs wrapped with tape – were turned out on an assembly-line basis. Some weapons were like knitting needles, honed to a point on each side. The weapons not used for self-defence were sold for cash to buy drugs and booze, or the owners contracted themselves out to commit murder.

An assailant would generally have some of his friends with him who would surround the victim. The perp would then move in and stab his victim, usually in the stomach or side, or hit him on the head. Then the assailant and his covering group would walk quickly away, leaving their victim seriously injured or to die, if that was the intention. No inmate ever witnessed such incidents, no one ever co-operated. If a perp was caught, he was brought before a trial board, but because inmates would never testify, there was little proof. Most often there would be no punishment, though it would really depend on the trial board of the associate warden, two officers and the chaplain. If they wanted to stick the inmate – if it was someone they were having constant problems with – they were free to treat the case as they saw fit. This was not like a trial on the outside and there was no appeal – an inmate convicted of murder in prison would spend the rest of his days in jail.

The major organised criminal was above all the petty feuds and random violence of prison life. He usually lived in a single cell, jogged and played a lot of handball, attended mass regularly and spent time in the 'chaplain's area'. The prison chaplain had made a lounge available for inmates to use for private conversation. Privacy was a precious commodity in prison, and the chaplain's area was meant to be a haven from the madness of the rest of Lewisburg. I frequented the chaplain's area, sometimes reading, often just talking with friends.

I had made so many mobster friends that I felt safe as long as I didn't try to be one myself. A mutual arrangement, based on respect, kept the friendship alive. I had many friends who were made men and when they got pressed and dressed for their families' visits, often there would be a button missing from their prison khaki shirts and they would rush in at the last minute to the only man with needle and thread – me. I would sew on a button for them and got the humorous name of being 'a button man for the mafia'.

I made small items in prison – two sets of tweezers were made into four small screwdrivers by breaking the two sides apart, sharpening each end to a different size and adding small pieces of wood for handles. Each cell could have a radio and headphones but had to use batteries bought in the prison commissary. I also made monotone headphones into stereo by making a small cut, pulling the wires out of the protective rubber cover, making a small incision on each of the interior wires, then connecting the wires themselves. For items like these, I was rewarded with food, even fillet steak.

Being in general population could be numbingly dull, so a job was valuable. Inmates not assigned a job were put on 'idle time', which meant they were on their block most of the day, apart from meal-times and one hour of release for exercise or 'yard time'. Some inmates had jobs in the kitchen or the general workshop, while connected criminals were assigned 'cushy' jobs.

I worked as the Visiting Room clerk at Lewisburg from October 1975 until June 1976 when the Visiting Room inmate assignment was abolished – I was the only inmate ever given the job. It was a position of huge importance. I met the families of the various gangsters and their lawyers from NYC and NY state, Philadelphia, New Jersey, Boston and Canada. I was strip-searched going back and forth to my prison job, with other prisoners going to and from the visiting room – four times per day in all. I went into the room in the early morning, then out for lunch and back after lunch, and then again when visiting hours were over at the end of each day.

Gangsters' families would arrange to meet me in the visiting room toilet and give me choice food to eat: meatballs, veal, all the best of Italian goods.

I insisted on the strip-search each time for my own protection because I was being approached all the time to bring money and drugs back into the prison.

CHAPTER 8
Safe in prison?

Lewisburg had its own community where there were bosses, workers, painters, plumbers, cooks, thieves, elders, hoods, enforcers, etc. Those who committed acts that violated the inner security could be sure of corrective punishment, which, in some cases, resulted in death. Usually, there were sit-downs where it was deemed necessary for the advantage of the population as a whole. Some would die because of their own weakness – drugs, debt or crimes of passion. Stealing was not tolerated – it was on a par with informing – and was punished, if repeated, with a death sentence.

Just because Joe Novoa and I were ex-cops didn't mean we were safe or given special treatment. Like the other 'good' criminals – city officials, mayors, priests, lawyers and doctors – we were cast into the whirlpool and had to sink or swim, as our own personal behaviour was accepted or rejected. We would become an easy target if we relaxed our usual highly adapted sense of survival and self-preservation for a single moment, and had to be on guard for the 'nuts' and 'cowboys' who wanted to make a name for themselves in the dog-eat-dog world of prison. It was stressful to people unused to physical violence to keep up a tough image to ward off conflict. Not everyone was capable of doing it. Some went out of their heads and were confined in padded cells. Some killed when there was no conflict, having struck out in a paranoid state of fear.

When sentenced, a judge gave over the convicted felon to the protection of the Justice Department for the period imposed in confinement. There was an impression given to some families that their son, father or brother would be safe, away from the city streets, the pushers, the pimps and other fellow criminals. They were safely locked away out of harm's way – or so they thought. For many, however, prison was as violent as the streets and for the white-collar criminals, it was something they had never experienced.

During my time in Lewisburg, fifteen prisoners were murdered. Many more were attacked and injured, though some attacks were never reported, for a variety of reasons. One attack, which involved me, was one of many unrevealed to the prison authorities. It began while Gerry Geaney was sharing his set of works with his cellmate Buffalo and a few others. For some unknown reason, Blue Eyes, an American Indian from Ohio, jumped up and pulled out a steel prison-made knife and attacked Geaney, who managed to take the shank from the Indian in a fierce struggle. Geaney received a long gash running down the inside of his left forearm, which continued around the top of his wrist, and also severed his leather watchband.

Geaney and Buffalo were housed next door to me, so Geaney ran, with his left arm up under his dark-blue sweatshirt, into my cell, before the news of the fight and the shank was broadcast to the cell block guards. The guards usually waited long enough not to get involved in the violence, and just picked up the injured or the lifeless remains. It was two hours before lock-up and Geaney needed stitches and bandages. The incident could not be revealed to the authorities as Geaney had an escape record from other prisons and would be held for the remainder of his sentence in solitary confinement, which could also impact on this type of living in any future judgement against him. Buffalo had some wax dental floss and he threaded one of my needles. Geaney consumed a bottle of hooch as an anaesthetic. Other inmates helped as I pushed the small stitches through Geaney's forearm, drawn together, tied and cut, as I had seen my surgeon father do. Band-aids supported the stitches.

The difficult part was to set the wrist in such a way that it would appear normal to the prison guards and yet not be moved for the four or five days it would need for the wound to start to heal. I remembered the only way to get blood stains out of a T-shirt was with the saliva of the person whose blood it was, so Geaney sucked at the shirt, until all the bloodstains came out. Inmates working in the hospital supplied liquid disinfectant, which was swabbed over the long length of the cut. Antibiotics and painkillers were collected from friends who were on the medication pill line. Geaney was put into his bunk with his left arm tied across the front of his chest to prevent movement and damage during sleep. He went to the work details to make the head count but a fellow prisoner did his work, saying he lost to Geaney in cards and had to pay him back. Other friends mopped his section of the large hall so he wouldn't be missed from his daily assignment, at least until his injured wrist section had healed.

Meanwhile, the Indian checked himself into 'the Hole' for safekeeping as Geaney had many friends from the Westies and the Woodside Irish Mob that were willing to retaliate on his behalf. Although the Indian did not say why he requested the protection of the segregation cell, he was aware of the usual run-of-the-mill excuses given that had worked in the past. This allowed time for a sit-down to take place, where all the views were aired and decisions were made about what the outcome of the attack would be. Death was not always a wise act as it could bring restrictions to the prison population and this would not be acceptable to the elders and the governing elite. Very few killings got the overall approval, as there were usually alternatives that were less complicated and less disruptive to the daily prison lifestyle. The Indian could be executed in his solitary cell as no one was beyond the forces of punishment if it was properly handled. He later requested, and got, a prison transfer to Marion in Illinois, but spent three months alone in the Lewisburg hole until it was worked out. It was a life-saving move. If he had returned to the general population, he could have been killed by those who might take the situation into their own hands, regardless of the decisions made by the leaders.

Geaney was paroled in 1979 from a sentence that was originally to run until 1994. When he was released from prison, I'd been out of Lewisburg for a couple of months. I gave him $100 and took him to the Westchester Shopping Mall where I bought him jeans and a black sweatshirt. I insisted he was clean of drugs and guns anytime he came to my basement apartment in the Upper West Bronx, because I was also on parole, so he always hid any guns and drugs before he came to see me and picked them up later.

I gave him a small leather case with a set of black rosary beads and a miniature detective's gold shield with my number on it – 7347 – to keep him safe. I had got to know his brother, a hard-working insurance salesman, who was supporting his mother in a nursing home. But Gerry was soon back to his old tricks and held up two banks in Queens when he was on parole. Then he met his ex-wife in a Woodside bar and followed her boyfriend into the toilet, put a gun up to his face and fired a bullet through both cheeks. The man, a member of the Westies, survived.

Geaney and an accomplice, William 'Machine Gun' Cody, an escaped convict, then picked up loan shark Leon Klinghoffer outside his fashionable Riverdale apartment pretending to be detectives.

Klinghoffer offered the two men $5,000 if they let him go, but the two kidnappers were looking for a $50,000 ransom. Klinghoffer was strangled with his own tie after a ransom attempt was bungled. Geaney was arrested in Brooklyn in October 1980, after his junkie girlfriend gave him up. She gave police his location and Gerry was arrested by the Joint Bank Robbery Task Force, made up of FBI agents and city bank specialist detectives.

When Geaney was arrested, he had my police shield on him but a detective friend, who was part of the arresting team, took the shield before FBI agents – who were also on the arresting team – could see it. He looked up the number in the police files and returned it to me with the inside story. Geaney was charged with the two bank robberies and the murder of Klinghoffer. He was on $25,000 bail for the attempted murder of his ex-wife's boyfriend when he was arrested, and was labelled a 'walking crime spree' by the Bronx DA, who sentenced him to life. Geaney was sent to Leavenworth Federal Prison where he died of kidney cancer. His mother was from Ireland and she used to make me soda bread when I first came out of prison. She lived to be ninety-eight. I have a painting Gerry Geaney made for me as an Easter card while he was in Leavenworth Prison. It hangs in a frame on my living-room wall.

On another occasion, an Italian hood named Paddy Polizzi had an argument with Vinnie Aloi, a New York made man. In the heat of the moment, Polizzi slapped Aloi across the face. This happened in the prison dining hall in the presence of many OC figures, including some of Polizzi's fellow mobsters from Boston. The witnesses were aware that Polizzi had committed a serious error by striking Aloi, whose crime family was much stronger than the Boston mafia family.

Vinnie Aloi was more than just a made man. He was acting boss of the Colombo crime family and was also the godson of Carlo

Gambino. The argument between Aloi and Polizzi caused a major row between the Colombo family and the Boston family, which could only be retracted by the ultimate sentence. No apologies were given and none would be acceptable. The secret and numerous sit-downs were well attended, but no blood was to be spilled inside the prison, as it would mean retaliation and would give the administration reason to transfer the Italian mobsters to different federal prisons. This had happened before when selected prisoners were taken in the middle of the night without any warning and transferred before any outside court or political connection could be alerted by their families, who could cite undue hardship of visiting their relatives in other parts of the country.

The result of the sit-downs was that Polizzi was allowed to live. Aloi could not do what he wanted to do while he was inside because of the great disruption it would cause to everyone else. Polizzi had to get new friends. Anyone from New York or Boston associating with him was taking a risk of being identified as being his friend. Polizzi's new friends were hillbillies and the odd black inmate – and I mean odd, as black prisoners were ruled by their own leaders, who had close business dealings with the Italians.

I was aware of Polizzi's situation and could not be seen with him, but I did bid him the time of day and, if the opportunity came my way to do him a kind turn, it was done happily, as I knew Polizzi did not have long to live.

Soon after, Polizzi was released to a halfway house in Boston. I was one of those who shook his hand and watched his smiling face as he left Lewisburg. A month or so later, word arrived that he had been shot six times in the head and his body dumped in the gutter in Boston's East End. He was last seen in a popular East End restaurant with two old pals. The official story was that Polizzi was skimming on Boston mafia loan-shark collections and was murdered by someone from his own mob. I, and many others, believed that the murder was committed by his own crime family because the Colombo family insisted that Aloi's insult had to be avenged.

I paid a trustee officer inmate with cigarettes to get me a list of each murder committed during my time in Lewisburg, which was typed up on the prison typewriter. I was thinking of someday writing my life story and thought this would come in handy for authentication. There was a range of motives for the murders. Some were crimes of passion as inmates fought for the services of young 'he/shes'. In Lewisburg, there was also an element of prison society labelled the 'PMNM list', which stood for 'Pay Me No Mind'. The sanity of these prisoners was questionable and they were responsible for many spur-of-the-moment murders.

On 18 March 1976, twenty-five-year-old Shaun Major* was stabbed several times in the chest. He was pronounced dead on arrival at the Evangelical Community Medical Center. Details of the murder were broadcast on all the local radio stations. It had taken place in G Block directly above where Joe and I lived. This young inmate was a pill head and was living in a two-bunk cell where one bunk was used for sexual favours, easily observed by others. On two occasions, Major asked me if I 'wanted to ball him' or 'buy greens, reds or blues'. Naturally, I declined all offers. Major's passing was a brutal multiple stabbing by two other inmates who were also high on pills.

A bloody shirt belonging to one of the killers was thrown away in the litter basket near my cell. Other blood-stained clothes were flushed away by a friend on the first floor, while the guards sealed off the second floor in a search for evidence. The clothes were picked up in the sewer system and led to the arrest of the killers. They were charged in outside court with murder, extending their stay within Lewisburg.

Nine days later, John Pryor was stabbed several times while in K-2 dormitory basement. He was taken to the Evangelical Medical Center, and placed on the critical list. Pryor spent several weeks in the intensive care unit, but survived the attempt on his life. Pryor was a prison informer and was involved with others in making hooch. He was giving up rival distilleries to the guards, resulting in widespread raids on the dormitory, which affected between 400 and 500 inmates. All their belongings were thrown about and personal mementoes, like family photos, were confiscated and destroyed. Bed boards (for bad backs), and items like extra blankets, socks, T-shirts, and underwear, were all confiscated. The guards knew exactly who they wanted, but they couldn't go directly to them as it would blow Pryor's identity. He was found out through a friendly guard who didn't like informers or all the extra work and effort involved in the searches and general shake-down operations. Pryor was transferred to another prison when he recovered.

The day after the attack on Pryor, Charlie Huff was burned to death – doused with flammable liquid and set on fire – while locked in his cell on the third floor of B Block. The lockbox was jammed and also ignited in an effort to make rescue by guards impossible. Huff was taken to the Evangelical Medical Center and later transferred by helicopter to the US Medical Center for federal prisoners in Springfield, Missouri, where he died because of complications from smoke inhalation. This incident was also given extensive coverage by local radio and news media.

Some of the prisoners in the cells next to Huff worked with prisoners who had access to paint thinner, which was moved into the cell next to Huff's the night before the attack. Nobody was ever convicted of the murder.

Huff had testified against people before coming to Lewisburg, and so was on the list of many who only needed the smallest excuse to kill him. He was housed near a few other dangerous prisoners. B Block was one step up the mental deficiency ladder from those in the open-cell type A Block.

Huff was not liked by his neighbours and, on one occasion, he was pointedly asked *not* to stir his coffee so loudly and vigorously because it disturbed the concentration of the man in the next cell, who was reading his book. He paid little heed to this request, until one day it became a command. If the disturbance continued, he would regret his lack of concern for those who had life sentences to serve. I think it was mainly because of the noise-making that he was killed. Everything inside was magnified a thousand times by those who were confined for life. Anything that unnecessarily disturbed an inmate's quiet time was serious enough to be punished by death.

Another prisoner, Dr Robert Abbott, a medical practitioner in civilian life, witnessed the incident and had a severe heart attack. Subsequently, he was transferred to the Federal Medical Facility at Lexington, Kentucky. Dr Abbott was eighty-three and had been sentenced to twenty years in 1975 for selling prescription pills and drugs to drug users in his home city. The FBI sent undercover agents into his offices to find that Dr Abbott never examined them for blood pressure, etc., but came to an agreed price to give them prescriptions for a variety of different federal government drugs and tablets. Abbott survived his heart attack, but he was in a more precarious position as he'd seen who committed the act and who had helped. If he were to testify, he would no doubt be murdered, an easy target for some much-needed money, drugs, cigarettes or even a bag of instant coffee. Dr Abbott was taken out of population and segregated until he recovered. He had few friends, though he and I used to discuss life and its various twists and turns from time to time in the grandstand wooden bench seats in the exercise yard.

Another prison conversationalist, Vince Yanni, was beaten on the head with a pipe while in his room in J Block, which was an 'honour' dormitory that consisted of private rooms that could not be locked because toilet facilities for that unit were in the hallway. Yanni was the inmate clerk in charge of the paint shop and decided whose cell would be painted and when. This would appear from an outsider's point of view to be a small position, but when an inmate lived every day within the close confines of four walls of a small cell, what colour it was became vitally important. A new colour and fresh paint could make a big difference to someone's mental well-being. Yanni refused one too many requests for a cell makeup and nearly lost his life. He never revealed who beat him, for he knew his life would be at risk if he did. Yanni's return to general prison population was ironed out with a sit-down before he came out, so that there would be no retaliatory measures.

On 12 April 1976, a search of B Block turned up an unspecified number of weapons: knives, axes, clubs, etc. Some of the shanks were more than thirty inches long. In addition, a sawn-off shotgun with shells and a fully loaded .38 calibre revolver were found. This search continued throughout the next day when the prison authorities decided that the FBI should conduct the investigation. The officials reasoned that there was no possibility of inmates being able to collect such an arsenal of large weapons without someone being paid to help. It was obvious that an escape was in the works. All the walls were checked for soft bricks, where bread was used to look like cement, while the bars in the blocks, cells and outer gates were also tested. It was thought the would-be escapees were from B Block because it had quite a number of lifers.

A few days later, a black inmate named David Bunk* was discovered in J Block, savagely mutilated. His throat had been ripped open to expose the inner cavity, which was described by hardened medical personnel as the most heinous butchery that they had ever seen – some had even become sick at the sight of his body. Bunk was a bully and had shaken down young Chinese prisoners for food, cigarettes and cash. In a few cases, he had assaulted the Chinese inmates and tried to rape others, as they were small in stature and he was a big, well-built man. His murder was carried out by a number of the close-knit Chinese group, with some taking a piece of his body as their section to slice into chunks. While he was dying, Bunk had scratched splinters out of the dormitory door, which was normally kept open. His killers had held the door closed with their bodies set against it, in what any passers-by would think was a regular chatty group of Chinese. The door was held closed until Bunk bled to death. His body was discovered when the guards were doing the evening head count.

More violent activity flared up on 15 May, but went almost unnoticed as I considered the regular stabbings quite normal. The incident happened on the second floor of C Block. Al Scipio was stabbed in the mouth, neck and shoulder. He was rushed to the Evangelical Medical Center where he received treatment and survived. I thought it seemed such a waste of time when one criminal tried to kill another and the authorities had to go to the trouble to save him. Again, of course, there was some good reason for the attack. The usual questions were asked about who, why and what the cause was but, more importantly, where the shank used had come from, and, given that it hadn't been left embedded in Scipio's body, where it was and when it would be used again. Shanks couldn't be flushed away, they were stashed away.

On the same day, an inmate named Mark Silver was brutally murdered on the third floor of C Block. He was stabbed twenty-one times and a crude, home-made sword was shoved into his back. It entered between the shoulder blades and protruded out about seven inches through his chest. He died immediately.

The previous day Silver had taken an X-ray of my lungs, as he was training to be a radiographer, but had found nothing. This was done as a favour by Silver to dispel my fear of cancer that had been plaguing me since my father's death in April 1976. Silver was a Jewish lad whose background and manner didn't show any street awareness or wisdom. I was impressed by Silver's sympathetic nature and his goodwill to his fellow prisoners. He was serving a five-year sentence and should never have been incarcerated with killers, gangsters, rapists and sociopaths. His death, unlike some of the other murders, was unwarranted. Many of the other prisoners murdered were killed with good reason and with the support of fellow inmates. The FBI caused quite an uproar of laughter inside the prison when they announced over the local radio station that they had found the weapon that had killed Silver. To the civilian listener, this would bring a sense of relief that the protectors of law and order had completed a thorough investigation and all was now well, but to those on the inside it was a clear case of misrepresentation as the weapon found was lodged in the body. It wasn't the only weapon used, but it was the only one found.

It was no safer for inmates in other US prisons. On 26 July 1977, Vinnie Papa was stabbed to death by three black inmates in Atlanta Federal Prison. He was the alleged mastermind behind the theft of 398 pounds of heroin and cocaine from the police property vault at 400 Broome Street (now a New York University dormitory) in six thefts between 1969 and 1972. The drugs were re-sold on the street and by the time the record theft was discovered in December 1972, the drugs – then valued at $73 million – had been replaced by flour and corn starch. This was discovered by the presence of flour beetles in the replaced substance. Taking advantage of the lax administrative procedures, someone had signed the register as Detective Joseph Nunziata, a member of the SIU, and used fictitious badge numbers to remove the drugs, which included the celebrated French Connection haul, the drugs from the Taft Hotel Case and my 100 Kilo Case seizure.

The six withdrawals formed no identifiable pattern, except that someone using the name Detective Nuzziato, or Nuzziata, using different shield numbers, had signed out the narcotics. Nunziata's name was apparently forged and further investigation showed that the idea of the rip-off had also been his because three years earlier, he had gone to author Robin Moore and suggested it as the plot for a novel. He had hoped to share in the profits of this book, but Moore declined to write it.

After the robbery, all narcotics detectives had to write their signatures with their left and right hands to be analysed. Handwriting analysis and a discovered fingerprint established that Detective Nunziata never actually signed the police register, but eight months before the thefts were discovered, Nunziata had been charged with corruption in an unrelated case and was found shot to death in his car. It was ruled a suicide, but Nunziata was shot in the chest, leading to speculation that he had been murdered. It was said, though, Nunziata had shot himself in the chest because he was too good-looking to shoot himself in the head. It was also rumoured that Nunziata was shot dead by rogue cop Vinnie Albano, using Nunziata's own service weapon so that it looked like suicide. Nunziata was a larger-than-life figure in police lore. He looked like the singer and actor Dean Martin and dressed very sharply. A Korean War veteran and tough street cop, he had been the star of the SIU and the NYPD. His name was spoken with the same reverence held for Popeye Egan and Sonny Grosso.

The loss of the Broome Street narcotics was probably the single most humiliating event to happen to any police force anywhere. Many suspects emerged in the theft, including major drug dealer

Vinnie Papa, Frank King (a retired narcotics detective), Pat Intrieri (a one-time decorated New York detective lieutenant who, upon his retirement, had become a bodyguard for one of Papa's sons), and Vinnie Albano (a corrupt cop who was murdered in 1985).

Frank King and Pat Intrieri resigned from the NYPD shortly after Nunziata's death to run a private investigation agency. Both became prime suspects in the Broome Street theft because of their association with Papa. King had previously never aroused any suspicion. His police record was clean but he had more money than he should have had, and was convicted of tax evasion. Intrieri also had more money than he earned as a police lieutenant and was sentenced to five years on income tax evasion.

Vinnie Albano, who had once been shot six times in the chest by an unidentified assailant, was never mentioned in the newspapers as a suspect in the Broome Street theft case, though the Brooklyn DA's office linked him to King and he had organised crime connections. He said he had become a policeman to make money. It was no secret, he let everyone know. As a cop, he never earned more than $30,000 a year. Nevertheless, the federal government prosecuted him for evading close to $200,000 dollars in tax. He owned an off-licence, a sweet shop, an ocean-front house, apartment buildings, a condominium in Florida and a yacht. He pleaded guilty to tax evasion and was sentenced to five years.

Anthony 'Gaspipe' Casso, a former head of the Lucchese family serving thirteen life sentences, pointed the finger at Albano as being behind the Broome Street theft. He claimed Albano had arranged with Lucchese associate Herbie 'Blue Eyes' Pate to steal the narcotics. The scheme involved Pate posing as a cop and presenting the right forged papers to withdraw the heroin and cocaine. According to Casso, Albano and Pate then sold the drugs to New York mobsters. The two became good friends and working associates but, after a time, Albano began accusing Pate of double-dealing and short-changing him, and they quickly became enemies.

Albano was a physically tough man with a bad temper and, one evening, he tried to run over Pate as he turned up for work. Pate jumped out of the way but Albano got out and began punching him, until Pate managed to pull a gun and shoot Albano dead. Albano's body was found rolled in a carpet and stuffed in the trunk of his car outside University Hospital in Staten Island.

Vinnie Papa was a lifelong drug dealer. Papa wasn't a flashy dresser, preferring dark jackets and trousers and plain or white unbuttoned shirts. He led a quiet family-oriented life, though he had a son from an extra-marital affair. He was not a made member of the Mafia, but knew and worked with major Italian crime figures. He was the perfect connection to buy and move the stolen Broome Street drugs and was considered a prime suspect by the task force. In February 1972 Papa was arrested as he drove away with Joe Di Napoli from the home of an associate in the Bronx. In the car was a suitcase that the two men had collected, which contained close to $1 million in new $100 bills. When questioned, Papa claimed that he and Di Napoli had found the money in a telephone booth and were bringing it to the police when they were arrested. It seemed more than a coincidence that the money in the suitcase in Papa's car had turned up not long after a consignment of drugs had mysteriously walked out of the property clerk's office. The money, along with information picked up from wiretaps, pointed directly at Papa and Frank King.

When Papa was arraigned before a judge, he requested legal aid, claiming he couldn't afford to hire a lawyer. He pleaded guilty to conspiracy to import narcotics and to tax evasion. As part of his plea bargain arrangement of five years, all the charges against his co-defendants were dismissed. While he was in prison, Papa was visited by prosecutors and asked to co-operate in the Broome Street Case. He refused and was brought before a grand jury. When he again refused to answer questions regarding his alleged purchase of the stolen narcotics, Papa was indicted for contempt. Prosecutor Tom Puccio was investigating leaks in the strike force in joint federal–state investigations and asked to see Papa in Atlanta. After providing what he thought was confidential information on four corrupt detectives in the SIU who were working with the strike force, the New York bosses apparently ordered Papa to be killed.

Papa heard that a murder contract had been put out on him. He pleaded with the bosses to remove the contract because the only names he'd given the grand jury were those of cops. The New York bosses advised him that giving any names to the grand jury was considered co-operating. Non-co-operation would have meant refusing to answer any questions by pleading the Fifth Amendment. Doing that would have increased his sentence by another six months every time, but because the federal government had arrested and indicted his son, Vincent Junior, Papa gave up the detectives' names, including that of Frank King.

Papa's lawyer tried to have him moved to a safer jail, but all attempts failed. Puccio tried one last time to get Papa to give up more of the crooked cops in the SIU, with a promise that he would move him to a safer prison, but Papa refused. On his way back to Atlanta, Papa took sick and was taken into Lewisburg Penitentiary Hospital where other connected friends worked. Through one, Papa sent out word that he wanted to see me because I was a close friend and fellow detective to the men whose names he had given. I was taken to his bedside in the hospital ward where we talked for about thirty minutes. I had never met him before. He was a man of less than medium height with swept-back salt-and-pepper hair. Vinnie Papa did not look like a gangster and could easily have been mistaken for a modest businessman. He looked troubled, though, and had reason to be. We talked about his situation and I promised that I would pass on his request for leniency to certain organised crime people. It was all to no avail. The contract wasn't lifted and a month later, he was murdered in Atlanta Federal Prison.

For some inmates, prison was just an extension of their street life and they continued their violent ways inside. For me, while I was no longer a cop, it was hard not to look at the violent occurrences through a cop's eyes. In my mind I looked at the evidence and the motive, though I never mentioned this to anyone except Joe Novoa. I tried not to be involved in these violent squabbles, but thinking about them and trying – in my mind – to solve the deaths helped keep me sane.

CHAPTER 9

The Quiet Man

On 19 April 1976, just moments after we'd finished our noon meal, approximately 95 per cent of the inmates employed in prison industry refused to return to their assigned jobs and, instead, assembled in the yard in peaceful protest. They were joined by many other inmates and they proceeded to sit down *en masse* and wait for someone in authority from the institution, the warden or his assistant, to come forward to speak to them regarding what they called the oppressive and degrading administrative practices carried out by the staff of the prison. In addition, they were seeking better food and educational facilities and an opportunity for a meaningful programme that would help prepare them for some future in society when they were released.

The only member of staff that came out was a lieutenant, who ordered them back to work, and when the men tried to negotiate, he ordered them back to their cells. All the men complied peacefully. The staff kept the men locked up in their cells for three days during which they were not allowed to go to the dining hall to eat and were fed sandwiches and Kool-Aid in their cells.

Novoa and I also had crackers and other small food items stored up, which helped us through the lean days and nights, but Joe ran out of cigarettes and his six or eight coffee drinks per day went up to ten or twelve. While Joe got more tense, I relaxed and caught up with some letter-writing and washed my prison whites. We never thought the sight of the large institutional grey walls could look so inviting, as it did the first morning after the lockup ended, with fried eggs for breakfast. The leaders of the protest were thrown into punishment cells. Nervous guards with pickaxe handles and automatic rifles patrolled the perimeter walls and gates, while the local and state police, backed up by military personnel, were camped on the 1,000-acre farm reservation, at the ready in case of a mass riot or attempted breakout.

Federal prison buses arrived and were loaded to capacity with the ringleaders, who were transferred to other long-distant prisons. Lines of guards stopped us from seeing the physical abuse inflicted on the leaders of the protest.

After the abolition of my visiting room job, I was designated a Central Monitoring Case and was given a job in the prison commissary as a clerk. Government employees and inmates staffed the prison commissary, a shop from which inmates bought products, such as toiletries, snacks and writing materials. Prisoners were not allowed to possess cash so, instead, they bought things through an account with money contributed by friends and family members, or earned as wages in the prison. I worked picking and filling out the order sheets. Each inmate had a brown account sheet with his photo, prison number and thumb print for identification.

I was trusted by many of the organised crime inmates, but I always had an ace up my sleeve, just in case. I made my prison money through these gangsters as I stored their cash funds in the files in the air-conditioned basement offices where I worked. If anything happened to me, the mob bosses would be out of cash, as no one else knew where it was stashed. It was an insurance policy that I had taken out for myself. The bosses protected themselves and their banker – me – by using their loobs as go-fors. If cash was needed, I made an arrangement for one of the loobs to buy certain items in the commissary into which I would conceal the money. There was no way the hidden money could be caught in the delivery stage and it was only after the goods had been delivered that there was more risk.

In March 1977 I spent three days and nights in solitary confinement as punishment for refusing to give up the name of Robert Schultz, who had signed a commissary order document – a photo album sent in to Johnny Dio – with the name of the approving prison officer and librarian, Mr Levine.

Schultz was a criminal lawyer who had been jailed for corruption and who spent much of his time with his friend, Eddie Rosner, another convicted criminal lawyer, in the law library, which was a hangout for those trying to find legal loopholes to help reduce their sentences. For many, this became an obsessive past-time. Novoa also hung out with Schultz and Rossner in the library, but I wasn't interested in working on my appeal.

I knew both lawyers and was on good terms with them. When I had received the album, which had been delivered to the prison, I went looking for Mr Levine to sign for it. I met Robert Schultz when I was trying to locate Levine, and I thought nothing about it when he offered to sign for the album. Knowing the legality of the matter, I told the prison board hearing that I had made the signature, but that I had not tried to forge it. I pointed out that it did not look anything like the real person's signature and that I had just scribbled the name, so, in effect, it was not a forgery. I also pointed out to the board – which had intended to bring me outside to a court to face forgery charges – that there was no self-gain and the photo album requested was not contraband, but a permissible item. It was all to no avail.

There were two types of punishment cells in Lewisburg: solitary and isolation. Solitary – 'the Hole' – was a dark cell, while isolation was a cell with a light. The solitary confinement cells were similar to other prison cells, but had a solid steel door that, when closed, left the cell in complete darkness. An observation window could be flipped open at any time by the guards to check on the inmate, then closed again, shutting out the light into the cell.

I spent my time in the Hole, dressed in a pair of cotton trousers, a short-sleeve cotton shirt, rubber sandals and no socks, in the unheated, windowless stripped-down cell, in an empty cell block, shivering under a single blanket. The cell had a toilet, basin and a bed frame without a mattress. A worn, soiled mattress was delivered to the cell each night at 9.30 p.m. and picked up at 6 a.m. The food was basic – bread and water. A day after I arrived, two Chinese prisoners were sent to the adjoining cells. The Chinese prisoners were on punishment for refusing to co-operate in the murder investigation of David Bunk. Through a small hole in the adjoining white-painted wall, which was blocked up with moist bread, the prisoner in the next cell inserted a straw and passed some granulated orange to me, which, when mixed with a little water, enabled me to make orange squash. I later learned that the prisoner was a friend of Benny Ong. I was very grateful for the gift. Some inmates came out of the Hole completely and utterly insane and I had some bad moments there, where in the numbing quietness and darkness I feared for my sanity. It is an experience I have never forgotten.

The length of the sentence in solitary was determined first of all by the seriousness of the incident and, secondly, by the inmate's attitude when inside the punishment block. Fr Duggan and my commissary supervisor, Mr Hardnock, spoke well of me and my work and wanted the charges dismissed and for me to be returned to my old commissary job and G Block. Meanwhile, I knew that if I gave the name of the person who had signed the actual form, I would not be able to go back into general population. This was not a problem, as I had kept my silence on more important matters.

After three days solitary, I was given a warning, reprimanded by the prison authorities and returned to my commissary job. I was welcomed back as a returning hero as everyone knew what had happened and why I was in solitary confinement. My stubborn streak had won me more respect. That night, some of the wiseguys sent around some well-cooked steak, with spaghetti and cheese, as a welcome back. It was devoured without trace in a matter of seconds.

When I was first jailed in Lewisburg, I was classified as 'close custody', which was later reduced to 'medium' and then to 'minimum security'. I applied to work on the prison farm as a commissary clerk, where I would then be housed. My application was turned down and I asked a friendly clerk why. I was told that it was possible just to walk off the prison farm, and I was considered a high-risk prisoner because I was from Ireland and might flee the country.

I applied again for a work position on the farm and was asked to present my case. I told the interviewing team that I intended to complete my sentence and had no intention of escaping from the prison or leaving the country. My previous work record in the prison was taken into account and the fact that I gave my word not to escape was also in my favour. Two and a half years after arriving in Lewisburg, on 5 May 1977, I was transferred to the Farm Camp, which meant I was out of the cells and would live in a huge, open dormitory, divided into cubicles for each prisoner.

To be transferred to the farm was a wonderful relief. A huge weight was lifted from my shoulders and I could finally relax. I would be out of danger – there were few violent criminals on the farm so the chances of being murdered waned. The farm was not like being in prison at all. I couldn't believe my luck when I saw my new abode. Each cubicle contained a bunk bed, desk and a small locker for extra clothes, and each had a full-sized window, that had blinds to close at night-time. I had the dormitory room-mates of my choice. The men assigned here had extraordinary freedom compared to the general prison. My diet improved when I moved because the farm encompassed over a thousand acres, with dairy cattle and all kinds of crops – corn, potatoes, onions, peas, etc. It had a meadow with cows.

The farm also supplied the Allenwood Correctional Facility, a minimum-security federal jail for white-collar criminals, which was about fifteen miles away. Joe Novoa was also transferred to the prison farm and housed in an adjacent cubicle. It was a reasonable cushy number compared to being in general population. Only prisoners thought to be a low security risk got to work and live on the farm. Prisoners with a reputation for violence or known killers – like Paulie Vario, Jimmy Burke, Benny Ong and Johnny Dio – would never have been given transfers to the farm. There was none of the cut-throat existence of the main prison, and the farm provided a great degree of safety and stability. I settled in quite comfortably, knowing that at least I was away from the worst of the prison population.

I continued working for the commissary on a part-time basis since the commissary only visited the camp once a week, but I also worked as the only clerk at the prison garage.

Being again in a trusted position, I worked with little or no supervision. On the farm there were five different employment sections where inmates worked most of the day. I found the garage filing system was in a bit of a mess and I devised and instituted a chronological filing system, recording the numerous purchase orders needed for the garage, and the forty-two trucks, transportation buses and other farm machinery. This was something I was good at and also enjoyed. It was so detailed and organised that it got a special meritorious award and I received a dollar bonus. My system was so efficient that prison guards and inmate clerks from the four other sections on the farm – the dairy, landscape, etc. – were taken up to spend two weeks in my garage office, so they could return to their own departments and set up the exact same filing system. I have to admit I was very proud of the system I introduced and I am sure this stood to me when I was applying for parole.

All five sections on the farm sent their requests in a mail bag and I was cleared to take these communications from the farm offices in and out through the prison security gates to the main offices each day. Using this method, I also delivered messages from organised criminals on the farm to OC gangsters in the main prison.

Reusing the method I had learned in the SIU, I would have my associates make out their reports, then I would first type extra carbon papers with their messages, then staple the message carbon in between the actual prison reports or requisitions. I did this service for mobsters like Charlie Brody, Johnny Dio, Vinnie Aloi, Paulie Vario and Bobby Maher. These were important and would be taken to the chaplain's office where the necessary carbon would be extracted. Usually someone would be there to receive the messages. They would bring the carbon paper back to their cells, hold it up to the light and read the message, then destroy it. I tried not to digest the content of the messages – I was not interested, and in any case the less I knew the better. What happened after the mobsters received their messages did not concern me. I really only did such things to beat the system and never smuggled anything other than the typed messages through the security gates. I was stopped almost every time and examined thoroughly, but nobody thought to examine the printed carbon papers.

Through my work in the garage I met William Terrell, another clerk, who was trying to lose weight. As I worked in the commissary, I was able to buy a lot of protein in the form of canned mixed nuts, which I supplied to Terrell, who soon shed eighty pounds. In this way, I made a good friend.

Terrell was a polite intellectual, with a touch of class – a quiet and non-assuming character. He only associated with the Italian made men and kept away from his old friends from outside, as he was always conscious that the guards made notes of prison friendships, old and new – for the authorities.

Known as Jimmy or Goldfinger, Terrell was one of the main drug dealers in Harlem until he was jailed for six years in 1973 for tax evasion. He was one of the first black gangsters to seize control of Harlem's heroin trade in the early 1970s from old-line Mafia figures. His brother Harry Terrell operated some of his business while Goldfinger was in jail, though one of his lieutenants, Nicky Barnes, inherited most of his network of suppliers. With his boss in jail, Barnes became one of the top members of Harlem's sinister 'Council of 12', modelled on the Italian crime families, which controlled nearly every criminal enterprise in Harlem. Barnes was convicted and faced jail in 1977, but flipped and ratted out his whole crew to keep himself out of prison.

While Goldfinger was in jail, a woman murdered his wife because she testified to a grand jury about the Harlem drug trade. Before he was released on parole, Goldfinger gave me his home phone number and told me that if there was ever a time in my life when I needed anything – money, work or advice – he would be delighted to be of assistance, as he would always consider me a good and trusted friend. At this time in my life, it was a great comfort to have a rich friend to offer assistance. Goldfinger, however, did not last long on the outside. He was shot nine times and his body was dumped in a drainage ditch in Yonkers in December 1978. He had $1,000 in his pockets, so robbery was ruled out as a motive.

Goldfinger's bodyguard later told me what had happened. He said a major South American drug dealer, whose father was in prison at the time, wanted Goldfinger dead because he had embarrassed him. The people that he was supplying cocaine and heroin to claimed that they couldn't get more than two hits from his drug supply, as it was cut too much. The South American drug dealers kidnapped Goldfinger's father and brother and held them until he came to meet them to give them the money that he owed. When he came, they released his family and then shot him. He was killed because, like many others in the game, he became too greedy. A detective friend, who was one of the investigators, verified this story to me.

Like many inmates, one of my biggest fears was dying in prison. I attended a prison funeral when I was on the farm. There were no family members present and I and three other inmates were 'volunteered' to be pallbearers. The dead inmate was serving twenty years for a bank robbery and had been killed by his cellmate who couldn't sleep because of his snoring. His cellmate had stuck a pencil in his ear, killing him. The killer had previously been a mental patient within the prison system and should not have been housed with the general population. The bank robber had been in prison most of his life and his family did not want his body. A simple coffin was transported on a truck and brought to the prison cemetery where there were about two dozen small headstones – a foot high and a few inches wide. A warden, chaplain and a senior member of staff were there as witnesses. A prison number was put on the headstone, but it was not the real number. This was in case family members might, at a later stage, come in and steal the body. The man was buried by complete strangers among complete strangers.

Gaspar Danka*, a Polish-American school custodian, taught me how to play solitaire to get through my many sleepless nights. Danka was jailed along with thirty-four other school custodians from New Jersey and Pennsylvania for taking bribes on school contracts. He was sick for the final six months of his sentence and I helped nurse him back to health. Like so many other inmates, Danka was afraid to go near the prison doctors. The doctors' mistakes were legendary. The inmates said the surgeons had a better record of committing crimes and getting away with it than the prisoners. Danka wrote to me after he was released, saying he had discovered that his illness had been a severe heart attack and that he had suffered major damage by not going to the doctor. He died within his first year of freedom.

One of the most important friends I had in Lewisburg was Charlie Brody, who I met again when I was assigned to the prison farm. Charlie Di Palermo, aka Charlie Beck or Charlie Brody, was a lifelong narcotics dealer for the Lucchese family.

Charlie got his alias from the bookmaker Steve Brody, the first man to jump off the Brooklyn Bridge and live. Steve Brody was the King of the Bowery, when the Bowery was the Golden Mile in old New York. The newspaper reports at the time gave Brody lots of publicity, and the tavern he opened shortly after his jump was a success. Hoax or not, Brody became famous, and his name for a time became slang – to 'pull a Brody' or 'do a Steve Brody' came to be understood as doing something flamboyant and dangerous. Charlie Di Palermo was notorious for his reckless and dangerous criminal career and so gained his moniker. His brothers Joseph and Peter were also top Mafiosi.

Those of us on the farm were deemed low-risk, and I was amazed that Brody was able to get a transfer there. Brody's organisation was next to impossible to penetrate until the DEA caught him in a sting operation. The DEA had evidence – telephone records and wiretaps – showing that Di Palermo was seeking a new heroin source in France, and so introduced him through an informant to three undercover agents posing as French heroin smugglers with an offer to sell twenty kilos of narcotics. The undercovers were two officers of the French National Police assigned to the DEA in New York and a French-speaking DEA agent. Ironically enough, one of the DEA agents involved in Brody's arrest was Mike Levine, the agent who had escorted me back to the USA from London.

From what I know, Charlie Brody protected me under instruction from Tom Di Bello and other mobsters and lawyers. Brody assured me that he would do all he could to make my prison stay as bearable as he could. He said that anyone or anything that became a problem to me became his problem too. He was my best friend, apart from my old partner, Joe Novoa, while I was in Lewisburg. Charlie Brody died on 26 July 2009. Before he passed away, he sent greetings to me through another former detective.

I often sat in a cubicle with Brody and several New York gangsters discussing life in general. I enjoyed their conversations and I used to tell them that their company and conversation was like good wine to be enjoyed fully; it had to be tasted in sips and that I'd had my sip for the day, but would be back tomorrow for another. Despite being an ex-detective, I was accepted by these people, but when 'business' conversations came up, I usually left, and they respected me for this. To the mobsters, I was a stand-up guy. They knew I was there by choice. This went for Joe Novoa too. Fellow police officers and New York gangsters trusted me as a man of my word. I was known to all of them as 'The Quiet Man' because I would not co-operate with the authorities. On one occasion sitting in Brody's cubicle with several New York mobsters Charlie turned around and, nodding towards me, said to his friends, 'I'd rather him as a partner than any one of you because he has something the government wants and he won't give it to them, but if any of you had it you'd be out of here in a flash!'

Many of the organised crime figures in Lewisburg treated me as one of their own. My new friends – Goldfinger, Brody, and 'Raffie C' Cuomo – made sure I received the same food they did: corn on the cob, pheasant and rice, steak and onions. Once when Fr Pat Duggan was visiting, he offered me a baloney sandwich. I laughed and said, 'Why should I eat baloney when I can have steak or pheasant?'

Boiled eggs – another favourite – were cooked in a large two-foot-high plastic bucket. About three-dozen eggs at a time were boiled with the aid of stingers. This would take some time, but there were always plenty of lookouts. Pheasants were also cooked on a nightly basis around autumn. Traps were set for the pheasants – milk boxes, which fell on them as they entered to eat the loose scattered corn. One night, a raid was conducted on the dormitory for narcotics and other contraband. Officer Hill picked up a laundry bag, put his arm deep inside, jumped back and shouted as two pheasants flew out and around the inside of the dormitory and out through an open window. The place was in an uproar of laughter because Officer Hill was very unpopular. He had the last laugh, though, as he put the owner of the laundry bag, a young hillbilly named Roy, in solitary confinement for three days. Nevertheless, that same night I received his pheasant, with rice, sweetcorn and gravy, in the usual small covered nut tin. On this occasion, Raffie C was the cook. He was a Lucchese family member, serving time for drug dealing.

Henry Hill, the self-proclaimed wiseguy, was also assigned to the prison farm and worked nearby as the dairy farm clerk. One night, he was filling in for a friend playing baseball. Novoa, some friends and I were watching the game and getting a laugh from the antics of the clumsy players. Hill tried so hard to be a star. He got to first base and then second, and his big chance came to run around third and race to home. Seeing he was not going to make it, he dived head first at the home base and slid over it. But in the midst of the high-rising sand, dust and the loud cheers, he could be heard sobbing, 'Oh, Jesus, I broke my arm. Oh, for fuck's sake my arm is broke!' This, of course, brought gales of mirth from the crowd watching, with inmates rolling around the grassy hillside in fits of laughter.

I got a large newspaper, wet it and folded it in a tight circular roll and put it around Hill's left wrist up to his elbow and tied it together with cord and a rubber band. This would prevent further movement or damage until he could get medical attention. His wrist was broken and Hill had a plaster cast on it for the next six months. He lived in a cubicle near to mine and, as he was left-handed, he asked me to write cards and short letters to his wife, family and girlfriend. I would kid Henry by asking him when he was going to write his book *My Life in the Mob*. I joked it could start with Hill asking Raffie C, 'Do you want a cup of coffee?' Or 'Can I light that cigarette for you?' Or 'Is that bed made up for your comfort, Charlie?' Or 'Can I steal any bread for you from the mess hall?'

Henry Hill was like many others who acted and talked like they were big-time gangsters, but they were only the runners for real made men.

CHAPTER 10

Freedom is never free

Every inmate dreams of the day when he will face the parole board for his parole hearing. The Lewisburg parole board was made up of three people, who would review a report about the prisoner that included their behaviour in prison, what they planned to do when they were released, and whether or not they were likely to commit more crime or were a danger to the public.

A prisoner normally attended a parole board hearing to say why he thought he should be released. Inmates practised responses they had crafted to convince the parole board that they were repentant and rehabilitated – even if they weren't – and were ready to take their place in society again. If all went well, the board could shorten a sentence or even release a prisoner outright. But the parole board could also choose to punish the applicant for his attitude or his unwillingness to confess and express remorse. This had happened Joe Novoa many times. Joe had a bad attitude to the parole board.

I attended my parole hearing in Lewisburg on 1 February 1978. Like most people, I told the parole board what they wanted to hear – that I had seen the errors of my ways. I said as a serving policeman, I had sometimes felt I was above the law and beyond reproach, but I had accepted my conviction for corruption at my trial. Much of this was true. I was sorry, especially for my personal conduct, and was genuinely remorseful for the hardship I had inflicted on my children and my parents. My father had died while I'd been in prison and I had not been able to see him or attend his funeral. I told the parole board I would like to be reconciled with my children and wanted nothing more than to see them under happier circumstances.

In the main prison, I had worked as a commissary clerk where I'd received excellent work reports. I was considered a very conscientious individual who took great pride in his work and was well-thought-of as an asset to that department. My work on the prison farm camp was also highly commended. I had an exemplary record in prison and I told the board that I hoped to continue in meaningful employment when I was released.

I felt my hearing had gone well, and I was right.

My parole date was set for 1 February 1979. My evaluation and recommendation for release noted that: '... the staff believes that Daly's prognosis for remaining in the community without violating the law is good and recommends that he be paroled through a community treatment center.'

Because I was given a parole date, Joe Novoa was also entitled to parole. Novoa and I copied the last couple of pages of both our trial minutes and gave them to our lawyers. It was stated in the trial minutes that I had been more deceitful than Novoa and that I had been sentenced to ten years, the same as Novoa.

Joe had applied for parole before, but he had always been antagonistic to trial judges and had been refused parole twice. He applied again and was refused, but when he gave his lawyer a copy of my trial minutes, in which the judge said he sentenced me to the same term as my accomplice, the lawyer was able to say that if I was entitled to parole, then Novoa should get the same deal. So, after being refused twice, Novoa was given parole and was to be released forthwith. He was housed in his own cubicle beside mine and, when he got the good news, we went back to his cubicle where we broke down and cried. Because he had been granted immediate parole, he was taken within hours, discharged and freed. I, however, had been given a parole date and had to wait until it arrived.

I remember the day of my release well. When my time came, I was up early as usual. There was an air of unreality about the events happening around me. The other prisoners in the dorm were aware I was being released. While everyone wished me well, they were also wondering when their turn would come. From the minute other prisoners knew I was being released, I became a different person. Although I was the focus of attention and conversation, my departure was discussed among them as if I had already left.

As the time approached, I could feel myself becoming nervous, wanting to get away. I'd packed my few belongings the night before and was having a last look around the dormitory when I felt the emotion hit me. My head was telling me, 'Get yourself together, you're nearly there, stay calm,' but my heart was ready to burst with sheer delight. I said goodbye to everyone, had a final round of handshakes and jokes along the lines of, 'We'll keep your bed for you, just in case,' and then I was out.

Joe arranged my flight home. I had made a lot of money in prison, around $2,500, and bought myself some shoes, a suit, a sports shirt and a small leather briefcase. I had passed through the town with one of the hacks, who allowed me to go into a local shop and buy the clothes and case, to be held in the shop for me for the future. When I was released, I told the taxi driver to take me to the shop, where I picked up my clothes. I changed into them right there and came out of the shop looking like a different man.

At Williamsport airport I became nervous when I saw all the

hacks from Lewisburg. I thought they were trying to catch Joe and me on a parole violation by us meeting together, as parolees are not allowed to meet while on parole. I asked one of the hacks what they were doing there and he told me they were picking up parole violators at Newark, so I relaxed. The airport only held about twenty-five people. I went to the little restaurant and ordered a hamburger. I sat down to eat and then said to myself, 'Well done!' Here I was – my first day of freedom – and I'd ordered a hamburger, which was nearly all we ever got to eat in prison. One of the things I took a long time to get over was the bland prison food.

Later, I flew to New York and presented myself to the Bryant Hotel, a halfway house for parolees. I would stay here until I could find meaningful employment. There were many other friends from Lewisburg there, including Jimmy Burke and his old protégé Tommy DeSimone. The Bryant Hotel halfway house was known as the 'Roach Hotel' because it was infested with cockroaches.

While in the Bryant, Jimmy Burke pulled off the $6 million Lufthansa heist, the largest robbery in American criminal history at the time. Burke and DeSimone were still resident in the halfway house and used this as their alibi. I was in the Bryant Hotel awaiting a release date when I read the papers and saw a sketch of a suspect who resembled Tommy DeSimone – Tommy had to take off his mask to be admitted to the cargo storage building and the police issued a rough sketch of a man they wanted to talk to. Tommy DeSimone disappeared soon after this.

The story circulated that Tommy was gunned down by the Gambinos for his murder of a made man, Billy Batts Bentvena, but it was thought in some circles that he was killed by Jimmy Burke, who was knocking off anyone connected to the Lufthansa heist. Tommy was the only robber identified, so he had to go. To this day, Tommy's body has never been found. Tommy was murdered by someone he trusted. That someone was probably Jimmy Burke, who was never found guilty of murder or even the Lufthansa robbery. The only thing they could do was put him in a maximum-security prison for fixing college basketball games. A friend took my greetings to Jimmy while he was there.

According to Henry Hill, Billy Batts was murdered because he insulted DeSimone in front of several people in a Queens bar. But it was thought that Batts was killed by Burke and DeSimone because Jimmy the Gent had taken over Batts' loan shark operation while Batts was in prison. Not wanting to return the business to Batts on his release, Jimmy Burke murdered him instead. Henry Hill made up the story of Batts insulting DeSimone because he was unaware of the real motive. He would never have known why Batts was murdered because he was not in Burke or DeSimone's confidence.

Hill bumped himself up to be a big-time gangster but he was a nobody, a hanger on. While in jail, Hill heard that Paul Vario was worried about Hill's ability to face a long sentence in silence. Hill became concerned – for about a day, then he started to sing.

He told all he heard about the Lufthansa heist and every other crime he knew anything or nothing about. The authorities pressed him about Jimmy Burke, who they suspected had engineered the JFK robbery. Henry and his family entered the Witness Protection Programme while Jimmy Burke was convicted in 1982 of fixing college basketball games as part of a gambling scam and was sentenced to twenty years. He was later charged with the murder of Richard Eaton based on evidence Hill gave the authorities and was given a life sentence. Hill testified that Burke had told him he killed Eaton for swindling him out of money. While he was convicted on Hill's evidence, it was a known fact that Burke would never have revealed any of his operations to Henry Hill.

Nicholas Pileggi wrote the bestselling *Wiseguy: Life in a Mafia Family* based on Henry Hill's life, which was the basis for the movie *Goodfellas* with Robert De Niro, Ray Liotta and Joe Pesci, as the three main characters – Jimmy Burke, Henry Hill and Tommy DeSimone.

Robert De Niro played the character of Jimmy Burke well. He did look like him, that same ruthless, charismatic guy. Joe Pesci played Tommy DeSimone. He was in character too. Pesci played him well. Tommy was a fiery guy, though a bit taller, a real tough guy. He was known as Tommy Two-guns. Henry Hill was a liar and a drug addict. I knew these guys. Hill was the only one alive, so he could lie away as much as he liked because the other main characters – Jimmy Burke, Tommy DeSimone and Paulie Vario – were dead.

Henry Hill left the Witness Protection Programme in the early 1990s. By now few of his enemies were left to track him down. The author contacted him for this publication, but he never replied. Henry Hill died on 12 June 2012 in a Los Angeles hospital aged sixty-nine. His partner and manager Lisa Caserta said years of heavy smoking combined with complications from a recent heart attack led to his death. She said Henry was with family members when he died, adding he 'went out pretty peacefully for a goodfella'.

PART III
RE-BORN

I would rather be carried by six, than judged by twelve.
An old cop proverb

CHAPTER 1

On the outside

When I was released on parole, it took a long time for me to readjust to civilian life. Prisoners often spoke about what they would do when they got out, crazy things like take a cruise with the wife – when they probably wouldn't be let out of the country – or normal things like have sex more than usual. I wanted to walk. I walked a lot in prison. In Lewisburg, the only sunlight was in the prison yard because the sun went down behind the walls, and people would walk alone there, lost in their own private thoughts. You did not interrupt them. A top mob guy, Frank Giordano, usually walked alone in the yard and was never interrupted but one day, with his permission, I walked with him and confided in him. After getting out of the Hole I told him I felt I was losing my mind, and that I could not go on. Prison was mind-numbingly boring. He advised me to come out to the yard and walk, take one step, then another and another. 'You will eventually walk through your anxiety,' he said. So that was part of my healing process. For months I went out and thought about the good times and happier moments in my life, and walked and walked as if I was on a mission.

And when I was released, I walked through the New York City streets until my feet were bleeding. I sat and watched children shout and run in the playground and even though I dislike dogs, I listened in delight to the noise of their bark. I sat for hours looking through the darkness at the stars. I walked from the East and West 50s from where I was staying, down to Wall Street, and old Manhattan and the waterfront. I walked from the East Side to the West Side. This was my therapy – day after day.

When I was tired, I would sit and watch people walking, jogging, hugging, and people rushing to and from work on their daily grind. Other released prisoners did similar things. It was just the freedom to be able to do this. I walked up from the Bryant Hotel on 52nd Street and Seventh Avenue to O'Donohue's pub on West 72nd Street, where Jack O'Donohue gave me the keys of his bar and grill so I could store clean clothes, razor and toothbrush, and take a shower. In the halfway house, I only kept the clothes I was wearing. When I slept at night, I kept my folded clothes under the sheets all night or they would be stolen.

The sound of subway trains screeching to a sudden stop in the huge underground stations was music to my ears. For five years, I hadn't heard a dog bark, a child cry or a female voice. I couldn't walk a mile in a straight line. I couldn't choose the clothes I wanted to wear. I wasn't outside after dark, and never saw the stars or the horizon. I couldn't pick the food I wanted to eat, couldn't switch off the light or even lock my own bedroom door (now I leave them all open). In prison I woke up feeling I was free, and in civilian life I now woke up sweating, thinking that I was back in prison.

Naturally, I knew it would take time to adjust to life outside prison. For prisoners released from confinement, it takes nine months to a year to establish some semblance of normality. When I was released, my immediate problem was how to earn a living. What would I do with my days? After all, twenty-four hours is a long time and, for the past seven years, everything I had done had been part of a prison's system. Now I had to fend for myself, provide money, lodgings and keep my mind and body healthy. I had to stay sane, confident and be aware of my skills, and ask myself where it would lead me to.

While in prison, I had been offered jobs in some valued positions by high-ranking people associated with unions like the Lathers Union, the Steel Workers Union and the Stage Hands Association. These were all seriously sought-after positions with union cards, which were known as 'ghost jobs' or 'no-show' jobs. I would get a salary without a day's work. I would be on the books, but didn't have to show up for work. As an ex-cop, there would always be work for me in the business.

My expertise was still wiretapping, which would be useful to my 'friends' to get information in various forms from those who were business associates. It could mean bugging places of work, home phones, cars, clubs and so on. These jobs would be worth it financially, but I knew it wouldn't be long before my usefulness became a danger. How long would it be before I knew too much, before I could also be useful to other interested parties, even the federal government? I couldn't see the job offers as a long-term benefit. I knew these types of jobs were not offered out of kindness, and I knew what had happened to my friend Frank Chin, the bugging expert. Chin had outlived his usefulness or crossed too many people and ended up dead.

One guy who offered me help was Benny Ong, the head of New York's Hip Sing Association. I went to the association's union hall in Chinatown and asked for Benny. The hall was an Asians-only place, so they were immediately suspicious of a white man. It was a world almost totally isolated from the larger American society. I obviously still looked like a cop, because the four Chinese in the hall would not speak to me, pretending they did not understand

English or know of Benny Ong. I informed them that I was a personal friend of Benny, who had asked me to visit him at this address. The men continued speaking in Chinese, pretending they did not understand. Finally, I took out my telephone address book and pointed out some Chinese writing scribbled by Ong, while we were in prison. One man immediately took the book and went out the union hall door at a sprint. He arrived back quickly, out of breath, and grabbed my left hand and said, 'Come with me, now. Hurry!'

He led me out through the door and to another building and upstairs into a kitchen where Benny Ong greeted me with open arms. It was just a social call, but Benny assured me of his help if I ever needed it. We had some food and tea and made some small talk about our lives. Then I said my goodbyes to Benny, assuring him that if I needed help, I would call again. It was the last time I saw Benny – a last visit of thanks for an old friendship. Benny Ong, 'the Godfather of Chinatown', died in 1994. A death in Chinatown was a joyous occasion and his funeral was one of the largest seen in New York. Benny was a top association man and when he died, to show respect and loyalty, the community had a brass band playing music all the way to the graveyard, followed by a fifty-Cadillac convoy. Many of the Cadillacs were empty except for a uniformed driver – befitting Chinese Tong tradition. I still have the address book in my possession with Benny Ong's greeting.

As I said, I was reasonably well off when I was released, with about $2,500 from the different jobs I had worked in prison. My trial lawyers, Field and Ernst, had also represented me in my motor accident claim, which led to my retirement from the NYPD. I initially tried to get three-quarters pay retirement, but had to settle for half-pay, as my accident occurred while driving home from police work and not in the line of duty. I went to my lawyer's office and talked about a temporary solution to my immediate future, as my parole stipulated I had to be officially employed. I handed over $2,000 and asked my lawyer to pay me $200 a week, so it would look like I was gainfully employed by Field and Ernst forthwith as an investigator.

I had also sent $500 from my prison account through my case worker to an old friend who I had worked with in the 7th Precinct. He was an ex-US Navy boxing champion and lived in the Bronx. However, he said he had been mugged and the money was stolen. His wife confessed to me that her husband had a drink problem and had drunk the money. To make up for her husband's transgressions, and knowing that my family had ostracised me and I didn't have a home to go to, she offered me a comfortable couch in the living room. For a small fee, she also supplied my meals.

With a proper address and legal employment, I was released from the Bryant Hotel. I became a boarder in my friend's house, where there were also eight children living. Through them, I got a job as an early-morning telephone operator for Cooper Elevators. My job was to open the offices at 6.30 a.m., get all the messages from the night-time phone answering service and then contact the two repair truck drivers before they left their homes to give them the addresses and jobs that needed their attention. Then I took the subway downtown to the law offices of Field and Ernst to begin my day's work there.

At the weekends, I took a bus to visit my children at the family home in upstate New York. Conor had enlisted in the US army and Finola, Conor's twin, had won a scholarship to Albany University. However, after a number of visits I could see that my return was not going well, and I decided not to continue visiting. I contacted another old friend, who was the Tri-state security officer for McDonald's Hamburger Company, who got me a weekend position working as a plain-clothes security guard for Ronald McDonald House, a cancer care home for children on West 86th Street in Manhattan.

I worked at Ronald McDonald House from Friday evening, when I finished my job at Field and Ernst, to Monday morning when I would take a cross-town bus back to Cooper Elevators' offices, where I started work again for another week. I was working day and night because now that I was free I found it hard to sleep. I never seemed to be tired, or maybe I did all the sleeping necessary when I was in prison. Work was a form of therapy – it stopped me thinking too much. Because when I could not sleep my mind was racing with overactive thoughts. I was worried about my future. I was now an ex-policeman, but I was also an ex-con and the chances of me getting gainful employment could be a problem.

At McDonald House I had a small bedroom in the building, which enabled me to be on duty twenty-four hours over the weekend. I contacted some old friends in the local precinct, and they would stop by and pick up several of the children who were receiving cancer treatment at the nearby Sloen Cancer Hospital on the West Side and take them for a drive in their unmarked police car, where they would turn on the siren and put out a stick-on-roof flashing red light. Many of the children had terminal cancer, but their day out with the NYPD was a highlight.

I can't put into words the horrendous feeling when one of the children died. As a father, it was horrifying. One girl made contact with me in 1981 just before I returned home to Ireland. Her name was Amy Fitzpatrick, from Florida, and her mother wanted to fulfil her last request, that she speak and thank me for all the happiness I had given her. Amy died within the week. She gave me a birthday gift of a lock of her long blonde hair, tied with a blue ribbon in a white envelope, that I have to this day.

Around Christmas 1979 I was given a full-time job in Field and Ernst, as an investigator. The firm gave me back the $2,000 I had originally given them and they agreed to continue paying me $200 a week. My parole officer was made aware of my full-time position.

With the unexpected return of my money, I moved out of my friend's household and rented a basement apartment a block away from Mr and Mrs Fitzgerald, an old couple from County Kerry. When Mrs Fitzgerald discovered I cooked my own dinner when I came home from work around 8 or 9 p.m., she offered to cook my meals for an extra small fee.

While working for Field and Ernst, I got a call from an old police friend – Frank King – who had found work in his own trial lawyers' offices a few blocks from where I worked. Frank wasn't doing so well. He had served his time in prison badly. People who saw him after his release were shocked by his appearance: his hands shook and he appeared ten years older. Frank was named as one of the guys who had ripped off the French Connection haul, but I don't think he had anything to do with it. He asked me for a small loan – so where was all this money he was supposed to have made from this big deal? It proves that most of these stories are just that – stories.

I told Frank I'd meet him during my lunch hour. I always kept a $100 bill folded up in each shoe in case of emergencies. I was walking on this for weeks so it was well flattened out. I slipped him the bill, not even looking at it. Frank rang me up the next day, saying he was nearly arrested for paying for a ninety-nine cent slice of pizza with a $100 bill! Frank was a good friend and an absolute gentleman. He has since died of cancer.

On my release from prison I decided to make up a resumé that I could give to any personnel office when applying for work. I was especially interested in finding out what I would get back from the NYPD Personnel Office as a future reference. Mainly I was interested in what they had to say about me to any other human resource office which would enquire about me. I was happy to see their response, which was quite positive. If anyone objected to me being hired by my law firm after being sentenced to a ten-year prison stretch, I would not have been appointed.

Release from jail was not the end of my problems. My marriage had been a victim of my imprisonment but, like many cops' marriages, the cracks had appeared a long time before.

Towards the end of 1979 I asked Rita to consider a divorce that we both could agree on and gave her a month to do this. When she couldn't come to a decision, I told her I would have to make the decision for all concerned and filed with the court for divorce. The procedure, however, took many years. I went back to the divorce court several times with no positive results, until a sympathetic female judge worked out an agreement and a time limit on my proposals to my wife. The judge made a stipulation that if the case was not back before her by a certain date, the divorce would be official and acted upon one year from that date. Rita did not return to the court and our divorce became official in 1981.

In the meantime, I had my parole transferred to Minneapolis in Minnesota and went to live with a woman I had met through my old friend Fr Pat Duggan, the chaplain in Lewisburg. I wrote letters and spoke by phone to my new lady friend, before visiting her, when we made the joint decision that I should move there.

Anthony Bouza, another old friend from New York, was chief of police in Minneapolis, and I approached him for a reference. Bouza had become deputy chief of the New York City Transit Police in 1976 and had been brought to Minneapolis by Mayor Donald Fraser, who wanted an outsider to head the police department following a series of scandals under his predecessor. Bouza willingly wrote me a letter of recommendation to prospective employers. Part of it read:

> *Like many fallible beings, Officer Daly stumbled and committed a serious error, for which he has paid dearly. I believe the crucible of that experience has deepened, matured and granted him insights he may not have otherwise developed. I find him an open, modest, capable, introspective person who is determined to overcome his mistakes and move forward. He strikes me as a very redeemable and potentially valuable employee.*

Because of his recommendation, I got a job as chief investigator for Leadens Investigators, Inc., whose owner was William Leadens, a retired Minneapolis police officer. I was employed as an investigator of fatal car crashes.

In the spring of 1981, after I was released from my two-year parole, I decided to return to Ireland. This was mainly because of my wife's refusal to allow our divorce to be settled. Despite having given her the family home, she continued to sue me at every turn. I realised I could never give her enough, so reluctantly I left the United States, my home for nearly thirty years. I was forty-eight and had spent more time in America than I had in the country of my birth.

CHAPTER 2
Home

When I returned to Ireland, I decided to write my life story in order to find some respite for myself. I wrote what came into my head as I sat alone in a caravan during the winter of 1981–1982, near the seaside village of Rossnowlagh, a few miles north of Ballyshannon. The popular beach was quiet during the winter and here I found peace and solitude. I sat for hours looking out the window of the caravan across the strand to the Atlantic Ocean. I found it difficult to sleep and had to be mentally and physically exhausted before I finally dozed off. I was depressed, and haunted by nightmares and overactive thoughts.

Reliving the story of my life was painful psychoanalysis. I wrote every day from lunchtime until darkness, barely eating in between. The writing was designed to calm my emotions: the high-tension existence that I was involved in on a daily basis as a policeman and then in prison, and the divorce and loss of my children. I took up golf, playing alone, sometimes three times a day – eighteen holes each time.

Part of me died when I realised that there was no future with my wife and family, but I lived the rest of my life because I was not going to permit any other person or circumstance to kill me.

It wasn't courage – it was stubborn defiance. I intended to survive against all the odds.

When I returned to Ireland to a quiet rural life, I was full of nervous tension. Often I would walk for hours, day and night, along the clifftop pathways that bordered the Atlantic Ocean. On a calm night I would think about throwing myself into the sea, but when there was a gale blowing, which could easily sweep me away, I would cling tightly to the sturdy stone walls and defy its power to take my life!

In Donegal I got involved in local and community issues and have become a respected member of my community. Most people knew something of my life in America. They had heard the rumours, but few people asked. I was a returned emigrant. I had made it good in America and had come back to my hometown to live out my retirement. That was enough. I was left alone and strangers were not welcome with questions.

In time, I renewed old friendships and made many new friends. In 1983 I was the founder of a campaign called Come Back to Erin, so named for the River Erne (pronounced Erin) that flows through Ballyshannon. With other local residents I mounted a campaign of letter-writing to thousands of people with ties to this lovely northwestern town, so they could re-meet old friends every year. Even local schoolchildren came onboard, writing overseas to suitable people. The festivities, timed for August, the busiest month for holidays in Ireland, included music, dancing, drama, golf, football and other activities, all designed to bring together the visitors, with or without Ballyshannon roots, and locals. However, it was not quite the success I had hoped or expected.

I made some trips to mainland Britain to visit friends and relations, and travelled through Wales, Chesterfield, Derbyshire and Cornwall. From my experience as a former policeman and private investigator, I was aware that I was being watched. This could have been because of my past convictions or the undying suspicions of the British Special Branch that I really had republican connections. At Larne ferry port I noticed that my car had been discreetly opened and searched when it was left unoccupied in the vehicle hold of the ferry. I found that both English and Irish men and women travelling on the ferry casually introduced themselves and struck up conversations. I noticed that I was photographed several times by people who were taking photos of each other and happened to get me in the photo. Civilians, posing as customs officers, always checked my car when I was returning to Ireland. On one trip to the city of York, what I thought were detectives from the British Special Branch pulled alongside my car and gave me a friendly eye and acknowledgement. These officers knew who I was and they were discreetly breaking their cover, letting me know they knew.

In NYC folklore, I am known as 'The Quiet Man'. Imagine all those people who in some way protected me – my physical security in prison. Who were they? To this day, my protectors are unknown. Never a word was said. It is a mystery I will take to the grave. Most of them, I am sure, have gone to their eternal rest. To all the 'unknowns' in my life, I give my silence! May they rest in peace.

CHAPTER 3

The 1751 Club

As a result of my car accident in 1973, I developed a fear of heights – especially anything above two storeys. For a time, I also had a fear of large crowds like those at football matches, parties, weddings, church meetings, airports, funerals, reunions, etc. I refused many invitations to events because of these fears. Some people, however, did not understand that I was not the same person they had once known.

When possible, I tried to visit New York and the reunion of the '1751 Club', though I can't go every year, mainly because I live in Ireland. The club was originally members of the Narcotics Bureau, active and retired. The term '1751' came from the old New York State Penal Law section under which they operated. Section 1751 related to the sale of narcotics or possession of narcotics over a certain weight. The charges were felonies and the expense accounts of narcotics detectives were based on the number of arrests affected per month – $100 per month maximum. Felonies were worth more than misdemeanours in terms of reimbursement, so everyone strived to make a felony arrest under Section 1751. Felonies were worth $25, while misdemeanours were worth $7.50. When the new penal law went into effect in 1965, they became Section 220.20. Because most of the old-timers worked when 1751 was in effect, they chose that name for the club. Every year, dozens of former detectives eat, drink and talk in celebration and remembrance of everything they have seen and done while members of the NYPD.

Former SIU detectives Eddie Mamet and Les Dana are the two main organisers of the annual dinner. Mamet retired from the NYPD as a captain; Les was an SIU detective and later formed his own private detective agency.

The first reunion of the 1751 Club I attended was in 1989, which, unknown to me, was organised in my honour. I travelled over 3,000 miles from Ireland to New York, my first time back in eight years. I was very excited and arrived in a blaze of glory. Everyone present had a tag saying, 'Hello! I'm Pete Daly.' I considered the joke to be a sign of respect, friendship and support.

About a year later, the 1751 Club had a special night for Joe Novoa. After our release, I lost contact with my old partner. I lived in the Bronx, while Joe lived in Brooklyn. He also went through a hard time on his release. Divorced and with nowhere to live, he took on menial jobs just to survive. For a time, he hit rock bottom, but his old friends from the NYPD got him back on the right road.

Eventually, through one of these old friends, the author Gerry Kelly, I was able to find Novoa. Kelly made some enquiries about Joe's whereabouts and found out where he lived. Joe attended several reunions of the 1751 Club before he died of natural causes in 2009. Gerry Kelly wrote a book about the narcotics theft from Broome Street entitled *Honor for Sale*. Many of the names of the main characters in the book were changed, although they were thinly disguised. However, my name remained unchanged and I asked Kelly why he hadn't altered it. He said it was because he had so much respect for me that he left my name as it was.

At its formation, there were over a hundred ex-detectives in the 1751 Club, but with time their numbers diminished. In 2007 the reunion was in the old 1st Precinct, now the NYPD Museum. In

2007, a retired detective who I had worked with and who had later become a judge called me aside and told me that a certain person had sent his best wishes to me for a long and healthy life – it was Charlie Brody, my old friend from Lewisburg. I told the judge that I was surprised and delighted, and asked him to return the good wishes in kind to one of many who could have easily arranged the end of my life, but didn't. Someone unknown to me made a connection with Tom Di Bella and Charlie Brody to protect me in prison. I will never know who that person (or persons) was. My silence against my fellow policemen bought their respect, and that saved my life.

My law enforcement friends have forgiven me my transgressions. To them, I was a loyal cop and a faithful friend; I had the chance to save myself at others' expense, but didn't. That meant a lot to old friends and colleagues.

My son Conor died in April 2013 of natural causes, and when Les Dana and Eddie Mamet heard the sad news, they decided that they would have the annual reunion in my honour. I was eighty in August 2013, and the chances of me making the long journey from Ireland were getting slimmer. I was driven 180 miles to Shannon airport, then flew to JFK where I was picked up by John Hartigan, my old friend and detective partner.

The author James Durney, along with RTÉ radio producer Ronan Kelly and researcher Mark McMeniman, flew from Dublin to JFK on 29 May 2013. All three attended the reunion, while Kelly and McMeniman were also to record an interview with me for RTÉ radio's *Documentary on One*. Mark McMeniman was a native of Ballyshannon and set up the interview. John Hartigan and I met them and Hartigan drove from JFK to Manhattan's Lower East Side, while Ronan Kelly recorded conversations between John and me. We were amazed at the changes in our old stomping ground. The Lower East Side was a far better place than we remembered it from our time as patrolmen.

Afterword

James Durney, January 2016
It was a great pleasure to sit in their company as Daly and Hartigan told stories and reminisced about the old days. For a time Pete Daly was back on the streets of his beloved New York City. He was transformed from a senior citizen to a young emigrant cop on the beat. The streets were bustling with people of all colours. One of the oldest neighbourhoods of the city, the Lower East Side, had long been a lower-class working neighbourhood and often a poor and ethnically diverse section of New York. Today, it has a predominantly Puerto Rican and Dominican community, although there are also sizeable Japanese, Bangladeshi and Chinese populations.

The Lower East Side is in the process of gentrification. Some of the old landmarks are still there. At East Houston Street Katz's Deli, a symbol of the neighbourhood's Jewish history, was dwarfed by modern development, while the Henry Street tenements no longer seemed as menacing as in Daly's day when it was described as the worst street in the city. The old 7th Precinct, where Daly and Hartigan were once patrolmen, has gone, demolished in the 1970s to be replaced by a modern building.

The two ex-cops marvelled at the changes and how safe-looking the streets were. They talked about street characters, arrests, beat patrols and cop friends, many since passed on.

The reunion of the 1751 Club was billed as a 'Pete Daly Night' and was held on 30 May 2013, at Incognito Italian Bistro at 30 West 18th Street, between Fifth and Sixth Avenues. I attended the event, along with Pete and about fifty other members. Daly was greeted with many 'Jaysus, Peter' or 'Top o' the morning, Peter' from his friends, including Eddie Mamet, Les Dana, Jim Mulligan, Kathy Burke, Stanley Tice, Sam Badillo and Lionel Tuckett. Daly and Mike Levine hugged warmly and, for Pete, it was quite emotional. Levine, who had not met Daly since he escorted him back from London in 1975, had a signed copy for Pete of his book *The Big White Lie*. It said, 'Welcome back to the US my old/new friend.' Levine said it took many years for him to go from an arresting officer to friend and 'that is the true joy of this strange life we all share'.

It is now over thirty years since Pete Daly left America, yet those two decades he spent in the police force and in the prison system have left their mark on him and continue to haunt his every living moment. Combat soldiers know this ordeal as post-traumatic stress. They might have served only a short time as a frontline soldier, but their experience remains with them forever. For Pete Daly, it is the same. He still thinks of himself as a policeman. It is something he will never lose.

The first time I met Pete Daly, he came up behind me in his car as if he was on a surveillance mission. We were to meet in a busy Irish midlands town. Both of us were driving, but he found me first. My cell phone rang. 'Is that you in the red van?' he asked, never having met me before. Old habits die hard, it seems. Even though he is long retired from the police department, in his heart Pete Daly is still a New York City cop. Nothing can erase the sense of pride and satisfaction his twelve years on the force brought him.

Over the course of writing this book, Pete Daly has changed. It took him a long time to trust me. At first, his revelations were painful to him but, over time, he mellowed, realising he was causing nobody any harm. He has kept his court case minutes; court appeal; parole hearing tapes; other personal file letters and the innumerable jottings and notes he has written over many years. Much of the information is in the public domain and many of the participants have passed on, but Pete is always conscious of hurting anyone mentioned in his story. It took me five years to convince him to co-operate on this book and another six years to write it. I have travelled with Pete to New York and all over his home area. He is a popular man in his hometown. Everyone knows him and recognises something of his story, but to his friends and neighbours it doesn't matter. Most mornings he drives to the nearby village of Belleek, has breakfast in his regular restaurant, collects some parcels for local businesses in Ballyshannon and then drives back home, where he delivers his few packages. When he is finished his rounds, Pete goes to his regular restaurant for dinner with friends and then goes for a walk around a local park before heading back to his house overlooking the bay.

We have had many conversations on the road his life has taken. There are things he still finds upsetting, some things he won't, or can't – for whatever reason – reveal. But he knows he has reached the end of the road. He has come full circle. I asked him many times did he have any regrets. His reply was:

'Of course, I was dishonest, but you have to make your own judgement. I was brought up to know right from wrong. My regrets are innumerable. It is all part of life. But I would die rather than inform on my police friends. The oath of office I took included loyalty. I gave up my family, my life and all that it meant to me. But I am lucky. Few people get to decide their fate.'

James Durney and Peter Daly, outside the old 1st Precinct building in Lower Manhattan, which housed SIU, now home to the NYPD Museum, May 2013.

Bibliography

Primary Sources

Official court and NY Police Department papers

Peter Daly's court case minutes; court appeal; parole hearing tapes; other personal file letters.

Extradition papers signed by Henry Kissinger, US Secretary of State.

Freedom of Information and Privacy Act; documents received from the USA State Department and the Government Agencies.

Appeal trial minutes of Joe Novoa.

Photographs

Copies of official NYPD photos from Peter Daly

Secondary Sources

Newspapers

Irish Daily Mirror
Irish Independent

Irish Press
Journal American
New York Daily News

Books

Bello, Stephen. *Doing Life: The extraordinary saga of America's greatest jailhouse lawyer* (New York: St. Martin's Press) 1982.

Berkow, Ira. *The Man Who Robbed The Pierre* (New York: Scribner) 1987.

Boyne, Sean. *Gunrunners: The covert arms trail to Ireland* (Dublin: O'Brien Press) 2006.

Breslin, Jimmy. *The Good Rat: A true story* (New York: Harper Perennial) 2008.

Burns, Sarah. *The Central Park Five* (New York: Vintage) 2012.

Carlo, Philip. *Gaspipe: Confessions of a Mafia boss* (New York: William Morrow) 2008.

Codella, Michael & Bennett, Bruce. *Alphaville. New York 1988: Welcome to heroin city* (New York: Thomas Dunne Books) 2010.

Conlon, Edward. *Blue Blood* (New York: Riverhead Books) 2004.

Demaris, Ovid. *The Last Mafioso: 'Jimmy the Weasel' Fratianno* (New York: Bantam) 1981.

English, T.J. *The Savage City: Race, murder and a generation on the edge* (New York: William Morrow) 2011.

Heaney, Frank & Machado, Gay. *Inside the Walls of Alcatraz* (Boulder: Bull Publishing) 1997.

Hoffman, William & Headley, Lake. *The Explosive Story of the Mafia's Most Notorious Hit Man Donald 'Tony the Greek' Frankos: Contract killer* (New York: Thunder's Mouth Press) 1993.

Kelly, Gerald E. *Honor for Sale* (New York: Sharon Publications) 1999.

Lardner, James & Reppetto, Thomas. *NYPD: A city and its police* (New York: Henry Holt & Co) 2000.

Levine, Michael. *Deep Cover: The inside story of how DEA infighting, incompetence and subterfuge lost us the biggest battle of the drug war* (Bloomington: iUniverse) 2000.

Leuci, Robert. *All the Centurions* (New York: William Morrow 2004.

Maas, Peter. *Serpico* (New York: Viking) 1973.

McAlary, Mike. *Good Cop, Bad Cop* (New York: Pocket Books) 1994.

McKenna, Thomas & Harrington, William. *Manhattan North Homicide* (New York: St. Martins Press) 1996.

Moore, Robin. *The French Connection* (London: Lyons Press) 2003.

O'Donnell, Ruan. *Special Category: The IRA in English prisons. Vol. 1: 1968–1978* (Dublin: Irish Academic Press) 2011.

Pileggi, Nicholas. *Wiseguy: Life in a Mafia family* (New York: Pocket Books) 1987.

Simon, David. *Homicide* (New York: Ballantine Books) 1992.

Wallance, Gregory. *Papa's Game* (New York: Rawson Wade Publishers) 1981.

Yevoli, Al. *Bed-Stuy: The way it was, the making of a cop* (Florida: publisher unknown) 2010.

Articles

el. 'Daly's Law', *Donegal Democrat,* (10 July 2003).

alph. 'French Connection Epilogue: Mob boss *New York Time* 21 February (2009).

Levine, Mike. 'Reverse Sting Operations – The American Hustle: The unethical use of reverse sting operations and the creation of crime' (essay, copy sent to author) 2014.

Walinsky, Adam. 'The Knapp Commission', *The Village Voice* (1 March 1973), Vol. XVIII, No. 9.

Wynne, Fiona. 'Goodbye Goodfella', *The Irish Sun* (14 June 2012).

ACKNOWLEDGEMENTS

This book would not have been written without the help and contributions of many people. I would like to thank Gerry Gough, for his patience and advice to both Peter and me; others whose advice and input were invaluable were former detectives Kathy Burke, Mike Levine, Bob Leuci, John Hartigan, Sam Badillo, Les Wolff, Lionel Tuckett, Joe Sanchez and Eddy Mamet; and my agent Peter O'Connell from TrueLit Agency, who believed in this work from the beginning.

Thanks also to journalists Marc McMenamin and Ronan Kelly, who accompanied Peter and me to New York in 2013, and John and Barbara Hartigan, my hosts for the May–June 2013 trip. This book also benefitted immensely from the editorial efforts of my friends and colleagues, Mario Corrigan and Karel Kiely. And thanks to the team at Hachette Ireland, especially Ciara Doorley and Joanna Smyth, and Anna Doble of Wiggin LLP.

Peter Daly would like to thank his family – Rita, Shane, Finola, Conor (RIP) and Evan – and all those who expressed kindness to him on the NYPD and in the variety of other circumstances throughout his life, whether in 'college' or civilian life.